SPSS® Introductory Guide:

Basic Statistics and Operations

SPSS® Introductory Guide:

Basic Statistics and Operations

Marija J. Norušis

Series Editors:
Norman H. Nie
C. Hadlai Hull

McGRAW-HILL BOOK COMPANY

New York St. Louis San Francisco Auckland Bogotá Hamburg
Johannesburg London Madrid Mexico Montreal New Delhi
Panama Paris São Paulo Singapore Sydney Tokyo Toronto

The SPSS® Batch System is distributed by

SPSS Inc.
Suite 3300
444 North Michigan Avenue
Chicago, Illinois 60611

Other SPSS Inc. Titles from McGraw-Hill Book Company:

SPSS, Second Edition
SPSS Update 7-9
SPSS Pocket Guide, Release 9
SPSS Primer

SPSS-11: The SPSS® Batch System for the DEC PDP-11®

SCSS: A Guide to the SCSS™ Conversational System
SCSS Short Guide: An Introduction to the SCSS™ Conversational System

IDA: A User's Guide to the IDA™ Interactive Data Analysis and Forecasting System

Please contact the Marketing Department of SPSS Inc. for information about the SPSS Batch System, the SPSS-11 System, the SCSS Conversational System, and the IDA Interactive Data Analysis and Forecasting System.

SPSS Inc.
Suite 3300
444 North Michigan Avenue
Chicago, Illinois 60611
(312) 329-2400

1234567890 SMSM 8987654321

ISBN 0-07-047528-8

This book was set in Times Roman by SPSS Inc. with the cooperation of Black Dot, Inc.

Library of Congress Catalog Card No.: 81-83771

Contents

Chapter 10   Statistical Models for Salary: Multiple Linear Regression Analysis   91

Preface

Through and through the world is infested with quantity: To talk sense is to talk quantities. It is no use saying the nation is large—How large? It is no use saying that radium is scarce—How scarce? You cannot evade quantity. You may fly to poetry and music, and quantity and number will face you in your rhythms and your octaves.

—Alfred North Whitehead

Quantity is as inescapable today as it was in Whitehead's time. Even those outside technical professions face a plethora of numbers when they look at a newspaper. The purpose of data analysis is to make it easier to deal with quantity—to simplify and summarize data and to illuminate patterns that are not immediately evident. This manual describes the SPSS Batch System, a computer program that can systematically handle the various components of data analysis.

The SPSS®System. Since 1969, the SPSS Batch System has enjoyed wide popularity as a tool for data analysis. A broad range of statistical analyses and data modification tasks are accomplished with a simple, English-like language. Results can be easily obtained with only minimal understanding of computer intricacies. This book is intended for novice users of the system and focuses on only the simple, most commonly used features and procedures:

- Frequency distributions and bar charts
- Descriptive statistics
- Crosstabulation and measures of association
- Descriptions of subpopulations
- Tests for equality of two means
- Scattergrams and correlations
- Oneway and multiway analysis of variance
- Nonparametric correlations and tests
- Bivariate and multiple regression

SPSS Graphics produced the pie, bar, and line charts in various chapters, but the operations of the graphics procedures are outside the scope of this manual. Some other procedures for tabulating and analyzing data that are available in the SPSS system but are not described here are

- Tabulation of multiple-response data
- Partial and canonical correlation
- Multivariate analysis of variance
- Discriminant analysis
- Factor analysis
- Survival analysis
- Box-Jenkins time series analysis
- Report writing

Similarly, while this text includes instructions for entering and defining data for analysis, for managing data files, and for transforming, selecting, sampling, and weighting data, it does not attempt to cover the full range of data and file management facilities available in SPSS. For those who want to extend their use of the system beyond the scope of this introduction, documentation can be found in *SPSS*, Second Edition, and *SPSS Update 7-9*, both published by McGraw-Hill Book Company. The computational methods used are described in *SPSS Statistical Algorithms*, available from SPSS, Inc. But the system and its documentation are continually being extended. Before obtaining other manuals, check with your computation center for information about the current release of SPSS being used there and the documentation for that release.

Using this text.   Although it is not meant to be a statistics text, this manual may be a useful supplement in courses that integrate the teaching of statistics and computing. Each chapter features a statistical problem and the SPSS output useful for its solution, followed by detailed information about the SPSS commands needed to obtain the analysis. Examples are taken from research papers in various disciplines. Published data were sufficient for the analyses except in Chapters 5 and 7, which required group variances not given in the original papers. For these examples, variances consistent with the published results were used. The data for Chapters 4, 10, and 11, and for the exercises in Appendix A, are available on the SPSS Batch System distribution tape. Consult your local installation staff for access.

The last chapter contains an extended example that reviews and summarizes many of the commands described in the previous chapters and also introduces some new features. This chapter should be consulted whenever more information about commands is desired. A summary of the syntax of SPSS commands presented in the text is given in Appendix B as a convenient reference guide.

Acknowledgments.   Most of the SPSS Inc. staff have participated either in the design and preparation of this manual or in creating and maintaining the system it documents. In particular, Keith Sours and Nancy Morrison wrote the operations sections and Chapter 11, Sue Shott assisted in the search for examples and in preparation of exercises, and Bob Gruen edited the text and saw it through production.

I am also grateful to Harry Roberts for many thoughtful comments and for permission to use and distribute the data file for exercises. Kenneth J. Barry, Kenneth Berk, Michael D. Biderman, and James S. Ford also reviewed the manuscript and offered useful suggestions. Finally, I wish to thank Rasa, Irena, and Linas, who provide copious advice for all aspects of my life.

—Marija J. Norušis

Chapter 1

Blue Mondays:
Data Entry and Tabulation

Although few people would dispute the effects of "rainy days and Mondays" on the body and spirit, only a limited number of scientific studies have investigated this relationship. A recently published paper (Rabkin et al., 1980) presents data that can be used to test hypotheses about the hazards of Mondays. These data, collected as part of the Manitoba Follow Up Study, established the day of the week for each of 152 cardiac deaths and whether the victim had a history of heart disease.

1.1 A FREQUENCY TABLE

A first step in analyzing the cardiac death data might be to count the number of deaths occurring on each day of the week. Figure 1.1 contains this information.

Figure 1.1 Frequency of cardiac death by day of the week

```
DAY        DAY OF THE WEEK
                                        RELATIVE  ADJUSTED    CUM
                              ABSOLUTE    FREQ       FREQ     FREQ
CATEGORY LABEL        CODE      FREQ      (PCT)     (PCT)    (PCT)
MONDAY                1.         38       23.5       25.0     25.0
TUESDAY               2.         17       10.5       11.2     36.2
WEDNESDAY             3.         16        9.9       10.5     46.7
THURSDAY              4.         29       17.9       19.1     65.8
FRIDAY                5.         15        9.3        9.9     75.7
SATURDAY              6.         17       10.5       11.2     86.8
SUNDAY                7.         20       12.3       13.2    100.0
UNKNOWN               9.         10        6.2      MISSING  100.0
                               _____    _____    _____
              TOTAL            162       100.0      100.0

VALID CASES    152    MISSING CASES    10
```

Each row of the frequency table describes a particular day of the week. The last row represents deaths for which the day of death is not known. (The original study had no cases with an unknown day of death; ten cases have been added here to illustrate missing data.) The first column *(category label)* gives the name of the day, while the second column contains the *code*, which is the symbol given to the computer to represent the day.

The number of people dying on each day is in column three *(absolute frequency)*. Monday is the most frequent death day with 38 of the deaths. These 38 deaths are 23.5%

(38/162) of all deaths. This *relative frequency* is in the fourth column. However, of the 162 people, 10 had an unknown day of death. The 38 deaths on Monday are 25.0% of the total deaths for which death dates are known (38/152). This *adjusted frequency* is in the fifth column.

The last column of the table contains the cumulative percentage. For a particular day, it is the sum of the adjusted percentages of that day and all other days that precede it in the table. For example, the cumulative percentage for Wednesday is 46.7. This is the percentage of cardiac deaths that occur on Monday, Tuesday, or Wednesday. It is calculated as

$$\frac{38}{152} + \frac{17}{152} + \frac{16}{152} = \frac{71}{152} = 46.7\%$$

1.2   Visual Displays

While the frequency table presents numbers that can be studied and compared, it is often useful to present results in a visually interpretable manner. Figure 1.2a is a pie chart of the data displayed in the previous frequency table. Each slice represents a day of the week. The size of the slice depends on the frequency of cardiac death for that day. One quarter of the pie (25%) represents Monday, since 25% of the deaths for which the day is known occurred on Monday.

Figure 1.2a   Frequency of cardiac death by day of the week (Pie chart from SPSS Graphics)

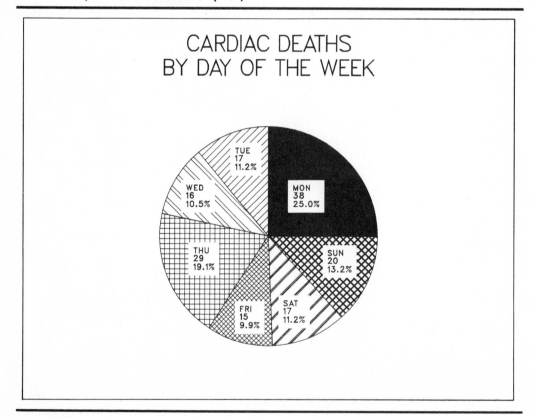

Another way of representing the data is with a bar chart, as shown in Figure 1.2b. Each line of asterisks corresponds to a day, and the length of the line is determined by the number of deaths observed on that day. The number of cases occurring on each day is given in parentheses.

Figure 1.2b   Frequency of cardiac death by day of the week
(Bar chart from SPSS procedure FREQUENCIES)

```
DAY        DAY OF THE WEEK

     CODE
          I
       1. ***************************************** (     38)
          I  MONDAY
          I
       2. ***************** (     17)
          I  TUESDAY
          I
       3. **************** (     16)
          I  WEDNESDAY
          I
       4. ***************************** (     29)
          I  THURSDAY
          I
       5. *************** (     15)
          I  FRIDAY
          I
       6. ***************** (     17)
          I  SATURDAY
          I
       7. ******************* (     20)
          I  SUNDAY
          I
          I........I.........I.........I.........I.........I
          0        10        20        30        40        50
          FREQUENCY

VALID CASES     152      MISSING CASES     10
```

Only values that actually occur in the data are represented in the bar chart from procedure FREQUENCIES. For example, if no deaths took place on Thursday, no space would be left for Thursday and the bar for Wednesday would be followed by the one for Friday. If numbers of cars per family are charted, it is possible for the line describing 6 cars and the one for 25 cars to be next to each other if no family had 7 to 24 cars. Therefore, you should pay attention to where categories with no cases may occur.

Although the basic information presented by frequency tables, pie charts, and bar charts is the same, the visual displays enliven the data. Differences among the days of the week are apparent at a glance, eliminating the need to pore over columns of numbers.

1.3   Why Monday?

The data displayed in the frequency table seem to support the notion that Monday is a notably hazardous day for cardiac death. Only Thursday approaches it in frequency of deaths.

When the cases are further subdivided according to whether or not they showed history of heart disease, additional interesting differences are found (see Figure 1.3). For people with a history of heart disease, only 18% of deaths occurred on Monday. If deaths were randomly distributed throughout the week, about 14% would be expected on any day. Thus, for people with previous heart problems, Monday is not particularly unusual. But for those with no previous history, 35% of the deaths were on Monday, 2 1/2 times the number expected. See Chapter 9 for further analysis of these data.

One possible explanation for the findings is that Mondays augur return to occupational anxieties, activity, and pollutants, factors that are stressful and may precipitate sudden death. Another, less intuitive, explanation is that neurophysiological function may have a seven-day cycle, with Mondays being a high or low. But one should be wary of explanations that are not directly supported by data. It is only too easy to find a clever rationalization for any statistical finding.

Figure 1.3   Cardiac death for day of week categorized by history of heart disease
(Bar chart from SPSS Graphics)

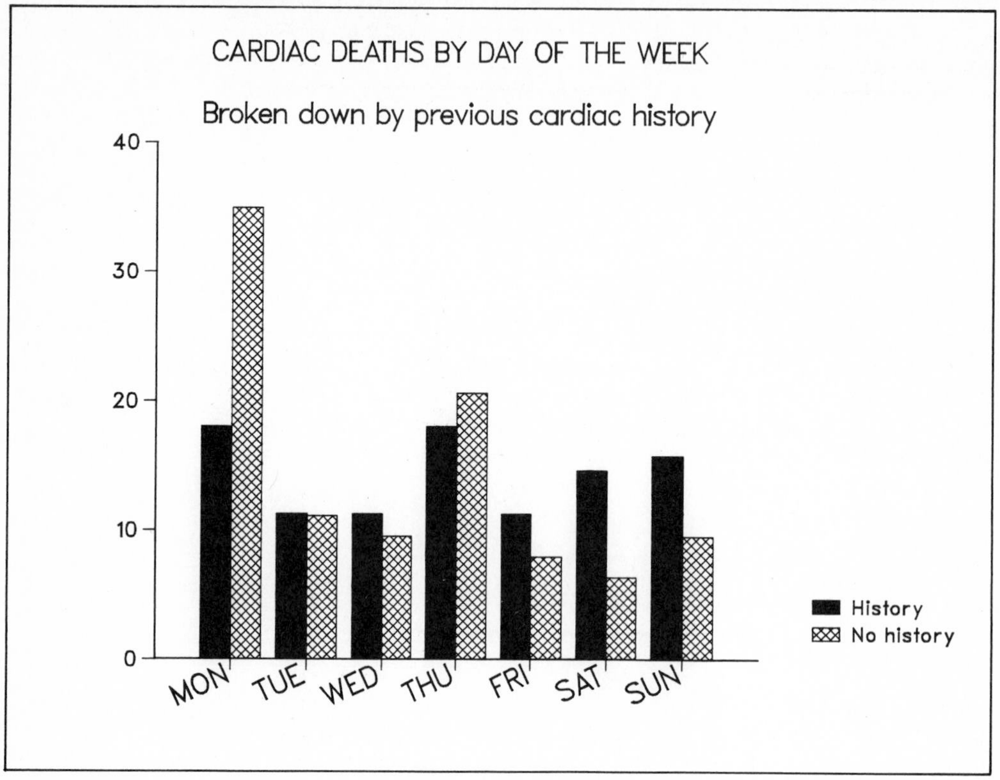

1.4   FROM PAPER INTO THE MACHINE

In order to easily tabulate the number of deaths on each day of the week and to pursue other types of analysis, the information on each death must be entered into the computer. Table 1.4 contains a facsimile of what the original data for the first six deaths might look like. Each line of the table is a *case* or *observation*. It contains measurements or *values* for a specific set of *variables*. For the first case, the value of the age variable is 54 and the value of the day variable is Monday. Each case has one and only one value for a particular variable. Note that "unknown" (or "missing") is an acceptable value for a variable, though it requires special treatment in analysis.

Table 1.4   Uncoded Data

ID	AGE	DAY	PREVIOUS HISTORY
1	54	Monday	Unknown
2	68	Saturday	Yes
3	73	Tuesday	No
4	85	Wednesday	No
5	66	Unknown	No
6	47	Thursday	Yes

The case is the basic unit for which measurements are taken. In this analysis, the case is a cardiac death. In studies of political opinion or brand preference, the case is most likely the individual respondent to a questionnaire. A case may be a larger unit such as a school, county, or nation; it may be a time period, such as a year or month in which measurements are obtained; or it may be an event such as an auto accident.

For any single analysis, the cases must be the same. If the unit of analysis is a county, all cases are counties, and the values of each variable are for individual counties. If the unit is a state, then all cases are states and the values of each variable are for states.

1.5   Preparing Data for Input

To enter observations into the computer, the values of the variables for each case must be typed using special machines and a special format.

One of the simplest ways to lighten the burden of data entry is to assign a number to represent each unique response. You can substantially decrease the number of symbols to be typed, especially for variables whose values are originally recorded as words (such as YES or NO), not numbers. For example, instead of typing the day of death for each case, you might use the coding scheme in Table 1.5.

Table 1.5   Coding scheme for day of the week

1=Monday	5=Friday
2=Tuesday	6=Saturday
3=Wednesday	7=Sunday
4=Thursday	9=Unknown

This coding scheme, and many others, is arbitrary. Any day can be designated as 1. Even the choice of the number 1 as a starting point is arbitrary; the coding symbols can just as well be the numbers 0 through 7 or any other eight unique numbers or letters. If you chose numbers, then the coding scheme is said to be *numeric*. If you choose letters or a mixture of numbers, letters, and special symbols, the codes are *alphanumeric*. In this example, a numeric coding scheme makes sense since choosing the first letter of each weekday leads to duplicates for Tuesday and Thursday and for Saturday and Sunday.

The values of the variable recording previous history of disease can also be easily coded. Two natural coding schemes are 0=None, 1=Yes, 9=Unknown or N=No, Y=Yes, U=Unknown. The latter scheme is chosen here to illustrate alphanumeric codes.

It is usually helpful to have at least one variable that uniquely identifies each case in the file. For the cardiac death data, that variable could be the name of each individual. But, since names are generally lengthy and not always unique, each case in this file is assigned an ID number.

Coding schemes should be selected carefully to insure that potentially useful information is not eliminated. For example, if one were planning to classify cardiac death victims according to those under age sixty and those sixty or over, it might be tempting to enter just two age values, one for the younger group, one for the older group. However, reasonable as this may be, it precludes subsequent regroupings. That is, it will not be possible to classify the cases into any other age categories without going back to the uncoded original values. Therefore it is a good idea to enter the actual age values and use the recoding capabilities available in SPSS to form age categories. Then none of the age information is lost. In general, data should be recorded and entered in as much detail as possible. The computer can always be used subsequently to classify responses into categories.

1.6 Recording the Data

The same first six cases in their coded format are shown in Table 1.6.

Table 1.6 Coded data

ID	AGE	DAY	PREVIOUS HISTORY
1	54	1	U
2	68	6	Y
3	73	2	N
4	85	3	N
5	66	9	N
6	47	4	Y

The data must now be placed on a computer-readable (known as *machine-readable*) medium. Data that can be read by a computer are stored on punched cards or as lines of data entered at a terminal and written onto a disk or tape. Each card or each line of machine-readable information is known as a *record*. Records in the form of cards have a maximum length of 80 columns. This historical restriction and the width of most terminal screens have dictated a tradition of reasonably short records even when the data are recorded on disk or tape which have fewer length limitations. Since there are only four variables in this example, all the information for a case can be stored on a single short record (multiple cases cannot go on the same record).

Each number or character is stored in a designated *column* on a record. Figure 1.6 shows the columns in which the cardiac data are recorded. The identification number is placed in columns 1 through 3. Three columns are used because there are more than one hundred cases. If the ID number is less than 100, leading zeros or blanks are used so that the last digit of the ID variable always occupies column three (that is, the data are right-justified in the columns). This is known as *fixed-column* format.

Column 4 is blank in this example to make for easier reading. Age occupies three columns to allow for centenarians and goes into columns 5-7. After age, a column is skipped and day of death goes into column 9. Finally, another column is skipped and history of heart disease goes into column 11.

Figure 1.6 Partial data file listing

```
12345678901   ◊ COLUMN INDEX (Not included in data file)

001 054 1 U
002 068 6 Y
003 073 2 N
004 085 3 N
005 066 9 N
006 047 4 Y
```

The selection of columns is arbitrary and is chosen for convenience. However, once the columns are chosen, the information for a particular variable is always kept in the same column(s). SPSS requires you to name the variable and to use that name instead of the original column location to refer to the data throughout the analysis.

When cases are written on machine-readable records, a *data file* is created. A data file is simply a collection of records with information stored the same way on each record.

1.7 Screening Data

A frequency table can serve purposes other than summarizing data. Unexpected codes in the table may indicate errors in data entry or coding. Cases with death dates coded as 0 or 8 are in error if the numbers 1 through 7 represent the days of the week and 9 stands for unknown. Since errors in the data should be eliminated as soon as possible, it is a good idea to run frequency tables as the first step in analyzing data.

Cases with values that are unusual but possibly correct can also be identified. For example, a tally of the number of cars in families may show a family with 25 cars. Although this is possible, especially if the survey didn't specify cars in working condition, it raises suspicion and should be examined to insure that the value is really correct.

Incorrect data values distort the results of statistical analyses, and correct but unusual values may require special treatment. Early identification of either is valuable.

1.8 Grouping Values for Tabulation

A frequency table of all values of a variable is a convenient way of summarizing a variable that has a relatively small number of distinct values. Variables such as sex, country, and astrological sign are necessarily limited in the number of values they can have. For variables that can take on many different values, such as income to the penny or weight in ounces, a tally of the cases with each observed value may not be very informative. In the worst situation, when all cases have different values, a frequency table is little more than an ordered list of those values.

To summarize variables that take on a large number of values, group them into intervals. For example, income can be collapsed into $5000 categories such as 0-4999, 5000-9999, 10,000-14,999, etc. (see Chapter 11 for the SPSS commands needed). Tabulating of the number of cases in each grouped category results in a more useful table.

1.9 THE SPSS JOB

Once the data file is created, you can create a set of commands telling SPSS what to do with the data, place those commands before the data file, and run a *job*. The SPSS job that was used to create Figure 1.1 is shown in Figure 1.9. Figure 1.9 does not include the machine-specific control commands used to access SPSS at your particular computer installation. Although these job control statements or operating system commands are very simple, you will have to contact somebody at your computer installation to learn how to access SPSS.

All SPSS jobs require two files: the data discussed in previous sections and the *command file*. The command file consists of SPSS commands entered into the computer either as cards or lines of input at a terminal in the same manner as data are entered. These commands declare the names variables will be known by, indicate where the information about a variable is located, specify whether to ignore a case if a variable has a certain value, assign a short label to a variable and to values for a variable, identify the type of statistical analysis to be performed, and tell SPSS when to start reading the data file. The commands must be entered in a sequence such that the computer always has the information needed to process the next command.

If you run a job using punched cards, or using commands and data in the same disk file, then the two files are essentially one, as is shown in Figure 1.9. However, the command file and data file are frequently stored in different locations. For a discussion of separate data files, see Chapter 11.

Figure 1.9   Sample SPSS job

```
DATA LIST         FIXED (1)/1 ID 1-3 AGE 5-7 DAY 9 HISTORY 11 (A)
N OF CASES        162
VAR LABELS        ID, CASE NUMBER/
                  AGE, AGE AT DEATH/
                  DAY, DAY OF THE WEEK/
                  HISTORY, HISTORY OF HEART DISEASE/
VALUE LABELS      DAY (1) MONDAY (2) TUESDAY (3) WEDNESDAY (4) THURSDAY
                      (5) FRIDAY (6) SATURDAY (7) SUNDAY (9) UNKNOWN/
                  HISTORY ('Y') PREVIOUS HISTORY ('N') NO HISTORY
                      ('U') UNKNOWN/
MISSING VALUES    DAY(9)/HISTORY('U')
PRINT FORMATS     HISTORY(A)
FREQUENCIES       GENERAL=DAY
READ INPUT DATA
001 054 1 U
002 068 6 Y
003 073 2 N
004 085 3 N
005 066 9 N
006 047 4 Y
... ...  . .
... ...  . .
... ...  . .
162 082 1 Y
FINISH
```

Each SPSS command is identified by a keyword that always begins in the first column of the input line. Following is a brief summary of the commands used in the job shown in Figure 1.9.

DATA LIST   Tells SPSS the names of the variables and the columns they occupy on a record. Keyword FIXED tells SPSS that the data values are always in the same location, and (1)/1 means there is one record per case. If the variable is alphanumeric, you must inform SPSS by following the column specifications with an A in parentheses. For example, variable HISTORY is read from column 11 on each record and is alphanumeric.

N OF CASES   Tells SPSS how many cases to expect. For Figure 1.1, SPSS is told to read 162 cases.

VAR LABELS   Gives a label of up to 40 characters to specified variables. DAY OF THE WEEK is a label for variable DAY. The variable name must be first, followed by one or more blanks or commas and the label, and is terminated with a slash (/).

VALUE LABELS   Associates a label of up to 20 characters with each value of a variable. The coding scheme for DAY in Table 1.5 is identified to SPSS in this command, with the value or code in parentheses followed by the label. A slash indicates that all the labels for one variable have been assigned. Note that the alphanumeric values for variable HISTORY are enclosed in apostrophes.

MISSING VALUES   Tells SPSS to flag the information as missing for a case when a 9 is encountered for DAY or a U is encountered for HISTORY. Note again that the slash terminates specifications for a variable.

PRINT FORMATS   Tells SPSS that you want the variable's values to be printed in a specific way. This specification reminds SPSS that variable HISTORY has alphanumeric values, not numeric values as SPSS generally assumes.

FREQUENCIES   Analyzes the data and generates the output in Figure 1.1. See the discussion beginning in Section 1.11 for information on how to run procedure FREQUENCIES.

READ INPUT DATA   Tells SPSS to begin reading the data. The lines of data immediately follow this command.

FINISH   Ends the SPSS run.

FREQUENCIES is known as a *procedure* since it takes the data you have defined and performs the analyses. Procedure commands must follow most other SPSS commands since they depend on the data being properly defined and labeled. The READ INPUT DATA command must immediately follow the first procedure command in an SPSS command file. For want of a better term, the commands other than FREQUENCIES shown in this example are known as *nonprocedure* commands. Other SPSS nonprocedure commands are discussed in the procedure chapters that follow, and a more complete summary is found in Chapter 11. The order of SPSS commands is described in Appendix B.

1.10   SPSS COMMAND STRUCTURE AND SYNTAX

An SPSS command line is subdivided into two components called *fields*. The first field occupies columns 1-15 and is called the *command field*. The second field occupies columns 16-80 and is called the *specification field*. You can continue a specification field by leaving columns 1-15 on the next line blank. However, variable names and SPSS command words *(keywords)* cannot be continued from one line to another. Continuation command lines make your SPSS command file more readable and less prone to error.

Consider the first line in Figure 1.9. DATA LIST is a command, and FIXED (1)/1 ID 1-3, begins the specification. The command DATA LIST must start in column 1, and the keywords DATA and LIST must be separated by a single blank.

A specification field can never start before column 16. But syntax requirements for the specifications are not as restrictive as for the command field. You can begin the specification field beyond column 16 and you can use the blank or comma to make the specifications more readable. The only restriction is that you insert at least one of these *delimiters* between specification elements (keywords, numbers, etc.) wherever SPSS might not be able to distinguish one from another. For example, DAY 9 tells SPSS that variable DAY is in column 9, but DAY9 is a valid variable name and SPSS has no way of knowing that you mean something else. Multiple blanks in a specification field are treated as single blanks. Thus, an alternative to the DATA LIST command in Figure 1.9 is

```
DATA LIST        FIXED (1)/1 ID       1-3,
                            AGE       5-7,
                            DAY         9,
                            HISTORY  11(A)
```

Names and Labels.   *Variable names* are composed of letters and/or numbers up to a maximum of eight characters and must begin with a letter. SALARY, VOTE81, X, and Q0001 are valid variable names; 1981, TREATMENT, and @DATE are not. You should choose variable names that describe the variable and are easy to remember because if you misspell a variable name, SPSS won't be able to recognize it as the same variable. Variable and value *labels* can be composed of any characters.

Delimiters.   *Common delimiters*—commas and blanks—can be inserted into specifications to improve legibility. *Special delimiters*—parentheses, slashes, and equals signs—must be specified exactly as they appear in the SPSS instructions. SPSS *keywords* must be spelled exactly as they appear in the instructions. *Alphanumeric values* must be enclosed in apostrophes when they appear in an SPSS command line.

Defaults.   For many specifications within SPSS, there are *defaults*, which are instructions SPSS assumes when you specify nothing. For example, the (1) specification following the FIXED keyword on the DATA LIST command means that you have one record per case. If you have more than one record per case, you must put that number in parentheses as shown. However, if you have only one record per case, you can leave this specification off and SPSS will assume that (1) is the intended specification.

1.11   RUNNING PROCEDURE FREQUENCIES

Procedure FREQUENCIES produces frequency tables, bar charts, and related statistics for numeric and alphanumeric variables.

Procedure FREQUENCIES requires only the GENERAL= subcommand to name the variables to be analyzed. Options are provided for handling missing values, reformatting tables, and printing bar charts. SPSS also prints eleven optional statistics including the measures of central tendency, dispersion, and shape described in Sections 2.11 through 2.13.

1.12   The GENERAL= Subcommand

Enter the command keyword FREQUENCIES beginning in column 1 and begin the GENERAL= subcommand keyword in column 16 or beyond. For example, to produce the table for the day of death variable discussed in this chapter, specify

```
FREQUENCIES     GENERAL=DAY
```

If you want more than one table, you can specify more than one variable, as in

```
FREQUENCIES     GENERAL=DAY,HISTORY
```

1.13   The OPTIONS Command for FREQUENCIES

Following your FREQUENCIES command specifications, you can enter the OPTIONS command keyword beginning in column 1 and a list of option numbers beginning in column 16 or beyond. These numbers correspond to content and format options for your tables. The following is a list of the most commonly used options; a complete list is found in Appendix B.

OPTION 1   Include cases with missing values.
OPTION 3   Limit output width to approximately 8 1/2 inches.
OPTION 5   Print tables in condensed format (see Figure 2.1b).
OPTION 7   Do not print frequency tables.
OPTION 8   Print a bar chart for each variable.
OPTION 10   Print tables in descending order of values.
OPTION 11   Print tables in descending order of frequency.
OPTION 12   Print tables in ascending order of frequency.

By default, FREQUENCIES prints the values in tables and bar charts in lowest to highest order of values. Option 10 reverses that order to highest to lowest. Option 11 orders the tables and bar charts based on the highest to lowest frequency of the values rather than the values themselves, and Option 12 orders them based on lowest to highest frequency.

1.14   Missing Values in Tables and Statistics

By default, SPSS includes cases with missing values in the frequency table, reports them as missing, and excludes them when calculating the cumulative percentage and statistics. Option 1 tells FREQUENCIES to ignore the missing-value status of any values. It should be used when you want frequencies for missing values included in a bar chart.

1.15   Bar Charts

Option 8 requests a bar chart for each variable. To request the bar chart shown in Figure 1.2b, specify

```
FREQUENCIES     GENERAL=DAY
OPTIONS         8
```

Use Option 7 to suppress the frequency tables if you want only bar charts or the statistics listed in Section 1.16.

1.16   The STATISTICS Command for FREQUENCIES

By default, FREQUENCIES prints only the tables. If you want statistics, enter the STATISTICS command keyword in column 1, followed by a list of numbers or the keyword ALL beginning in column 16 or beyond and corresponding to the desired statistics. The numbers in parentheses in the following list are the sections in Chapter 2 where the statistics are discussed.

STATISTIC 1	Mean (2.11)
STATISTIC 2	Standard error (2.15)
STATISTIC 3	Median (2.11)
STATISTIC 4	Mode (2.11)
STATISTIC 5	Standard deviation (2.12)
STATISTIC 6	Variance (2.12)
STATISTIC 7	Kurtosis (2.13)
STATISTIC 8	Skewness (2.13)
STATISTIC 9	Range (2.12)
STATISTIC 10	Minimum (2.12)
STATISTIC 11	Maximum (2.12)
ALL	All statistics

Chapter 2

Telling the Whole Truth
and Nothing But:
Descriptive Statistics

Survey data that rely on voluntary information are subject to many sources of error. People deliberately distort the truth, inadvertently fail to recall events correctly, or refuse to participate. Refusals influence survey results by failing to provide information about a particular type of person—one who refuses to answer surveys at all or avoids certain types of questions. For example, if college graduates tend to be unwilling to be bothered by pollsters, results of surveys will be biased.

One possible way to examine the veracity of responses is to compare them to official records. Systematic differences between the two sources jeopardize the usefulness of the survey. Unfortunately, for many sensitive questions such as illicit drug use, abortion history, or even income, official records are usually unavailable.

Wyner (1980) examined the differences between the true and self-reported numbers of arrests obtained from 79 former heroin addicts enrolled in the Vera Institute of Justice Supported Employment Experiment. As part of their regular quarterly interviews, participants were asked about their arrest histories in New York City. The self-reported value was compared to arrest record data coded from New York City Police Department arrest sheets. The goal of the study was not only to quantify the extent of error but also to identify factors related to inaccurate responses.

2.1 EXAMINING THE DATA

Figure 2.1a shows bar charts for the three variables—true number of arrests, reported arrests, and the discrepancy between the two. From a bar chart it is possible to see the *shape* of the distribution, that is how likely the different values are, how much spread or *variability* there is among the values, and typical values or *measures of central tendency*. Such characteristics are important because of the direct insight they provide into the data and because many statistical procedures are based on assumptions about the underlying distributions of variables.

Figure 2.1a   Reported and true arrests
(Bar charts from SPSS Graphics)

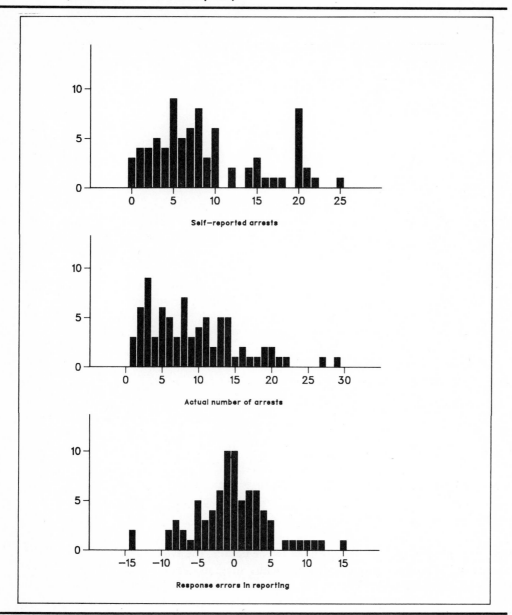

The distributions of the reported and true number of arrests have a similar shape. Most participants have 15 or fewer arrests. The distributions are fairly flat, without an obvious central value or concentration of values. The distribution of self-reported values has a peak at 20 arrests, while the true number of arrests has a somewhat longer right tail due to the cases with 27 and 29 arrests. The reported arrest values have more peaks than do the true arrest data. The peaks at 5, 10, and 20 arrests arouse the suspicion that people are likely to report their arrest records to round numbers. Examination of the true arrest records shows no corresponding peaks at multiples of 5 and supports the hypothesis that people report round numbers. The most frequently occurring value in the self-report distribution is 5; in the true distribution it is 3.

Figure 2.1b Error in reported arrests
(Condensed frequency table from SPSS procedure FREQUENCIES)

ERRORS   REPORTED ARRESTS MINUS ACTUAL ARRESTS

CODE	FREQ	ADJ PCT	CUM PCT	CODE	FREQ	ADJ PCT	CUM PCT	CODE	FREQ	ADJ PCT	CUM PCT
-14.	2	3	3	-2.	6	8	35	7.	1	1	92
-9.	2	3	5	-1.	10	13	48	8.	1	1	94
-8.	3	4	9	0.	10	13	61	9.	1	1	95
-7.	2	3	11	1.	5	6	67	10.	1	1	96
-6.	1	1	13	2.	6	8	75	11.	1	1	97
-5.	5	6	19	3.	6	8	82	12.	1	1	99
-4.	3	4	23	4.	4	5	87	15.	1	1	100
-3.	4	5	28	5.	3	4	91				

VALID CASES   79   MISSING CASES   0

The distribution of the differences between reported and true number of arrests is not as irregularly shaped as the two distributions from which it is derived. It has two adjacent peak values, -1 and 0. Most cases cluster around the peak values with cases far from these values being infrequent. Figure 2.1b is a condensed frequency table for the response errors (the adjusted and cumulative percents are rounded to the nearest integer). Almost 47% of the sample (37 cases) reported their arrest record to within two arrests of the true value. Only 22% (17 cases) misrepresented their records by more than 5 arrests. Underreporting is somewhat more likely than exaggeration, with 39% of the cases overestimating and 48% of the cases underestimating.

2.2 THE NORMAL DISTRIBUTION

For many variables, most observations are concentrated near the middle of the distribution, and as distance from the central concentration increases, the frequency of observation decreases. Such distributions are often described as "bell-shaped." An example is the *normal* distribution (see Figure 2.2). A broad range of observed phenomena in nature and in society are approximately normally distributed. For example, variables such as height, weight, and blood pressure are approximately normally distributed. The normal distribution is by far the most important theoretical distribution in statistics and serves as a reference point for describing the form of many distributions of sample data.

The normal distribution is symmetric: when it is folded in the center, the two sides are identical. Three measures of central tendency—the mean, median, and mode (Section 2.11)—coincide exactly. As shown in Figure 2.2, 95% of all observations fall within two standard deviations (σ) of the mean (μ), and 68% within one standard deviation. The exact theoretical proportion of cases falling into various regions of the normal curve can be found in tables given in most introductory statistics textbooks.

Figure 2.2 A normal curve

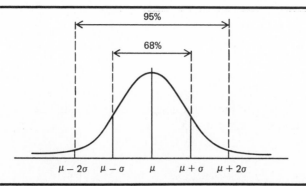

2.3 SUMMARIZING THE DATA

Although frequency tables and bar charts (Chapter 1) are a useful way of summarizing and displaying data, further condensation and description is often desirable. A variety of summary measures that convey information about the data in single numbers can be computed. The choice of summary measure, or *statistic*, as it is often called, depends upon characteristics of the data as well as of the statistic. One important characteristic of the data that must be considered is the *level of measurement* of each variable being studied.

2.4 LEVELS OF MEASUREMENT

Measurement is the assignment of numbers or codes to observations. Levels of measurement are distinguished by ordering and distance properties. A computer does not know what measurement underlies the values it is given. You must determine the level of measurement of your data and apply appropriate statistical techniques.

The traditional classification of levels of measurement into nominal, ordinal, interval, and ratio was developed by S. S. Stevens (1946). This remains the basic typology and is the one used throughout this manual. Variations exist, however, and issues concerning the statistical effect of ignoring levels of measurement are debated. See, for example, Borgatta and Bohrnstedt (1980).

2.5 Nominal Measurement

The nominal level of measurement is the "lowest" in the typology because no assumptions are made about relations between the values being assigned. Each value defines a distinct category and serves merely as a label or name (hence, "nominal" level) for the category. For instance, the birthplace of an individual is a nominal variable. For most purposes, there is no inherent ordering among cities or towns. Although cities can be ordered according to size, density, or air pollution, a city thought of as "place of birth" is a concept that is normally not tied to any order. When numeric values are attached to nominal categories, they are merely identifiers. None of the properties of numbers such as relative size, addition, or multiplication, can be applied to these numerically coded categories. Therefore, statistics that assume ordering or meaningful numerical distances between the values do not ordinarily give useful information.

2.6 Ordinal Measurement

When it is possible to rank or order all categories according to some criterion, the ordinal level of measurement is achieved. For instance, classification of employees as clerical, supervisory, and managerial is an ordering according to responsibilities or skills. Each category has a position lower or higher than another category. Furthermore, knowing that supervisory is higher than clerical and that managerial is higher than supervisory automatically means that managerial is higher than clerical. However, nothing is known about how much higher; no distance is measured. Ordering is the sole mathematical property applicable to ordinal measurements, and the use of numeric values does not imply that any other property of numbers is applicable.

2.7 Interval Measurement

In addition to order, interval measurements have the property that distance between values is meaningful. A thermometer, for example, measures temperature in degrees which are the same size at any point on the scale. The difference between 20 and 21°C is the same as the difference between 5 and 6°C. However, an interval scale does not have an inherently determined zero point. In the familiar Celsius and Fahrenheit systems, 0° is determined by an agreed-upon definition, not by the absence of heat. Consequently, interval-level measurement allows us to study differences between items but not their proportionate magnitudes. That is, it is incorrect to say that an 80°F day is twice as hot as a 40°F day.

2.8   Ratio Measurement

Ratio measurements have all the ordering and distance properties of an interval scale. In addition, a zero point can be meaningfully designated. In measuring physical distances between objects using feet or meters, a zero distance is naturally defined as the absence of any distance. The existence of a zero point means that ratio comparisons can be made. For example, it is quite meaningful to say that a 6-foot-tall adult is twice as tall as a 3-foot-tall child or that a 500-meter race is five times as long as a 100-meter race.

Because ratio measurements satisfy all the properties of the real number system, any mathematical manipulations appropriate for real numbers can be applied to ratio measures. However, the existence of a zero point is seldom critical for statistical analyses.

2.9   The Special Case of Dichotomies

A *dichotomous* variable has only two possible categories or values, such as sex. While some dichotomies are based on a natural ordering (pass or fail), many are not (male or female). Yet a dichotomy can be treated as an ordinal measure. Although a rank may not be inherent, either order of the categories satisfies mathematical requirements. The requirements of a distance measure based on equal-sized intervals is also satisfied because there is only one interval. Consequently, a dichotomy can be treated as a nominal, ordinal, or interval measurement, depending upon the research situation.

2.10   SUMMARY STATISTICS

Figure 2.10 contains a variety of summary statistics that are useful in describing the distributions of reported arrests, true number of arrests, and the discrepancy. The statistics can be grouped into three categories according to what they quantify: central tendency, dispersion, and shape.

Figure 2.10   Statistics describing arrest data

```
VARIABLE   TRUE       ACTUAL NUMBER OF ARRESTS

MEAN            9.253                   STD ERROR       0.703          STD DEV         6.248
VARIANCE       39.038                   KURTOSIS        0.597          SKEWNESS        0.908
RANGE          28.000                   MINIMUM         1.000          MAXIMUM        29.000
SUM           731.000

VALID OBSERVATIONS -      79                       MISSING OBSERVATIONS -        0


- - - - - - - - - - - - - - - - - - - - - - - - - - - - - - - - - - - - - - - - - - - - -


VARIABLE   SELF       SELF-REPORTED ARRESTS

MEAN            8.962                   STD ERROR       0.727          STD DEV         6.458
VARIANCE       41.704                   KURTOSIS       -0.485          SKEWNESS        0.750
RANGE          25.000                   MINIMUM         0.0            MAXIMUM        25.000
SUM           708.000

VALID OBSERVATIONS -      79                       MISSING OBSERVATIONS -        0


- - - - - - - - - - - - - - - - - - - - - - - - - - - - - - - - - - - - - - - - - - - - -


VARIABLE   ERRORS     REPORTED ARRESTS MINUS ACTUAL ARRESTS

MEAN           -0.291                   STD ERROR       0.587          STD DEV         5.216
VARIANCE       27.209                   KURTOSIS        1.102          SKEWNESS        0.125
RANGE          29.000                   MINIMUM       -14.000          MAXIMUM        15.000
SUM           -23.000

VALID OBSERVATIONS -      79                       MISSING OBSERVATIONS -        0
```

2.11   Measures of Central Tendency

The mean, median, and mode are frequently used to describe the location of a distribution. The *mode* is the most frequently occurring value (or values). From Figure 2.1a, for the true number of arrests the mode is 3; for the self-reported values it is 5. The distribution of the difference between the true and self-reported values is multi-modal. That is, it has more than one mode since the values −1 and 0 occur with equal frequency. The mode can be used for data measured at any level. It is usually not the preferred measure for interval and ordinal data since it ignores much of the available information.

The *median* is a number above and below which one half of the observations fall. For example, if there are 79 observations the median is the 40th largest observation. When there is an even number of observations, no unique center value exists, so the mean of the two middle observations is usually taken as the median value. The median is 0 for the differences, 8 for the true arrests, and 7 for reported arrests. For ordinal data the median is usually a good measure of central tendency since it makes use of the ranking information. The median should not be used for nominal data since ranking of the observations is not possible. (See Section 2.19 for details on the computation of the median in SPSS.)

The *mean*, also called the arithmetic average, is the sum of the value of all observations divided by the number of observations. Thus

$$\bar{X} = \sum_{i=1}^{N} \frac{X_i}{N}$$

where N is the number of cases and X_i is the value of the variable for the ith case. Since the mean utilizes the distance between observations, the measurements should be interval or ratio. Mean race, religion, and auto color are meaningless.

The three measures of central tendency need not give the same answers. For example, the mean number of true arrests is 9.25 (from Figure 2.10). The median is 8, while the mode is 3. The arithmetic mean is greatly influenced by outlying observations, while the median is not. Adding a single case with 400 arrests would increase the mean from 9.25 to 14.1, but it would not affect the median. Therefore, if there are values far removed from the rest of the observations, the median may be a better measure of central tendency than the mean.

For symmetric distributions, the observed mean, median, and mode are usually close in value. The mean of the differences between reported and true arrest values is −0.291. The median is 0, and the modes are −1 and 0. All three measures give similar estimates of central tendency in this case.

2.12   Measures of Dispersion

Two distributions can have the same values for measures of central tendency yet be very dissimilar in other respects. For example, if the true number of arrests for five cases in two methadone clinics is

CLINIC A: 0, 1, 10, 14, 20
CLINIC B: 8, 8, 9, 10, 10

the mean number of arrests (9) is the same in both. However, even a cursory examination of the data indicates that the two clinics are different. In the second clinic, all cases have fairly comparable arrest records while in the first the records are quite disparate. A quick and useful index of dissimilarity, or dispersion, is the *range*. It is the difference between the *maximum* and *minimum* observed values. For clinic B the range is 2, while for clinic A it is 20. Since the range is computed only from the minimum and maximum values, it is sensitive to extreme values.

Although the range is a useful index of dispersion, especially for ordinal data, it does not take into account the distribution of observations between the maximum and minimum. A commonly used measure of variation that is based on all observations is the *variance*. For a sample, the variance is computed by summing the squared differences from the mean for all observations, and then dividing by one less than the number of observations. In mathematical notation this is

$$S^2 = \sum_{i=1}^{N} \frac{(X_i - \bar{X})^2}{N - 1}$$

If all observations are identical—that is, if there is no variation—the variance is 0. The more spread out they are, the greater the variance. For the methadone clinic example previously considered, the sample variance for clinic A is 73, while for clinic B it is 1.

The square root of the variance is termed the *standard deviation*. The standard deviation is expressed in the same units of measurement as the observations, while the variance is in the units squared. This is an appealing property since it is much clearer to think of variability in terms of the number of arrests instead of the number of arrests squared.

2.13 Measures of Shape

A distribution that is not symmetric but has more of a "tail" toward one end of the distribution than the other is called *skewed*. If the tail is toward larger values, the distribution is positively skewed or skewed to the right. If the tail is toward smaller values, the distribution is negatively skewed or skewed to the left.

Another characteristic of the form of a distribution is called *kurtosis*, the extent to which, for a given standard deviation, observations cluster around a central point. If cases within a distribution cluster more than those in the normal distribution (that is, the distribution is more peaked), the distribution is called *leptokurtic*. A leptokurtic distribution also tends to have more observations straggling into the extreme tails than does a normal distribution. If cases cluster less than in the normal distribution (that is, it is flatter), the distribution is termed *platykurtic*.

Although examination of a bar chart provides some indication of possible skewness and kurtosis, it is often desirable to compute formal indices that measure them. Values for skewness and kurtosis are 0 if the observed distribution is exactly normal. Positive values for skewness indicate a positive skew, while positive values for kurtosis indicate a distribution that is more peaked than normal. For samples from a normal distribution, measures of skewness and kurtosis typically will not be exactly zero but will fluctuate about zero because of sampling variation.

2.14 Standard Scores

It is often desirable to describe the relative position of an observation within a distribution. Knowing that a score of 80 is obtained in a competitive examination conveys little information about the performance of the exam-taker. Different reactions would be elicited depending on whether 80 is the lowest, the median, or the highest score.

One way of describing the location of a case in a distribution is to calculate its *standard score*. This score, sometimes called the Z-score, indicates how many standard deviations above or below the mean an observation falls. It is calculated by finding the difference between the value of a particular observation X_i and the mean of the distribution, and then dividing this difference by the standard deviation:

$$Z_i = \frac{X_i - \overline{X}}{S}$$

The mean of Z-scores is 0, and the standard deviation is 1.

For example, a participant with 5 actual arrests would have a Z-score of $(5-9.25)/6.25$, or -0.68. Since the score is negative, the case had fewer arrests than the average for the individuals studied.

Standardization permits comparison of scores from different distributions. For example, an individual with a Z-score of -0.68 for actual arrests and 1.01 for the difference between reported and actual arrests has fewer arrests than the average but reported an exaggerated number.

When the distribution of a variable is approximately normal and the mean and variance are known or are estimated from large samples, the Z-score of an observation provides more specific locational information. For example, if actual arrests and response error were normally distributed, 75 percent of cases would have more arrests than the example individual but only 16 percent would have exaggerated as much (75 percent of a normal curve lies above a Z-score of -0.68, and 16 percent lies above a score of 1.01).

2.15   Who Lies?

The distribution of the difference between reported and actual arrests indicates that response error exists. Although observing a mean close to zero is comforting, misrepresentation is obvious. What then are the characteristics that influence willingness to be truthful?

Wyner identifies three factors that are related to inaccuracies: the number of arrests before 1960, the number of multiple-charge arrests, and the perceived desirability of being arrested. The first factor is related to a frequently encountered difficulty—the more distant an event in time, the less likely it is to be correctly recalled. The second factor, underreporting of multiple charge arrests, is probably mediated by the general social undesirability of serious arrests. Finally, persons who view arrest records as laudatory are likely to inflate their accomplishments.

2.16   RUNNING PROCEDURE CONDESCRIPTIVE

Procedure CONDESCRIPTIVE produces all the statistics provided by procedure FREQUENCIES, except the median and the mode, and provides a compact table of statistics for a number of variables. CONDESCRIPTIVE is particularly well-suited for continuous, interval-level or ratio-level variables. It does not print tables or bar charts. However, if you want statistical summaries of a long list of variables, CONDESCRIPTIVE prints the summaries several to the page whereas FREQUENCIES prints them on separate pages even when you suppress the tables.

There is no subcommand for CONDESCRIPTIVE. Simply enter the command beginning in column 1 and your variable list (or the keyword ALL) beginning in column 16 or beyond. For example, to produce the output shown in Figure 2.10, specify

```
CONDESCRIPTIVE TRUE SELF ERRORS
```

2.17   The OPTIONS Command for CONDESCRIPTIVE

By default, procedure CONDESCRIPTIVE excludes cases with missing values from computation of the statistics and prints all available variable labels. To override these defaults, include an OPTIONS command following your CONDESCRIPTIVE command

and specify the number(s) of the options you want. The following is a list of the most commonly used options; a complete list is found in Appendix B.

OPTION 1 Include cases with missing values.
OPTION 2 Do not print variable labels.

2.18 The STATISTICS Command for CONDESCRIPTIVE

By default, CONDESCRIPTIVE prints all the following statistics. If you want to limit the output to a few, enter the STATISTICS command and the numbers corresponding to the following statistics.

STATISTIC 1 Mean
STATISTIC 2 Standard error
STATISTIC 5 Standard deviation
STATISTIC 6 Variance
STATISTIC 7 Kurtosis
STATISTIC 8 Skewness
STATISTIC 9 Range
STATISTIC 10 Minimum
STATISTIC 11 Maximum
STATISTIC 12 Sum
ALL   All statistics (the default)

2.19 Median and Mode Computation

When SPSS computes the *median,* it uses an algorithm based on the assumption that the original measurement was continuous and interval level but that the cases were subsequently grouped into categories. It computes the median by interpolation, assuming that the observed value is the midpoint of an interval of length 1. If this is not the case, you should determine the median by using the cumulative percentages in the frequency table to locate the category containing the middle case.

When SPSS computes the *mode,* if two or more values tie in having the greatest number of cases, the lowest numerical value is reported as the mode.

2.20 CONDESCRIPTIVE and Other SPSS Commands

The complete SPSS command file used to produce the output in Figure 2.10 is

```
RUN NAME        ARREST HISTORY
DATA LIST       FIXED(1)/1 TRUE 1-2 SELF 4-5
COMPUTE         ERRORS = SELF - TRUE
VAR LABELS      TRUE, ACTUAL NUMBER OF ARRESTS/
                SELF, SELF-REPORTED ARRESTS/
                ERRORS, REPORTED ARRESTS MINUS ACTUAL ARRESTS/
CONDESCRIPTIVE TRUE SELF ERRORS
READ INPUT DATA
01 01
01 02
 ...
 ...
 ...
27 21
20 18
END INPUT DATA
FINISH
```

DATA LIST. Specifies that there is one record per case with two variables. The variable named TRUE is recorded in columns 1 and 2, and the variable named SELF is in columns 4 and 5.

COMPUTE.   Creates a new variable called ERRORS by subtracting the actual number of arrests of each participant from the number reported by the participant. The COMPUTE command creates a new variable that is an arithmetic function of one or more existing variables. The new variable can be computed by adding, subtracting, dividing, multiplying, or in some other way transforming variables. (See Chapter 11 for a discussion of this command.)

VAR LABELS.   Assigns labels to all three variables. Note that the command comes after the COMPUTE command because variable ERRORS cannot be given a label before SPSS is told to create that variable.

CONDESCRIPTIVE.   Requests descriptive statistics for the three variables.

READ INPUT DATA.   Tells SPSS to begin reading the data.

END INPUT DATA.   Signals the end of the data lines. In most implementations of SPSS, this command can be used instead of the N OF CASES command (Section 1.9) to indicate how many data lines are included in the command file.

FINISH.   Ends the SPSS job.

Chapter 3

Lost Letters in Cities and Towns: Crosstabulation and Measures of Association

Newspapers headline murders in subway stations, robberies on crowded main streets, suicides cheered by onlookers. All are indications of social irresponsibility and apathy said to characterize city residents. Since overcrowding, decreased sense of community, and other urban problems are usually blamed, one might ask whether small town residents are more responsible and less apathetic than their urban counterparts.

Hansson and Slade (1977) used the "Lost Letter Technique" to test the hypothesis that altruism is higher in small towns than in cities, unless the person needing assistance is a social deviant. In this technique, stamped and addressed letters are "lost" and the rate at which they are returned is examined. A total of 216 letters were lost in Hansson and Slade's experiment. Half were dropped within the city limits of Tulsa, Oklahoma, the others in 51 small towns within a 50-mile radius of Tulsa. The letters were addressed to three fictitious people at a post office box in Tulsa: M. J. Davis; Dandee Davis, c/o Pink Panther Lounge; and M. J. Davis, c/o Friends of the Communist Party. The first person is considered a normal "control," the second is a person whose occupation is questionable, and the third is a subversive or political deviant.

3.1 CROSSTABULATION

To see whether the return rate is similar for the three addresses, the letters found and mailed and those not mailed must be tallied separately for each address. Figure 3.1 is a *crosstabulation* of address type and response. The number of cases (letters) with each distinct combination of values of the two variables is displayed in each *cell* of the table, together with various percentages. These cell entries provide information about relationships between the variables.

Figure 3.1   Crosstabulation of status of letter by address

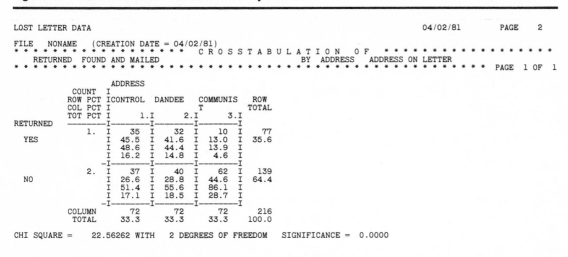

```
LOST LETTER DATA                                           04/02/81      PAGE   2
FILE   NONAME   (CREATION DATE = 04/02/81)
* * * * * * * * * * * * * * * *   C R O S S T A B U L A T I O N   O F   * * * * * * * * * * * * * * * * *
    RETURNED  FOUND AND MAILED                    BY  ADDRESS   ADDRESS ON LETTER
* * * * * * * * * * * * * * * * * * * * * * * * * * * * * * * * * * * * * * * * * *  PAGE  1 OF  1

                   ADDRESS
            COUNT I
            ROW PCT ICONTROL  DANDEE   COMMUNIS   ROW
            COL PCT I                     T      TOTAL
            TOT PCT I      1.I      2.I      3.I
RETURNED     ---------I---------I---------I---------I
          1.  I     35 I     32 I     10 I    77
   YES       I   45.5 I   41.6 I   13.0 I  35.6
             I   48.6 I   44.4 I   13.9 I
             I   16.2 I   14.8 I    4.6 I
           -I---------I---------I---------I
          2.  I     37 I     40 I     62 I   139
   NO        I   26.6 I   28.8 I   44.6 I  64.4
             I   51.4 I   55.6 I   86.1 I
             I   17.1 I   18.5 I   28.7 I
           -I---------I---------I---------I
            COLUMN     72       72       72     216
            TOTAL    33.3     33.3     33.3   100.0

CHI SQUARE =    22.56262 WITH   2 DEGREES OF FREEDOM   SIGNIFICANCE =   0.0000
```

In Figure 3.1, the address is called the *column* variable since each address is displayed in a column of the table. Similarly, the status of the letter, whether it was returned or not, is called the *row* variable. With three categories of the column variable and two of the row, there are 6 cells in the table.

3.2   Cell Contents and Marginals

The first entry in the table is the number of cases or *frequency* in that cell. It is labeled as COUNT in the key printed in the upper left corner of the table. For example, 35 letters addressed to the control were returned, 62 letters addressed to the Communist were not returned. The second entry in the table is the *row percentage* (ROW PCT). It is the percentage of all cases in a row that fall into a particular cell. Of the 77 letters returned, 45.5% were addressed to the control, 41.6% to Dandee, and 13.0% to the Communist.

The *column percentage* (COL PCT), the third item in each cell, is the percentage of all cases in a column that occur in a cell. For example 48.6% of the letters addressed to the control were returned and 51.4% were not. The return rate for Dandee is similar (44.4%), while that for the Communist address is markedly lower (13.9%).

The last entry in the table is the *table percentage* (TOT PCT). The number of cases in the cell is expressed as a percentage of the total number of cases in the table. The 35 letters returned to the control represent 16.2% of the 216 letters in the experiment.

The numbers to the right and below the table are known as *marginals*. They are the counts and percentages for the row and column variables taken separately. In Figure 3.1, the row marginals show that 77 (35.6%) of the letters were returned, while 139 (64.4%) were not.

3.3   Choosing Percentages

Row, column, and table percentages convey different types of information, so it is important to choose carefully among them.

In this example, the row percentage indicates the distribution of address types for returned and not returned letters. It conveys no direct information about the return rate. Whether all letters had been returned or only one letter in each category, the row percentages for the first row of Table 3.1 would have been identical—33.3%, 33.3%, 33.3%. If differing numbers of letters had been "lost" for each address type, this would influence the interpretation of the row percentages. That is, if twice as many letters were addressed to the control, an identical return rate for all letters would give row percentages of 50%, 25%, 25%. However, this does not indicate that the return rate is higher for the controls.

The column percentage is the percentage of letters returned and not returned for each address. By looking at column percentages across rows, one can compare return rates for the address types. Interpretation of this comparison would not be affected if unequal numbers of letters had been addressed to each category.

Since it is always possible to interchange the rows and columns of any table, general rules about when to use row and column percentages cannot be given. They depend on the nature of the two variables. If one of the two variables is under experimental control, it is termed an *independent* variable. This variable is hypothesized to affect the response, or *dependent* variable. If variables can be classified as dependent and independent, the following guideline may be helpful: If the independent variable is the row variable, select row percentages; if the independent variable is the column variable, select column percentages. In this example the dependent variable is the status of the letter, whether it was mailed or not. The type of address is the independent variable. Since the independent variable is the column variable in Figure 3.1, column percentages should be used for comparisons of return rates.

3.4   Adding A Control Variable

Since Figure 3.1 combines results from both the city and the towns, differences between the locations cannot be seen. Two separate tables, one for the city and one for the towns, are required. Figure 3.4 shows crosstabulations of response and address for each of the locations. SPSS produces a separate table for each value of the location ("control") variable.

Figure 3.4   Crosstabulations of status of letter by address controlled for location

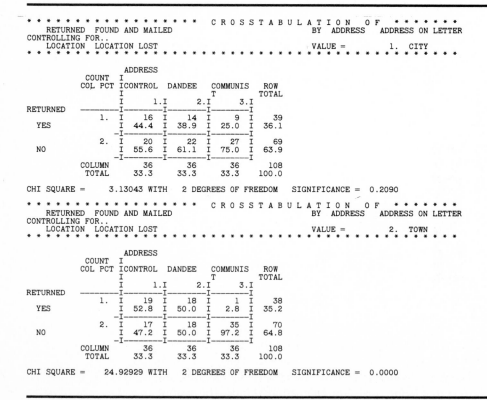

```
* * * * * * * * * * * * * * * * * *   C R O S S T A B U L A T I O N   O F  * * * * * * *
     RETURNED  FOUND AND MAILED                        BY  ADDRESS   ADDRESS ON LETTER
CONTROLLING FOR..
     LOCATION  LOCATION LOST                                VALUE =        1. CITY
* * * * * * * * * * * * * * * * * * * * * * * * * * * * * * * * * * * * * * * * * * * * *

                  ADDRESS
          COUNT  I
          COL PCT ICONTROL  DANDEE   COMMUNIS   ROW
                 I                   T          TOTAL
                 I     1.I      2.I       3.I
RETURNED  --------I--------I--------I--------I
            1.  I    16  I    14  I     9  I     39
   YES          I  44.4  I  38.9  I  25.0  I   36.1
             ---I--------I--------I--------I
            2.  I    20  I    22  I    27  I     69
   NO           I  55.6  I  61.1  I  75.0  I   63.9
             ---I--------I--------I--------I
          COLUMN      36       36       36     108
           TOTAL    33.3     33.3     33.3   100.0

CHI SQUARE =    3.13043 WITH   2 DEGREES OF FREEDOM   SIGNIFICANCE =  0.2090

* * * * * * * * * * * * * * * * * *   C R O S S T A B U L A T I O N   O F  * * * * * * *
     RETURNED  FOUND AND MAILED                        BY  ADDRESS   ADDRESS ON LETTER
CONTROLLING FOR..
     LOCATION  LOCATION LOST                                VALUE =        2. TOWN
* * * * * * * * * * * * * * * * * * * * * * * * * * * * * * * * * * * * * * * * * * * * *

                  ADDRESS
          COUNT  I
          COL PCT ICONTROL  DANDEE   COMMUNIS   ROW
                 I                   T          TOTAL
                 I     1.I      2.I       3.I
RETURNED  --------I--------I--------I--------I
            1.  I    19  I    18  I     1  I     38
   YES          I  52.8  I  50.0  I   2.8  I   35.2
             ---I--------I--------I--------I
            2.  I    17  I    18  I    35  I     70
   NO           I  47.2  I  50.0  I  97.2  I   64.8
             ---I--------I--------I--------I
          COLUMN      36       36       36     108
           TOTAL    33.3     33.3     33.3   100.0

CHI SQUARE =   24.92929 WITH   2 DEGREES OF FREEDOM   SIGNIFICANCE =  0.0000
```

These tables show interesting differences between cities and towns. Although the overall return rates are close, 36.1% for the city and 35.2% for the towns, there are striking differences between the addresses. Only 2.8% of the Communist letters were returned in towns, while 25.0% of them were returned in Tulsa. (At least two of the Communist letters were forwarded by small town residents to the FBI for punitive action!) The return rates for both the control (52.8%) and Dandee (50.0%) are higher in towns.

The results support the hypothesis that, in small towns, suspected social deviance influences the positive response more than in big cities, although it is surprising that Dandee and the Pink Panther Lounge were deemed worthy of as much assistance as they received. If the Communist letter is excluded, inhabitants of small towns are somewhat more helpful than city residents, returning 51% of the other letters, in comparison to the city's 42%.

3.5 GRAPHICAL REPRESENTATION OF CROSSTABULATIONS

As with frequency tables, visual representation of a crosstabulation often simplifies the search for associations. Figure 3.5 is a bar chart of letters returned from the crosstabulations shown in Figure 3.4.

Figure 3.5   Status of letter by address by location (Bar chart from SPSS Graphics)

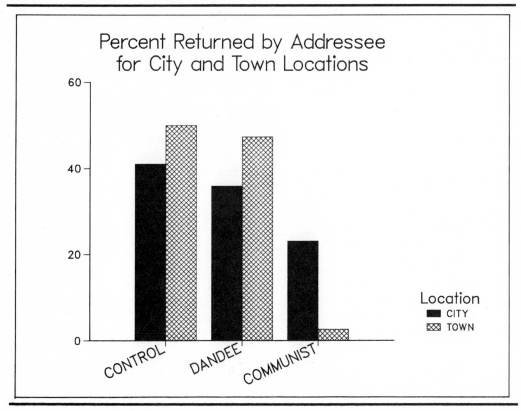

In a bar chart, the length of each bar represents the frequencies or percentages for each category of a variable. In Figure 3.5, the percentages plotted are the column percentages shown in Figure 3.4 for the returned letters only. This chart clearly shows that the return rates for the control and Dandee are high compared to the return rate for the

Communist. Also, it demonstrates more vividly than the crosstabulation that the town residents' return rates for the control and Dandee are higher than for city residents but that the reverse is true for the Communist.

3.6   USING CROSSTABULATION FOR DATA SCREENING

Errors and unusual values in data entry can sometimes be identified using crosstabulation. For example, a case coded as a male with a history of three pregnancies would not be identified as suspicious using procedure FREQUENCIES to produce tables of sex and of number of pregnancies. When considered separately, the code for male is acceptable for variable sex and the value 3 is acceptable for number of pregnancies. Jointly, however, the combination is noteworthy.

Whenever possible, crosstabulations of related variables should be obtained so that anomalies can be identified and corrected before further statistical analysis of the data.

3.7   CROSSTABULATION STATISTICS

Although examination of the various row and column percentages in a crosstabulation is a useful first step in studying the relationship between two variables, it does not allow for quantification or testing of that relationship. For these purposes, it is useful to consider various indexes that measure the extent of association, as well as statistical tests of the hypothesis that there is no association.

3.8   The Chi-Square Test of Independence

The hypothesis that two variables of a crosstabulation are *independent* of each other is often of interest to researchers. Two variables are by definition independent if the probability that a case falls into a given cell is simply the product of the marginal probabilities of the two categories defining the cell.

For example in Figure 3.1, if returns of the letter and address type are independent, the probability of a letter being returned to a Communist is the product of the probability of a letter being returned and the probability of a letter being addressed to a Communist. From the table, 35.6% of the letters were returned and 33.3% of the letters were addressed to a friend of the Communist party. Thus, if address type and status of the letter are independent, the probability of a letter being returned to the Communist is estimated to be

P(return) P(Communist)$=0.356 \times 0.333 = 0.119$

The *expected* number of cases in that cell is 25.7, which is 11.9% of the 216 cases in the sample. From the table, the *observed* number of letters returned to the Communist is 10 (4.6%), nearly 16 fewer than expected if the two variables are independent.

To construct a statistical test of the independence hypothesis, the above calculations are repeated for each cell in the table. The probability, under independence, of an observation falling into cell (ij) is estimated by

$$P(\text{row} = i \text{ and column} = j) = \left(\frac{\text{count in row } i}{N}\right)\left(\frac{\text{count in column } j}{N}\right)$$

To obtain the expected number of observations in cell (ij), the probability is multiplied by the total sample size

$$E_{ij} = N\left(\frac{\text{count in row } i}{N}\right)\left(\frac{\text{count in column } j}{N}\right)$$

$$= \frac{(\text{count in row } i)(\text{count in column } j)}{N}$$

Table 3.8 contains the observed and expected frequencies, and the *residuals*, which are the observed minus the expected frequencies for the data in Figure 3.1.

Table 3.8   Observed, Expected, and Residual Values

		CONTROL	DANDEE	COMMUNIST
RETURNED	observed	35	32	10
	expected	25.7	25.7	25.7
	residual	9.3	6.3	−15.7
NOT RETURNED	observed	37	40	62
	expected	46.3	46.3	46.3
	residual	−9.3	−6.3	15.7

A statistic often used to test the hypothesis that the row and column variables are independent is the *Pearson chi-square*. It is calculated by summing over all cells the squared residuals divided by the expected frequencies.

$$\chi^2 = \sum_i \sum_j \frac{(O_{ij} - E_{ij})^2}{E_{ij}}$$

The calculated chi-square can be compared to the critical points of the theoretical chi-square distribution to produce an estimate of how likely (or unlikely) the observed chi-square value is if the two variables are in fact independent. Since the value of chi-square depends on the numbers of rows and columns of the table being examined, one must know the *degrees of freedom* for the table. The degrees of freedom can be viewed as the number of cells of a table that can be arbitrarily filled when the row and column totals (marginals) are fixed. For an R by C table, the degrees of freedom are $(R-1)\times(C-1)$ since once $(R-1)$ rows and $(C-1)$ columns are filled, frequencies in the remaining row and column cells must be chosen so that marginal totals are maintained.

   In this example, the degrees of freedom are two (1×2) and the chi-square value is 22.56 (see Figure 3.1). If type of address and return rate are independent, the probability that a random sample would result in a chi-square value of at least that magnitude is less than 0.00005. SPSS prints 0.0000, the probability rounded to 4 decimals. The value printed on the SPSS output is the probability of obtaining the observed result or one more extreme if the two variables are independent. This probability is also known as the *observed significance level* of the test. If the probability is small enough (usually less than 0.05 or 0.01), the hypothesis that the two variables are independent is rejected.

   Since the observed significance level for Figure 3.1 is very small, based on the combined city and town data, the hypothesis that address type and return rate are independent is rejected. When the chi-square test is calculated for the city and town data separately (Figure 3.4), different results are obtained for the two. The observed significance level of the city data is 0.209, so the independence hypothesis is not rejected. For the towns, the observed significance level is less than 0.00005, leading to rejection of the hypothesis that address and return rate are independent. These results support the theory that city and town residents respond differently.

   The chi-square test is a test of independence; it provides little information about the strength or form of the association between two variables. The magnitude of the observed chi-square depends not only on the goodness of fit of the independence model, but also on the sample size. If the sample size for a particular table increases *n*-fold, other things remaining equal, so does the chi-square value. Thus, large chi-square values can arise in applications where residuals are small relative to expected frequencies but where the sample size is large.

Certain conditions must be met for the chi-square distribution to be a good approximation to the distribution of the statistic in the equation given above. The data must be random samples from multinomial distributions and the expected values must not be too small. It has been recommended that all expected frequencies be at least five. Recent studies indicate that this recommendation is probably too stringent and can be relaxed (Everitt, 1977). If there are cells with expected values less than 5, SPSS prints the number of such cells and the minimum expected value.

In hope of improving the approximation in the case of a 2 by 2 table, *Yates' correction for continuity* is sometimes applied. Yates' correction for continuity involves subtracting 0.5 from the positive differences between observed and expected frequencies (the residuals) and adding 0.5 to the negative differences before squaring. For a discussion of some of the controversy regarding the merits of this correction, see Conover (1974) and Mantel (1974).

An alternative test for the 2 by 2 table can be based on the hypergeometric distribution. Exact probabilities of obtaining the observed results if the two variables are independent and the marginals fixed are calculated. This is called *Fisher's exact test*. It is most useful when the total sample size and the expected values are small. SPSS calculates Fisher's exact test when the sample size in a 2 by 2 table is 20 or less.

3.9   Measures of Association

In many research situations, the strength and nature of the dependence of variables is of central concern. Indexes that attempt to quantify the relationship between variables in a cross-classification are called *measures of association*. No single measure adequately summarizes all possible types of association. Measures vary in their interpretation and in the way they define perfect and intermediate association. These measures also differ in the way they are affected by various factors such as marginals. For example, many measures are "margin sensitive" in that they are influenced by the marginal distributions of the rows and columns. Such measures reflect information about the margins along with information about association.

A particular measure may have a low value for a given table, not because the two variables are not related, but because they are not related in the way to which the measure is sensitive. No single measure is best for all situations. The type of data, the hypothesis of interest, as well as the properties of the various measures must all be considered when selecting an index of association for a given table. It is not, however, reasonable to compute a large number of measures and then to report the most impressive as if it were the only one examined.

The measures of association available in SPSS CROSSTABS are computed only from bivariate tables (see Figure 3.4). For example, if three dichotomous variables are specified in the table, two sets of measures are computed, one for each subtable produced by the values of the controlling variable. In general, if relationships among more than two variables are to be studied, examination of bivariate tables is only a first step. For an extensive discussion of various more sophisticated multivariate procedures for the analysis of qualitative data, see Fienberg (1977), Everitt (1977), and Haberman (1978).

3.10   Nominal Measures

Consider measures that assume only that both variables in the table are nominally measured. As such, these measures can only provide some indication of the strength of association between variables; they cannot indicate direction, nor anything about the nature of the relationship. The measures provided are of two types: those based on the chi-square statistic and those that follow the logic of proportional reduction in error denoted PRE.

3.11 Chi-Square Based Measures

As explained above, the chi-square statistic itself is not a good measure of the degree of association between two variables. But its widespread use in tests of independence has encouraged the use of measures of association based upon it. Each of these measures based on the chi-square attempts to modify the chi-square statistic to minimize the influence of sample size and degrees of freedom as well as to restrict the range of values of the measure to those between 0 and 1. Without such adjustments, comparison of chi-square values from tables with varying dimensions and sample sizes is meaningless.

The *phi-coefficient* modifies the chi-square by dividing it by the sample size and taking the square root of the result:

$$\phi = \sqrt{\frac{\chi^2}{N}}$$

For tables in which one of the dimensions is greater than 2, phi need not lie between 0 and 1 since the chi-square value can be greater than the sample size. To obtain a measure that must lie between 0 and 1, Pearson suggested the use of

$$C = \sqrt{\frac{\chi^2}{\chi^2 + N}}$$

which is called the *coefficient of contingency*. Although the value of this measure is always between 0 and 1, it cannot generally attain the upper limit of 1. The maximum it can reach depends upon the number of rows and columns. For example, in a 4 by 4 table, the maximum value of C is 0.87.

Cramér introduced the following variant:

$$V = \sqrt{\frac{\chi^2}{N(k - 1)}}$$

where k is the smaller of the number of rows and columns. *Cramér's V* can attain the maximum of 1 for tables of any dimensions. If one of the table dimensions is 2, V and phi are identical.

The chi-square based measures are hard to interpret. Although, when properly standardized, they can be used to compare strength of association in several tables, the "strength of association" being compared is not easily related to intuitive ideas about what association should mean.

3.12 Proportional Reduction in Error

Common alternatives to chi-square based measurements are those based on the idea of *proportional reduction in error* (PRE) introduced by Goodman and Kruskal (1954). With PRE measures, the meaning of association is clearer. They are all essentially ratios of a measure of error made in predicting the values of one variable based first on knowledge of that variable alone and the same measure of error applied to predictions based on knowledge of an additional variable.

For example, consider Figure 3.12, a crosstabulation of depth of hypnosis and success in treatment of migraine headaches by suggestion (Cedercreutz (1978)). To predict the results of treatment when no other information is available, the best guess is the outcome category with the largest proportion of observations (the modal category). In Figure 3.12, "no change" is the largest outcome category, with 45% of the subjects. The estimate of the probability of incorrect classification is 1 minus the probability of the modal category:

$$P(1) = 1 - 0.45 = 0.55$$

Figure 3.12   Depth of Hypnosis and Success of Treatment

```
* * * * * * * * * * * * * * * * * *   C R O S S T A B U L A T I O N   O F   * * * * * * * * * * * * * * * * * * *
     HYPNOSIS  DEPTH OF HYPNOSIS                                    BY  MIGRAINE  OUTCOME
* * * * * * * * * * * * * * * * * * * * * * * * * * * * * * * * * * * * * * * * * * * * * * * * * *  PAGE  1 OF  1

                      MIGRAINE
             COUNT  I
             TOT PCT ICURED     BETTER   NO          ROW
                    I                    CHANGE      TOTAL
                    I      1.I      2.I      3.I
 HYPNOSIS    ───────I────────I────────I────────I
                1.  I    13  I     5  I     0  I       18
    DEEP          I  13.0  I   5.0  I   0.0  I     18.0
                 -I────────I────────I────────I
                2.  I    10  I    26  I    17  I       53
    MEDIUM        I  10.0  I  26.0  I  17.0  I     53.0
                 -I────────I────────I────────I
                3.  I     0  I     1  I    28  I       29
    LIGHT         I   0.0  I   1.0  I  28.0  I     29.0
                 -I────────I────────I────────I
             COLUMN      23        32        45       100
             TOTAL     23.0      32.0      45.0     100.0

     1 OUT OF    9 ( 11.1%) OF THE VALID CELLS HAVE EXPECTED CELL FREQUENCY LESS THAN 5.0.
 MINIMUM EXPECTED CELL FREQUENCY =   4.140
 CHI SQUARE =     65.52519 WITH   4 DEGREES OF FREEDOM   SIGNIFICANCE =  0.0000
 CRAMER'S V =    0.57239
 CONTINGENCY COEFFICIENT =     0.62918
 LAMBDA (ASYMMETRIC) =  0.29787 WITH HYPNOSIS DEPENDENT.          =  0.40000 WITH MIGRAINE DEPENDENT.
 LAMBDA (SYMMETRIC) =  0.35294
 UNCERTAINTY COEFFICIENT (ASYMMETRIC) =  0.36537 WITH HYPNOSIS DEPENDENT.          =  0.34547 WITH MIGRAINE DEPENDENT.
 UNCERTAINTY COEFFICIENT (SYMMETRIC) =  0.35514
```

Information about the depth of hypnosis can be used to improve the classification rule. For each hypnosis category the outcome category that occurs most frequently for that hypnosis level is predicted. Thus, "no change" is predicted for participants achieving a "light" level of hypnosis, "better" for those achieving a "medium" level, and "cured" for those achieving a "deep" level.

The probability of error when depth of hypnosis is used to predict outcome is the sum of the probabilities of all the cells that are not row modes. That is,

$$P(2) = 0.05 + 0.10 + 0.17 + 0.01 = 0.33$$

Goodman and Kruskal's *lambda*, with outcome as the predicted (dependent) variable, is calculated as

$$\lambda_{outcome} = \frac{P(1) - P(2)}{P(1)} = \frac{0.55 - 0.33}{0.55} = 0.40$$

A 40% reduction in error is obtained when depth of hypnosis is used to predict outcome.

Lambda always ranges between 0 and 1. A value of 0 means the independent variable is of no help in predicting the dependent variable. A value of 1 means that knowledge of the independent variable perfectly specifies the categories of the dependent variable (perfection can occur only when each row has at most one nonzero cell). When the two variables are independent, lambda is 0; but a lambda of 0 need not imply statistical independence. As with all measures of association, lambda is constructed to measure association in a very specific way; in particular, lambda reflects the reduction in error when values of one variable are used to predict values of the other. If this particular type of association is absent, lambda is 0. Other measures of association may find association of a different kind even when lambda is zero. A measure of association sensitive to every imaginable type of association does not exist.

For a particular table, two different lambdas can be computed, one having the row variable as the predictor and the other using the column variable. The two do not usually have identical values, so care should be taken to specify which is the dependent variable, that is, the variable whose prediction is of primary interest. In some applications, there is no clear emphasis on one or the other variable as dependent. Then, a symmetric version of lambda can be computed. It is based on predicting the row variable and the column variable with equal frequency. When the lambda statistic is requested, SPSS prints the symmetric lambda as well as the two asymmetric lambdas.

3.13   Uncertainty Measures

The *uncertainty coefficient* can also be considered a PRE measure since it defines the relative reduction in uncertainty about one variable when the second is known (Theil, 1967). Based on information theory, the uncertainty in the distribution of variable Y is

$$U(Y) = -\sum_j P(Y_j) \log P(Y_j)$$

The uncertainty in the joint distribution of X and Y is

$$U(Y,X) = -\sum_i \sum_j P(Y_j,X_i) \log P(Y_j,X_i)$$

The uncertainty of Y given X is then defined as

$$U(Y|X) = U(Y,X) - U(X)$$

Finally, the relative reduction in uncertainty of Y given X is

$$U_Y = \frac{U(Y) - U(Y|X)}{U(Y)}$$

A symmetric version of the coefficient is

$$U = \frac{2(U(Y) + U(X) - U(Y,X))}{U(Y) + U(X)}$$

The multiplication of the numerator by two is used to normalize the coefficient so that it lies between 0 and 1.

3.14   Ordinal Measures

Although relationships among ordinal variables can be examined using nominal measures, there are measures that reflect the additional information available from ranking. Consideration of the kind of relationships that may exist between two ordered variables leads to the notion of direction of relationship and to the concept of *correlation*. Variables are positively correlated if cases with low values for one variable also tend to have low values for the other and cases with high values on one also tend to be high on the other. Negatively correlated variables show the opposite relationship: the higher the first variable, the lower the second tends to be.

Several measures of association for a table of two ordered variables are based on consideration of all possible *pairs* of cases or observations and examination of their ranking on the two variables. A pair of cases is *concordant* if both variables' values of one case are higher (or both are lower) than the corresponding values of the other case. The pair is *discordant* if one variable's value for a case is larger than the corresponding values for the other case while the direction is reversed for the second variable. When the two cases have identical values on one or on both variables, they are *tied*.

Thus, for any given pair of cases with measurements on variables X and Y, the pair may be concordant, discordant or tied in one of three ways: they may be tied on X but not on Y, they may be tied on Y but not on X, or they may be tied on both variables.

When data are arranged in crosstabulated form, the number of concordant, discordant, and tied pairs can be easily calculated since all possible pairs can be conveniently determined.

If the preponderance of pairs is concordant, the association is said to be positive; as ranks of variable X increase (or decrease), so do ranks of variable Y. If the majority of pairs is discordant, the association is negative; as ranks of one variable increase, those of the other tend to decrease. If concordant and discordant pairs are equally likely, no association is said to exist.

The ordinal measures presented here all have the same numerator: the number of concordant pairs (P) minus the number of discordant pairs (Q) calculated for all distinct pairs of observations. They differ primarily in the way in which $P-Q$ is normalized. The simplest measure involves subtracting Q from P and dividing by the total number of pairs. If there are no pairs with ties, this measure (Kendall's tau-a) is in the range from -1 to $+1$. If there are ties, the range of possible values is narrower; the actual range depends on the number of ties. Since all observations within the same row are tied, so also those in the same column, the resulting tau-a measures are difficult to interpret.

A measure that attempts to normalize $P-Q$ by considering ties on each of the variables of a pair separately but not ties on both variables of a pair is *tau-b*:

$$\tau_b = \frac{P - Q}{\sqrt{(P + Q + T_X)(P + Q + T_Y)}}$$

where T_X is the number of pairs tied on X but not on Y, and T_Y is the number of pairs tied on Y but not on X. If no marginal frequency is 0, tau-b can attain positive or negative 1 only for a square table.

A measure that can attain, or nearly attain, 1 or -1 for any R by C table is *tau-c*.

$$\tau_c = \frac{2m(P - Q)}{N^2(m - 1)}$$

where m is the smaller of the number of rows and columns. The coefficients tau-b and tau-c do not differ much in value if each margin contains approximately equal frequencies.

Goodman and Kruskal's *gamma* is closely related to the tau statistics.

$$G = \frac{P - Q}{P + Q}$$

Gamma can be thought of as the probability that a random pair of observations is concordant minus the probability that the pair is discordant, assuming the absence of ties. The absolute value of gamma is the proportional reduction in error between guessing concordant and discordant ranking depending on which occurs more often and guessing ranking of each pair according to the outcome of the toss of a fair coin. Gamma is 1 if all observations are concentrated in an upper-left to lower-right diagonal of the table. In the case of independence, gamma is 0. However, the converse (that a gamma of 0 necessarily implies independence) need not be true except in the 2 by 2 table.

In the computation of gamma, no distinction is made between the independent and dependent variable; the variables are treated symmetrically. Somers (1962) proposed an asymmetric extension of gamma that differs only in the inclusion of the number of pairs not tied on the independent variable (X) in the denominator. Somers' d is

$$d_Y = \frac{P - Q}{P + Q + T_Y}$$

The coefficient d_Y indicates the proportionate excess of concordant pairs over discordant pairs among pairs not tied on the independent variable. The symmetric variant of Somers' d uses for the denominator the average value of the denominators of the two asymmetric coefficients.

3.15 Measures Involving Interval Data

If the two variables in the table are measured on an interval scale, various coefficients that make use of this additional information can be calculated. A useful symmetric coefficient that measures the strength of the *linear* relationship is the Pearson correlation coefficient or r. It can take on values from -1 to $+1$ indicating negative or positive linear correlation. Further description, including a PRE interpretation, is found in Chapter 6 on scatterplots.

The *eta* coefficient is appropriate for data in which the dependent variable is measured on an interval scale and the independent variable on a nominal or ordinal scale. When squared, eta can be interpreted as the proportion of the total variability in the dependent variable that can be accounted for by knowing the values of the independent variable. The measure is asymmetric and does not assume a linear relationship between the variables.

3.16 RUNNING PROCEDURE CROSSTABS

Procedure CROSSTABS produces 2- to *n*-way tables and related statistical measures for numeric and alphanumeric variables. For most applications, procedure CROSSTABS requires only the TABLES= subcommand to set up row, column, and control variables. This is known as the *general mode* of CROSSTABS. Options are provided for handling missing values, suppressing cell percentages and labels, reordering rows, and printing an index of tables. SPSS also prints eleven optional statistics including the chi-square and the measures of association described in Sections 3.7 through 3.15.

If your variables are integer-valued and you want certain options and statistics that are otherwise unavailable (see Sections 3.18 through 3.22), you can provide CROSS-TABS with additional information with the VARIABLES= subcommand as shown in Section 3.23. This is known as the *integer mode* of CROSSTABS.

3.17 The TABLES= Subcommand

Enter the command keyword CROSSTABS beginning in column 1 and begin the TABLES= subcommand keyword in column 16 or beyond. The first variable named is the row variable and the variable named after the keyword BY is the column variable. To produce the crosstabulation shown in Figure 3.1, specify

```
CROSSTABS       TABLES=RETURNED BY ADDRESS
```

If you have a control variable, enter its name after a second keyword BY. To produce the crosstabulations shown in Figure 3.4, specify

```
CROSSTABS       TABLES=RETURNED BY ADDRESS BY LOCATION
```

SPSS produces a bivariate table (or *subtable*) of the variables RETURNED by ADDRESS for each value of variable LOCATION. In general mode, you can specify up to 8 control variables (that is, there can be up to 9 BYs). However, each new level further subdivides previous divisions, so you may create a large number of subtables with many empty cells unless you are working with a very large data file.

If any table or subtable is too large to appear on a single page, it is segmented and printed on successive pages until complete.

You can specify a variable list in any or all of the row, column, and control variable positions. For example, to produce tables of RETURNED by ADDRESS and RETURNED by LOCATION, specify

```
CROSSTABS       TABLES=RETURNED BY ADDRESS,LOCATION
```

the order in which tables are requested is unimportant except that SPSS prints them in the order specified.

3.18   The OPTIONS Command for CROSSTABS

Following your CROSSTABS command specifications, you can enter the OPTIONS command keyword beginning in column 1 and a list of integer numbers beginning in column 16 or beyond. These numbers correspond to content and format options for your tables. The following is a list of the most commonly used options; a complete list is found in Appendix B.

OPTION 1   Include cases with missing values.
OPTION 2   Do not print labels.
OPTION 3   Do not print row percentages.
OPTION 4   Do not print column percentages.
OPTION 5   Do not print total percentages.
OPTION 6   Do not print value labels, but print variable labels—available only in integer mode.
OPTION 7   Include missing values in the tables but do not include the cases in calculating percentages or statistics—available only in integer mode.
OPTION 8   Order row variable values highest to lowest—available only in integer mode.
OPTION 9   Print an index of the tables.

3.19   Missing-Value Treatment Options

Unless you specify otherwise, SPSS excludes a case from any table if it has a missing value on any variable in the table. Option 1 tells CROSSTABS to ignore the missing-value status of any values and to include the cases in all tables as if the values were valid. Option 7 is available only if you are running CROSSTABS in integer mode as described in Section 3.23. This option tells CROSSTABS to include missing values in the tables (flagged with an M) but not to use cases with missing values in calculating row and column percentages and the statistics.

3.20   Cell Percentage Options

Options 3, 4, and 5 tell CROSSTABS not to print row, column, and total percentages respectively. For example, to produce the table in Figure 3.4, specify

```
CROSSTABS       TABLES=RETURNED BY ADDRESS BY LOCATION
OPTIONS         3,5
```

where Options 3 and 5 restrict cell contents to the count and the column percentage.

3.21   Table Formatting Options

Option 2 tells CROSSTABS not to print either variable or value labels. Option 6 is available only in integer mode (see Section 3.23) and suppresses printing of value labels but not variable labels. Using either of these options speeds printing of the tables, but some information is naturally lost.

Option 8 is also available only in integer mode. This option tells CROSSTABS to print the tables with the values of the row variable ordered highest to lowest. By default, CROSSTABS prints the values in lowest to highest order.

Option 9 instructs SPSS to print an index of all tables printed and the page on which they appear. This is very helpful when you are requesting a large number of tables.

3.22   The STATISTICS Command for CROSSTABS

By default, CROSSTABS prints only the tables. If you want statistics calculated on those tables, request them with the STATISTICS command. Enter the STATISTICS command keyword in column 1 followed by a list of numbers beginning in column 16 or beyond corresponding to the desired statistics. The order in which you specify the statistics numbers does not affect the order in which CROSSTABS prints them. The numbers in parentheses in the following list are the section numbers where the statistics are discussed.

STATISTIC 1   Chi-square (3.8)
STATISTIC 2   Phi for 2 × 2 tables, Cramér's *V* for larger tables (3.11)
STATISTIC 3   Contingency coefficient (3.11)
STATISTIC 4   Lambda, symmetric and asymmetric (3.12)
STATISTIC 5   Uncertainty coefficient (3.13)
STATISTIC 6   Kendall's tau-*b* (3.14)
STATISTIC 7   Kendall's tau-*c* (3.14)
STATISTIC 8   Gamma—partial and zero-order available only in integer mode (3.14)
STATISTIC 9   Somers' *d*, symmetric and asymmetric (3.14)

For example, to produce the output shown in Figure 3.4, specify

```
CROSSTABS     TABLES=RETURNED BY ADDRESS BY LOCATION
OPTIONS       3,5
STATISTICS    1
```

These statistics are computed only from the bivariate table or subtable as explained in Section 3.9. Therefore, the two chi-square values printed in Figure 3.4 are based on the separate subtables created by the two values of control variable LOCATION.

3.23   The VARIABLES= Subcommand for Integer Mode

If you want to use Options 6, 7, or 8 (Sections 3.19 and 3.21) or obtain the partial and zero-order gamma available with Statistic 8 (Section 3.22), you must run CROSSTABS in integer mode and your data must be coded with integer values.

To specify integer mode CROSSTABS, precede your TABLES= subcommand with a VARIABLES= subcommand that names the variables with their lowest and highest values enclosed in parentheses and separated by commas. If you want the same highest and lowest values used for two or more variables, you can specify those values just once, following the last of the variables to which they apply. For example, to construct the same example shown in Section 3.22, specify

```
CROSSTABS     VARIABLES=RETURNED,LOCATION(1,2) ADDRESS(1,3)/
              TABLES=RETURNED BY ADDRESS BY LOCATION
OPTIONS       3,5
STATISTICS    1
```

All variables named in the TABLES= subcommand must be specified first on the VARIABLES= subcommand. The order makes no difference. In fact, as the example shows, you may want to group variables that have the same lowest and highest values.

In integer mode, you are restricted to 6 control levels (7 BYs).

3.24 CROSSTABS and Other SPSS Commands

The complete SPSS command file used to produce the table and statistics shown in Figure 3.4 is

```
RUN NAME        LOST LETTER DATA
DATA LIST       FIXED/1 ADDRESS RETURNED LOCATION 1-3
VAR LABELS      ADDRESS,ADDRESS ON LETTER/
                RETURNED,FOUND AND MAILED/
                LOCATION,LOCATION LOST/
VALUE LABELS    ADDRESS (1) CONTROL (2) DANDEE (3) COMMUNIST/
                RETURNED (1) YES (2) NO/
                LOCATION (1) CITY (2) TOWN/
CROSSTABS       TABLES=RETURNED BY ADDRESS BY LOCATION
OPTIONS         3,5
STATISTICS      1
READ INPUT DATA
[data records]
END INPUT DATA
FINISH
```

DATA LIST. The three single-column variables named ADDRESS, RETURNED, and LOCATION are recorded in the first three columns of each data record. Note that SPSS allows you to specify a list of variables, then a range of columns to be divided equally among those variables. (See Chapter 11 for more information on DATA LIST specifications.) Because no decimal places are recorded on the data or implied in the DATA LIST command, you could use CROSSTABS integer mode as shown in Section 3.23.

VAR LABELS, VALUE LABELS. The variable and value labels are not being suppressed in this example and therefore appear on the output as they are specified on the VAR LABELS and VALUE LABELS commands. Since the amount of print space is limited, note that CROSSTABS will print only the first 16 characters of the value labels. For the column variable, long value labels are split after the eighth character and printed on two lines. If you know this, you can specify your value labels in more pleasing manner, as in

```
DATA LIST        FIXED/1 HYPNOSIS MIGRAINE 1-2
VAR LABELS       HYPNOSIS DEPTH OF HYPNOSIS/
                 MIGRAINE OUTCOME/
VALUE LABELS     HYPNOSIS(1)DEEP(2)MEDIUM(3)LIGHT/
                 MIGRAINE(1)CURED(2)BETTER(3)NO        CHANGE/
CROSSTABS        TABLES=HYPNOSIS BY MIGRAINE
OPTIONS          3,4
STATISTICS       1,2,3,4,5
READ INPUT DATA
[data records]
END INPUT DATA
FINISH
```

These are the basic commands used to produce the output shown in Figure 3.12.

3.25 ENTERING CROSSTABULATED DATA

Frequently, you already have a crosstabulation that you want to present in a different way or for which you want to produce additional statistics. You can enter the crosstabulated data rather than the original observations into SPSS and proceed with your analysis. Each cell of the table is considered a case. For each case (cell of the table), enter the cell counts along with the values of the row, column, and control variables. Define this file as you would any other data file. Then use the WEIGHT command to specify that each case should be counted as many times as specified by the cell frequency.

For example, to reproduce the table in Figure 3.1 from the crosstabulated data, use the following SPSS command file.

```
RUN NAME        ENTERING THE TABLE OF RETURNED BY ADDRESS
DATA LIST       FIXED/1 FREQ 1-5 RETURNED 7 ADDRESS 9
WEIGHT          FREQ
VAR LABELS      RETURNED,FOUND AND MAILED/
                ADDRESS,ADDRESS ON LETTER/
VALUE LABELS    RETURNED (1) YES (2) NO/
                ADDRESS (1) CONTROL (2) DANDEE (3) COMMUNIST/
CROSSTABS       TABLES=RETURNED BY ADDRESS
STATISTICS      1
READ INPUT DATA
    35 1 1
    37 2 1
    32 1 2
    40 2 2
    10 1 3
    62 2 3
END INPUT DATA
FINISH
```

DATA LIST.   Each cell of the table is entered as a case. The cell frequency is entered in columns 1 through 5 and is defined as variable FREQ. The value of RETURNED for each cell is entered in column 7, and the value of ADDRESS in column 9. So, the first line of data represents the first cell of the table where RETURNED has the value 1 and ADDRESS the value 1. The second line of data is the second cell in the first column of the table, and so forth.

WEIGHT.   The WEIGHT command defines FREQ, the cell frequencies, as the weight variable. The value of this variable for each case is then used as a *replication factor:* SPSS reads the single case as though it were reading a number of separate cases equal to the replication factor. For example, the first case is counted as 35 cases in the table requested on the CROSSTABS command. The WEIGHT command allows you to represent the original data from the crosstabulated data.

Other Data Definition Commands.   You can assign variable and value labels to crosstabulated data with the VAR LABELS and VALUE LABELS commands. You can also use the PRINT FORMATS command to specify the number of decimal positions that you want printed for the values. If you have included values in the crosstabulated data that you now want excluded from the table, use the MISSING VALUES command to specify the values to be excluded.

CROSSTABS.   As usual, the CROSSTABS command specifies the desired crosstabulation. If you want to rearrange the variables in the crosstabulated input data or drop certain variables from the table, you can do so by specifying only the variables that you want and in the order that you want. For example, you can define ADDRESS as the row variable and RETURNED as the column variable by specifying

```
CROSSTABS       TABLES=ADDRESS BY RETURNED
```

Chapter 4

Breaking Down Discrimination: Describing Subpopulation Differences

The 1964 Civil Rights Act prohibits discrimination in the workplace based on sex or race. Employers who violate the act, by unfair hiring or advancement, are liable for prosecution. Numerous lawsuits have been filed on behalf of women, blacks, and other groups offered equal protection under the law.

The courts have ruled that statistics can be used as *prima facie* evidence of discrimination, and many lawsuits depend heavily on complex statistical analyses, which attempt to demonstrate that similarly qualified individuals are not treated equally. Identifying and measuring of all variables that legitimately influence promotion and hiring is difficult, if not impossible, especially for nonroutine jobs. Years of schooling and prior work experience can be quantified, but what about the more intangible attributes such as enthusiasm and creativity? How are they to be objectively measured so as not to become convenient smoke screens to conceal discrimination?

4.1 SEARCHING FOR DISCRIMINATION

In this chapter, employee records for 474 individuals hired between 1969 and 1971 by a bank engaged in EEO litigation are analyzed. Two types of unfair employment practices are of particular interest: shunting (placing some employees in lower job categories than others with similar qualifications) and salary and promotion inequities.

Although extensive and intricate statistical analyses are usually involved in studies of this kind (see, for example, Roberts, 1980), the discussion here is necessarily limited. The SPSS BREAKDOWN procedure is used to calculate average salaries for groups of employees based on race and sex. Additional grouping variables are introduced to help "explain" some of the observed variability in salary.

4.2 Who Does What?

Figure 4.2 is a crosstabulation of an individual's beginning job category at the time of hiring and a variable recording combined sex and race characteristics. The first three job classifications contain 64% of the white males (adding column percents), 94% of the white females and nonwhite males, and all of the nonwhite females. Seventeen percent of white males are in the college trainee program, compared to 4% of the white females.

Figure 4.2   Crosstabulation of job category by sex-race

```
               SEXRACE
        COUNT I
        COL PCT IWHITE   NONWHITE WHITE    NONWHITE  ROW
        TOT PCT IMALES   MALES    FEMALES  FEMALES   TOTAL
               I    1.I     2.I     3.I      4.I
JOBCAT         ---------I--------I--------I---------I
          1.   I   75 I   35 I    85 I    32 I    227
CLERICAL       I 38.7 I 54.7 I  48.3 I  80.0 I   47.9
               I 15.8 I  7.4 I  17.9 I   6.8 I
               -I--------I--------I--------I---------I
          2.   I   35 I   12 I    81 I     8 I    136
OFFICE TRAINEE I 18.0 I 18.8 I  46.0 I  20.0 I   28.7
               I  7.4 I  2.5 I  17.1 I   1.7 I
               -I--------I--------I--------I---------I
          3.   I   14 I   13 I     0 I     0 I     27
SECURITY OFFICE I  7.2 I 20.3 I   0.0 I   0.0 I    5.7
               I  3.0 I  2.7 I   0.0 I   0.0 I
               -I--------I--------I--------I---------I
          4.   I   33 I    1 I     7 I     0 I     41
COLLEGE TRAINEE I 17.0 I  1.6 I   4.0 I   0.0 I    8.6
               I  7.0 I  0.2 I   1.5 I   0.0 I
               -I--------I--------I--------I---------I
          5.   I   28 I    2 I     2 I     0 I     32
EXEMPT EMPLOYEE I 14.4 I  3.1 I   1.1 I   0.0 I    6.8
               I  5.9 I  0.4 I   0.4 I   0.0 I
               -I--------I--------I--------I---------I
          6.   I    3 I    1 I     1 I     0 I      5
MBA TRAINEE    I  1.5 I  1.6 I   0.6 I   0.0 I    1.1
               I  0.6 I  0.2 I   0.2 I   0.0 I
               -I--------I--------I--------I---------I
          7.   I    6 I    0 I     0 I     0 I      6
TECHNICAL      I  3.1 I  0.0 I   0.0 I   0.0 I    1.3
               I  1.3 I  0.0 I   0.0 I   0.0 I
               -I--------I--------I--------I---------I
        COLUMN     194     64      176       40       474
        TOTAL     40.9   13.5     37.1      8.4    100.0
```

Although these observations are interesting, they do not imply discriminatory placement into beginning job categories because the qualifications of the various groups are not necessarily similar. If women and nonwhites are at least as qualified as white males in the same beginning job categories, discrimination may be suspected.

4.3   Level of Education

One easily measured employment qualification is years of education. Figure 4.3a shows the average years of education for the entire sample (labeled FOR ENTIRE POPULATION) and then for each of the two sexes (labeled SEX and MALES or FEMALES) and then for each of the two race categories within each sex category (labeled MINORITY and WHITE or NONWHITE).

Figure 4.3a   Education broken down by race within sex

```
- - - - - - - - - - - - - - - -  D E S C R I P T I O N   O F   S U B P O P U L A T I O N S  - - - - - - - - - - - - - - - - - -
CRITERION VARIABLE    EDLEVEL    EDUCATIONAL LEVEL
   BROKEN DOWN BY     SEX        SEX OF EMPLOYEE
             BY       MINORITY   MINORITY CLASSIFICATION
- - - - - - - - - - - - - - - - - - - - - - - - - - - - - - - - - - - - - - - - - - - - - - - - - - - - - - - -
VARIABLE                       CODE   VALUE LABEL              SUM        MEAN      STD DEV    VARIANCE          N
FOR ENTIRE POPULATION                                    6395.0000    13.4916     2.8848      8.3223     (   474)

SEX                             0.    MALES            3723.0000    14.4302     2.9793      8.8764     (   258)
   MINORITY                     0.    WHITE            2895.0000    14.9227     2.8484      8.1132     (   194)
   MINORITY                     1.    NONWHITE          828.0000    12.9375     2.8888      8.3452     (    64)

SEX                             1.    FEMALES          2672.0000    12.3704     2.3192      5.3785     (   216)
   MINORITY                     0.    WHITE            2172.0000    12.3409     2.4066      5.7917     (   176)
   MINORITY                     1.    NONWHITE          500.0000    12.5000     1.9081      3.6410     (    40)

   TOTAL CASES =     474
```

The entire sample has an average of 13.49 years of education. Males have more years of education than females—an average of 14.43 years compared to 12.37. White males have the highest level of education, almost 15 years, which is 2 years more than nonwhite males and approximately 2.5 years more than either group of females.

Figure 4.3b Education by sex-race and job category

```
* * * * * * * * * * * * * * *   C R O S S — — B R E A K D O W N   O F   * * * * * * * * * * * * * * * * * *
     JOBCAT    EMPLOYMENT CATEGORY                     BY   SEXRACE
* * * * * * * * * * * * * * * * * * * * * * * * * * * * * * * * * * * * * * * * * * * * * * * *
VARIABLE AVERAGED...    EDLEVEL   EDUCATIONAL LEVEL
* * * * * * * * * * * * * * * * * * * * * * * * * * * * * * * * * * * * * * * * *  PAGE  1 OF  1
                        SEXRACE
           MEAN I
           COUNT I   WHITE       NONWHITE    WHITE       NONWHITE
           STD DEV I  MALES       MALES       FEMALES     FEMALES     ROW
                 I      1   I       2   I       3   I       4   I    TOTAL
JOBCAT        ---I----------I----------I----------I----------I
           1 I   13.87 I   13.77 I   11.46 I   12.63 I   12.78
  CLERICAL    I      75 I      35 I      85 I      32 I      227
             I    2.30 I    2.31 I    2.43 I    2.12 I     2.56
            -I----------I----------I----------I----------I
           2 I   13.89 I   12.58 I   12.81 I   12.00 I   13.02
  OFFICE TRAINEE I    35 I      12 I      81 I       8 I      136
             I    1.41 I    2.61 I    1.93 I    0.0  I     1.89
            -I----------I----------I----------I----------I
           3 I   10.29 I   10.08 I    0.0  I    0.0  I   10.19
  SECURITY OFFICE I   14 I      13 I       0 I       0 I       27
             I    2.05 I    2.47 I    0.0  I    0.0  I     2.22
            -I----------I----------I----------I----------I
           4 I   17.21 I   17.00 I   16.00 I    0.0  I   17.00
  COLLEGE TRAINEE I   33 I       1 I       7 I       0 I       41
             I    1.34 I    0.0  I    0.0  I    0.0  I     1.28
            -I----------I----------I----------I----------I
           5 I   17.61 I   14.00 I   16.00 I    0.0  I   17.28
  EXEMPT EMPLOYEE I   28 I       2 I       2 I       0 I       32
             I    1.77 I    2.83 I    0.0  I    0.0  I     1.97
            -I----------I----------I----------I----------I
           6 I   18.33 I   19.00 I   16.00 I    0.0  I   18.00
  MBA TRAINEE I       3 I       1 I       1 I       0 I        5
             I    1.15 I    0.0  I    0.0  I    0.0  I     1.41
            -I----------I----------I----------I----------I
           7 I   18.17 I    0.0  I    0.0  I    0.0  I   18.17
  TECHNICAL  I       6 I       0 I       0 I       0 I        6
             I    1.47 I    0.0  I    0.0  I    0.0  I     1.47
            -I----------I----------I----------I----------I
  COLUMN TOTAL   14.92     12.94     12.34     12.50     13.49
                   194        64       176        40       474
                  2.85      2.89      2.41      1.91      2.88
```

In Figure 4.3b, the cases are further subdivided by their combined sex-race characteristics and by their inital job category. For each of the cells in the table, the average years of education, the standard deviation, and number of cases are printed. White males have the highest average years of education in all job categories, except MBA trainees where the single nonwhite male MBA trainee has 19 years of education. From this table, it does not appear that females and nonwhites are overeducated when compared to white males in similar job categories. It is important to note that group means provide information about a particular class of employees. It is possible for discrimination not to exist for the class as a whole, yet for some individuals within a class to be victims and some to be beneficiaries of discrimination.

4.4 Beginning Salaries

The average beginning salary for the 474 persons hired in 1969-1971 is $6,806. The distribution by the four sex-race categories is shown in Figure 4.4a.

Figure 4.4a Beginning salary by sex-race

```
- - - - - - - - - - - - - - - -   D E S C R I P T I O N   O F   S U B P O P U L A T I O N S   - - - - - - - - - - - - - - - -
CRITERION VARIABLE    SALBEG    BEGINNING SALARY
   BROKEN DOWN BY     SEXRACE
- - - - - - - - - - - - - - - - - - - - - - - - - - - - - - - - - - - - - - - - - - - - - - - - - - - - - - - - -

VARIABLE              CODE    VALUE LABEL              SUM           MEAN        STD DEV       VARIANCE          N

FOR ENTIRE POPULATION                              3226250.0000    6806.4346   3148.2553   9911511.1934    (  474)

SEXRACE                1.    WHITE MALES           1675680.0000    8637.5258   3871.1017  14985428.3750    (  194)
SEXRACE                2.    NONWHITE MALES         419424.0000    6553.5000   2228.1436   4964624.0000    (   64)
SEXRACE                3.    WHITE FEMALES          939926.0000    5340.4886   1225.9605   1502979.0742    (  176)
SEXRACE                4.    NONWHITE FEMALES       191220.0000    4780.5000    771.4188    595086.9231    (   40)

   TOTAL CASES =     474
```

White males have the highest beginning salaries—an average of $8,638—followed by nonwhite males. Since the men are in higher job categories than females, this difference is not surprising.

Figure 4.4b   Beginning salary by sex-race and job category

```
* * * * * * * * * * * * * * * * * * * * * * * * * * * * * * * * * * * * * * * * * * * * * * * * * * * * *
VARIABLE AVERAGED...    SALBEG    BEGINNING SALARY
* * * * * * * * * * * * * * * * * * * * * * * * * * * * * * * * * * * * * * * * * *  PAGE  1 OF  1

                    SEXRACE
            MEAN I
                 I   WHITE      NONWHITE    WHITE      NONWHITE
                 I   MALES      MALES       FEMALES    FEMALES     ROW
                 I        1 I        2 I        3 I        4 I   TOTAL
JOBCAT    -------I----------I----------I----------I----------I
           1 I   6553.44 I   6230.74 I   5147.32 I   4828.13 I  5733.95
  CLERICAL     I          I          I          I          I      227
           -I----------I----------I----------I----------I
           2 I   6262.29 I   5610.00 I   5208.89 I   4590.00 I  5478.97
OFFICE TRAINEE I          I          I          I          I      136
           -I----------I----------I----------I----------I
           3 I   6102.86 I   5953.84 I      0.0 I      0.0 I  6031.11
SECURITY OFFICE I         I          I          I          I       27
           -I----------I----------I----------I----------I
           4 I  10467.63 I  11496.00 I   7326.86 I      0.0 I  9956.48
COLLEGE TRAINEE I         I          I          I          I       41
           -I----------I----------I----------I----------I
           5 I  13255.29 I  15570.00 I  10998.00 I      0.0 I 13258.88
EXEMPT EMPLOYEE I         I          I          I          I       32
           -I----------I----------I----------I----------I
           6 I  14332.00 I  13992.00 I   7200.00 I      0.0 I 12837.60
  MBA TRAINEE  I          I          I          I          I        5
           -I----------I----------I----------I----------I
           7 I  19996.00 I      0.0 I      0.0 I      0.0 I 19996.00
  TECHNICAL    I          I          I          I          I        6
           -I----------I----------I----------I----------I
  COLUMN TOTAL     8637.52    6553.50    5340.49    4780.50    6806.43
                      194         64        176         40        474
```

Beginning salaries subdivided by the race, sex, and job category of the employees are shown in Figure 4.4b. For most of the job categories, white males have higher beginning salaries than the other groups. There is a $1400 salary difference between white males and white females in the clerical jobs, and a $1000 difference in the general office trainee classification. In the college trainee program, white males averaged over $3000 more than white females. However from Figure 4.3b, it can be seen that white females in the college trainee program had only an undergraduate degree, while white males had an average of 17.2 years of schooling.

4.5   Introducing More Variables

The differences in mean beginning salaries between males and females are somewhat suspect. It is, however, unwise to conclude that salary discrimination exists since several important variables, such as years of prior experience, have not been considered. It is necessary to control (or to adjust statistically) for other relevant variables. Crossclassifying cases by the variables of interest and comparing salaries across the subgroups is one way of achieving the control. However, as the number of variables increases, the number of cases in each cell rapidly diminishes, with resulting difficulties in making statistically meaningful comparisons. To circumvent these problems, regression methods are used which achieve the control or adjustment by specifying certain statistical relations that may describe what is happening. Regression methods are described in Chapter 10.

4.6   RUNNING PROCEDURE BREAKDOWN

Procedure BREAKDOWN prints sums, means, standard deviations, and variances of a variable within subgroups defined by another variable. For example, it provides income statistics broken down by sex, age group, level of education, etc. For most applications, you need to specify only the TABLES= subcommand to name the variables. This is known as the *general mode* of BREAKDOWN. Options are provided for handling missing values and for requesting modified tabular formats.

If your data are integer-valued and you want the special crosstabulation-like format, you can use the VARIABLES= and CROSSBREAK= subcommands as shown beginning in Sections 4.9 and 4.10.

4.7   The TABLES= Subcommand

Enter the BREAKDOWN command beginning in column 1 and the TABLES= subcommand and specifications in column 16 or beyond. The variable list for the TABLES= subcommand is of the form *varname* BY *varname*. Means, standard deviations, etc., of the first variable are computed for the categories defined by the variable list to the right of keyword BY. For example, to produce the table shown in Figure 4.4a, specify

```
BREAKDOWN      TABLES=SALBEG BY SEXRACE
```

Additional grouping variables can be specified by entering additional BY keywords followed by the variable names. For example, to summarize education for race within each sex category as shown in Figure 4.3a, specify

```
BREAKDOWN      TABLES=EDLEVEL BY SEX BY MINORITY
```

You can specify multiple variables in any of the dimensions. If you specify multiple variables, SPSS produces separate tables for each variable named. For example, to summarize beginning and current salaries by sex-race and then by job category, specify

```
BREAKDOWN      TABLES=SALBEG,SALNOW BY SEXRACE,JOBCAT
```

4.8   The OPTIONS Command for BREAKDOWN

Following your BREAKDOWN command, you can request special missing-value treatment options. Enter the OPTIONS command beginning in column 1 and one of the following numbers in column 16. A complete list of options is found in Appendix B.

OPTION 1   Include cases with missing values.
OPTION 2   Include cases with missing values on the control (BY) variables only.

Unless you specify otherwise, cases with missing values for any variable in a table are excluded. Option 1 directs SPSS to include all cases regardless of the missing-value status and consider all values valid. Option 2 excludes cases with missing values for the variable or variables named to the left of the first BY only; missing-value categories will appear for control variables.

4.9   The VARIABLES= and CROSSBREAK= Subcommands

To print the alternative crosstabulation-like format shown in Figures 4.3b and 4.4b, use the VARIABLES= subcommand to name the variables and give their ranges and the CROSSBREAK= subcommand to specify the tables in the same manner as shown for the TABLES= subcommand in Section 4.7. For example, to produce the output shown in Figure 4.3b, specify

```
BREAKDOWN      VARIABLES=EDLEVEL(LO,HI) SEXRACE(1,4) JOBCAT(1,7)/
               CROSSBREAK=EDLEVEL BY JOBCAT BY SEXRACE
```

All variables you intend to use in a table must be named on the VARIABLES= subcommand, each with a minimum and maximum value specified in parentheses following the variable name. This is the *integer mode* of BREAKDOWN. Keywords LO (or LOWEST) and HI (or HIGHEST) can be used to specify the minimum and maximum for dependent variables. If you specify values for the minimum or maximum, any case with a value outside the limits is eliminated from the table.

4.10 Special Options for CROSSBREAK

There are four options that apply to the CROSSBREAK= format only. By default, SPSS prints the mean, frequency (count), sum, and standard deviation in each cell of the table unless you use one or more of the following options.

OPTION 5   Don't print cell frequencies.
OPTION 6   Don't print sums.
OPTION 7   Don't print standard deviations.
OPTION 8   Don't print value labels.

For example, the table shown in Figure 4.3b is a result of Option 6, and the table shown in Figure 4.4b is specified by

```
BREAKDOWN      VARIABLES=SALBEG(LO,HI) SEXRACE(1,4) JOBCAT(1,7)/
               CROSSBREAK=SALBEG BY JOBCAT BY SEXRACE
OPTIONS        5,6,7
```

4.11   The STATISTICS Command for BREAKDOWN

You can request several optional statistics with BREAKDOWN, including an analysis of variance table. Enter the STATISTICS command keyword in column 1 followed by a list of numbers beginning in column 16 or beyond corresponding to the desired statistics. A complete list of the optional statistics available is found in Appendix B.

4.12   BREAKDOWN and Other SPSS Commands

A complete SPSS command file used to generate Figures 4.3a and 4.4b is

```
GET FILE       BANK
COMPUTE        SEXRACE=1
IF             (MINORITY EQ 1 AND SEX EQ 0) SEXRACE=2
IF             (MINORITY EQ 0 AND SEX EQ 1) SEXRACE=3
IF             (MINORITY EQ 1 AND SEX EQ 1) SEXRACE=4
VALUE LABELS   SEXRACE (1) WHITE MALES (2) NONWHITE MALES
               (3) WHITE FEMALES (4) NONWHITE FEMALES/
BREAKDOWN      TABLES=EDLEVEL BY SEX BY MINORITY
VALUE LABELS   SEXRACE (1) WHITE    MALES (2) NONWHITEMALES
               (3) WHITE    FEMALES (4) NONWHITEFEMALES/
BREAKDOWN      VARIABLES=SALBEG(LO,HI) SEXRACE(1,4) JOBCAT(1,7)/
               CROSSBREAK=SALBEG BY JOBCAT BY SEXRACE
OPTIONS        5,6,7
```

GET FILE.   The GET FILE command is used to read an SPSS system file that contains the bank data along with variable labels, value labels, missing-value declarations, etc., supplied in a previous run with a SAVE FILE command. It is a substitute for reading and defining raw data using DATA LIST, VAR LABELS, etc. The SAVE FILE and GET FILE commands are described in Chapter 11.

COMPUTE and IF.   The COMPUTE command and the three IF commands are used to create a single four-category variable that combines the sex and race variables already on the file. The COMPUTE command sets new variable SEXRACE to 1, which will be the white male category. The value is then changed to 2 for nonwhite males, to 3 for white females, and to 4 for nonwhite females in the respective IF commands. Refer to Chapter 11 for an additional discussion of the COMPUTE and IF commands.

VALUE LABELS.   Two sets of value labels are assigned to new variable SEXRACE. The first set is used in the standard BREAKDOWN table shown in Figure 4.3a, and the second set is specially formatted to print well in the CROSSBREAK tables in Figures 4.3b and 4.4b in exactly the manner described for CROSSTABS in Chapter 3.

Chapter 5

Selling Canary Crunch to Junior: Testing Hypotheses About Differences in Means

Television advertising directed to children is responsible for billions of dollars in sales as well as innumerable episodes of parent-child conflict. Consumer groups comparing TV ads to "Nazi propaganda methods," continue to pressure the Federal Trade Commission and the Federal Communications Commission to restrict the nature and number of commercials aired during children's programs. To regulate advertising, it is important to identify the types of commercials that are particularly seductive to children.

Miller and Busch (1979) conducted an experiment to compare the effects of three types of commercials on boys and girls of various ages and races. Two of the commercial types are host selling, in which a character in the program recommends the product, and premium sales, which entice the viewer with goodies tucked inside. Children were exposed to one of the commercial types under carefully supervised conditions. The criteria used to establish effectiveness were scores on a test that measured recall of the commercial's contents and the actual selection of the product when faced with a choice.

5.1 TESTING HYPOTHESES

Two of the hypotheses tested in the advertising experiment are that children's recall of contents is the same for the two types of commercials and that selection of the product is not influenced by commercial type. Consider each in turn.

The first part of the table in Figure 5.1 contains basic descriptive statistics for the recall scores of children viewing host and premium commercials for a cereal called Canary Crunch. The 66 children exposed to the host format (Group 1) had a mean recall score of 17.42, while the 82 children lured with premiums had a score of 16.78. The standard deviations show that scores for the first group were somewhat more variable than those for the second.

Figure 5.1   Recall scores by commercial type

```
- - - - - - - - - - - - - - - - - - - - - - - - - - - T - T E S T - - - - - - - - - - - - - - - - - - - - - - - - - - - - - -
```

					*		* POOLED VARIANCE ESTIMATE		* SEPARATE VARIANCE ESTIMATE		
GROUP 1 – TYPE	EQ	1.											
GROUP 2 – TYPE	EQ	2.				*		*			*		
VARIABLE	NUMBER OF CASES	MEAN	STANDARD DEVIATION	STANDARD ERROR		* F VALUE	2–TAIL PROB.	* T VALUE	DEGREES OF FREEDOM	2–TAIL PROB.	* T VALUE	DEGREES OF FREEDOM	2–TAIL PROB.
RECALL COMMERCIAL RECALL SCORE						*		*			*		
GROUP 1	66	17.4240	2.804	0.345		*		*			*		
						* 2.57	0.000	* 1.71	146	0.089	* 1.63	103.95	0.106
GROUP 2	82	16.7803	1.750	0.193		*		*			*		

If one is willing to restrict the conclusions to the 148 children included in the study, it is safe to say that the children who viewed the host commercial correctly answered more questions about the contents than did the children who viewed the premium commercial. However, this statement is not very satisfying. What is needed is some type of statement about the effectiveness of the two commercial types for all children—or at least some larger group of children—not just those actually studied.

5.2   Samples and Populations

The totality of all cases about which conclusions are desired is called a *population*, while the observations actually included in the study are the *sample*. The children in this experiment can be considered a sample from the population of all 5- to 12-year-old children in the United States.

Statistics helps draw inferences about populations based on observations from random samples (samples in which the characteristics and relationships of interest are independent of the probabilities of being included in the sample). The necessity of good experimental design cannot be overemphasized. Unless precautions are taken to insure that the sample is from the population of interest, and that the cases are chosen and observed without bias, the results obtained from statistical analyses may be misleading. For example, if a sample contains only affluent suburban children, conclusions about all children may be unwarranted.

If an entire population is observed, it can be characterized by the various measures of central tendency, dispersion, and shape described in Chapter 2. The results describe the population exactly. If, however, one obtains information from a random sample, the results serve as *estimates* of the unknown population values, termed *parameters*. Special notation is used to identify population values and distinguish them from sample values. The mean of a population is denoted by μ, the variance by σ^2. The symbols $\overline{X}$ and S^2 are reserved for the mean and variance of samples.

Because of sampling variation, results obtained from a sample typically differ from those that would be obtained if the entire population is studied. Therefore, it is useful to know what can actually be said about the unknown population parameters based on results from samples.

5.3   Sampling Distributions

It is useful to consider what would happen if many random samples were selected from the population, and each sample were used to estimate population parameters. Ordinarily, a researcher works with a single sample, so the idea of repeated sampling is a conceptual tool. Imagine that the researcher takes 1000 samples of size N and each time calculates the mean. These estimates have a distribution, and their mean and variance can be calculated. The 1000 estimates are a sample of possible values that can be obtained.

The theoretical distribution of all possible values of a statistic obtained from a population is called the *sampling distribution* of the statistic. The mean of the sampling distribution is called the *expected value* of the statistic. The standard deviation is termed the *standard error*. The sampling distributions of most commonly used statistics calculated from random samples are tabulated and readily accessible. Knowing the sampling distribution of a statistic is very important for hypothesis testing.

5.4 Sampling Distribution of the Mean

Consider the sampling distribution of the sample mean, a commonly used statistic. If the variable being examined is itself normally distributed, the sampling distribution of the sample means is also normal. Even if the distribution of the variable is not normal, the distribution of means of sufficiently large samples will be approximately normal. This is a major reason why the normal distribution is very important for statistical inference. The mean of the sampling distribution is μ, the population mean. The standard error is

$$\sigma_{\bar{X}} = \frac{\sigma}{\sqrt{N}}$$

where σ is the standard deviation of the variable, and N is the sample size. The larger the sample size, the smaller the variability of the distribution of means.

In a sample, the standard error of the mean is estimated using

$$S_{\bar{X}} = \frac{S}{\sqrt{N}}$$

where S is the *sample* standard deviation. This value is printed when Statistic 2 is requested in procedures FREQUENCIES and CONDESCRIPTIVE and is part of the output shown in Figure 5.1.

The standard error of the mean depends on both the sample standard deviation and the sample size. As the size of a sample increases, the standard error decreases. This is intuitively clear, since the more data are gathered, the more confident you can be that the sample mean is not too far from the population mean. Also, as the standard deviation of the observations decreases, the standard error also decreases.

5.5 THE TWO-SAMPLE T TEST

Consider again whether there is evidence that host and premium commercials differ in their influence on children's ability to recall their contents correctly. The question is not whether the two sample means are equal, but whether the two population means are equal.

To test the hypothesis that, in the population, recall scores for the two commercial types are the same, the following statistic is calculated:

$$t = \frac{\bar{X}_1 - \bar{X}_2}{\sqrt{S_1^2/N_1 + S_2^2/N_2}}$$

The symbol $\bar{X}_1$ represents the sample mean of group 1, S_1^2 the variance, and N_1 the sample size. The *observed significance level* associated with this statistic is the probability that a difference at least as large as the one observed would occur if the two population means (μ_1 and μ_2) are equal. If this probability is small enough, usually less than 0.05, or 0.01, the hypothesis that the population means are equal is rejected.

The t value and its associated probability value are given in Figure 5.1 in the section labeled SEPARATE VARIANCE ESTIMATE. The probability of observing a difference at least as large as the one in the sample when $\mu_1 = \mu_2$ is estimated about 0.106. Since this probability is greater than 0.05, the hypothesis that in the population mean recall scores are equal for the two commercials is not rejected. The entry under degrees of freedom is a function of the sample size in the two groups and is used together with the t value in establishing the observed significance level.

Another statistic based on the t distribution can be used to test the equality of means hypothesis. It is called the *pooled variance t test,* since it is based on the assumption that the population variances in the two groups are equal, and it is obtained using a pooled estimate of that common variance. From the output in Figure 5.1, the pooled t test value for the study is 1.71. The degrees of freedom for the pooled t test are 146, the sum of the sample sizes in both groups minus 2. If the pooled variance t test is used when the population variances are not equal, the probability level associated with the statistic may be in error. The amount of error depends on the inequality of the sample sizes and of the variances. Use of the separate variance t value when the population variances are equal will usually result in an observed significance level somewhat larger than it should be. For large sample sizes the discrepancy between the two methods is small. In general, it is a good idea to use the *separate variance t test* whenever there is suspicion that the variances are unequal.

In this example, the separate variance t test is used since the variance in the first group is more than double the variance in the second group. The F value in Figure 5.1 is the ratio of the larger sample variance to the smaller. It is used to test the hypothesis that the two population variances are equal. If the observed significance level for the F test is small, the hypothesis that the population variances are equal is rejected, and the separate variance t test for means should be used.

5.6 Significance Levels

The common-sense interpretation when a small observed significance level is found is straightforward: it appears unlikely that the two population means are equal. Of course, the possibility exists that the means are equal and the observed difference is due to chance. The observed significance level is the probability that a difference at least as large as the one observed would have arisen if the means are really equal.

When the observed significance level is too large to reject the equality hypothesis, the two population means may indeed be equal, or the means may be unequal but the difference cannot be detected. Failure to detect can be due to a true difference that is very small. For example, if a new cancer drug prolongs survival time by only one day when compared to the standard treatment, it is unlikely that such a difference will be detected, especially if survival times vary substantially and the additional day represents a small increment. Failure to identify such a small difference may not be a great loss, unless the new drug has other properties that make it appealing. The actual increase in life span may not be of much practical significance.

There are other reasons why real differences may not be found. If the sample sizes in the two groups are small, or the variability large, even substantial differences may not be detected.

Significant t values are obtained when the numerator of the t statistic is large when compared to the denominator. The numerator is the difference between the sample means, and the denominator depends on the standard deviations and sample sizes of the two groups. For a given standard deviation, the larger the sample size, the smaller the denominator. Thus, a difference of a given magnitude may be significant if obtained with a sample size of 100, but not significant with a sample size of 25.

5.7   One-Tailed vs. Two-Tailed Tests

In the output in Figure 5.1, all probabilities are labeled as two-tailed. That corresponds to a test of the alternative hypothesis that the two means are not equal, the direction of the difference not being specified. For example, there would be interest in detecting a true difference in either direction, favoring the host commercial or the premium commercial. In applications where one is interested in detecting a difference in one direction—such as interest in whether a new "miracle" drug is better than the current treatment—a so-called one-tailed test can be performed. The procedure is the same as previously outlined, but the resulting probability value is divided by two. This is an adjustment for the fact that the equality hypothesis is rejected only when the difference between the two means is sufficiently large and in the direction of interest. In a two-tailed test, the equality hypothesis is rejected for large positive or negative values of the statistic.

5.8   What's the Difference?

It appears that the format of a commercial has no significant effect on children's ability or willingness to recall product information. Children viewing both host and premium commercials had a high degree of recall as measured by scores on a 20-point scale. Hype about the premium does not seem to detract from remembering details about the product.

It is possible that the recall scores obtained in the experiment are higher than would be observed in a routine television viewing situation since the commercials were viewed in a program shown at school. Commercials may be more appealing when they replace geography lessons.

5.9   USING PROCEDURE CROSSTABS TO TEST HYPOTHESES

The T-TEST procedure is used to test hypotheses about the equality of two means for variables measured on an interval or ratio scale. Procedure CROSSTABS and the chi-square statistic can be used to test hypotheses about a dichotomous variable, such as selection or nonselection of a cereal.

Although recall scores are one indication of the effectiveness of a commercial, the real test of success is measured by children's selection of the product when faced with a choice. Figure 5.9 is a crosstabulation showing the number of children and (column) percentages of children who selected Canary Crunch when allowed to choose between it and three other cereals. The advertised brand was chosen by 54.0% of the children tempted with premiums, while only 37.9% of the children who viewed the host commercial chose Canary Crunch. How does one allow for chance in interpreting this difference?

Figure 5.9   Choosing the cereal

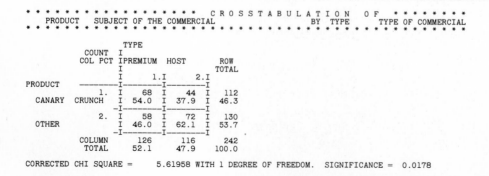

The probability of 0.0178 associated with the chi-square statistic in Figure 5.9 is the probability that a difference at least as large as the one observed would occur in the sample if in the population there is no difference in the selection of the product between the two commercial formats. Since the probability is small, the hypothesis of no difference between the two formats is rejected.

It appears that the premium commercial is more effective than the host format in persuading children to select the advertised product when faced with a choice. Again, in more realistic situations, the premium commercial may not be as effective as suggested by the experimental results. Premium commercials must compete with other premium commercials and will not be as memorable. Also, in this experiment, children were faced with the product selection problem immediately after viewing the commercials. Usually, the time interval between the two events will be longer and the appeal of the premium somewhat less vivid.

5.10   INDEPENDENT VS. PAIRED SAMPLES

Several factors contribute to the observed difference in response between two groups. Part of the observed difference in recall scores between the host and premium formats may be attributable to commercial type. Another component is due to innate differences between individuals. Not all children have the same recall capabilities, so even if the type of commercial does not affect recall, differences between the two groups will probably be observed due to differences between the children within the two groups.

One method of minimizing the influence of individual variation is to choose the two groups so that the children within them are comparable on characteristics that can influence recall ability. If twins are available, and can be divided between the experimental groups, differences in age, race, socioeconomic status, etc. between the groups can be eliminated. However, if twins respond to commercials differently than other people, the generalizability of the results may be limited.

Another frequently used experimental design is to expose the same individual to both types of commercials. The subject-to-subject variability then has substantially less effect on between-commercial comparisons. However, care must be taken to insure that the sequential administration of treatments does not influence response by providing a practice effect, decreased attention span for the second treatment, or other carryover effects. Both designs are called *paired samples* designs since for each subject there is a corresponding pair in the other group (In the second design a person is paired with himself or herself).

5.11   Analysis of Paired Data

Although the interpretation of the significance of results from paired experiments is the same as those from the two independent samples discussed previously, the actual computations are different. For each pair of cases, the difference in the responses is calculated. The statistic used to test the hypothesis that, in the population, the difference is zero is:

$$t = \frac{\overline{D}}{S_D/\sqrt{N}}$$

where $\overline{D}$ is the observed difference between the two means and S_D is the standard deviation of the differences of the paired observations. The sampling distribution of t, if the differences are normally distributed with a mean of zero, is Student's t with $N-1$ degrees of freedom, where N is the number of pairs. If the pairing is effective, the standard error of the difference will be smaller than the standard error obtained if two independent samples with N subjects each were chosen. However, if the variables chosen for pairing do not affect the responses under study, pairing may result in a test that is less powerful since true differences can be detected less frequently.

5.12   Further Analysis of the Arrest Data

In Chapter 2, actual and self-reported arrest data for 79 cases were examined. The experiment is paired since the two variables were obtained for each subject. To test the hypothesis that in the population there is no difference between the mean reported arrests and mean actual arrests, the results in Figure 5.12 are used. The t value is the mean difference divided by the standard error of the difference ($-0.29/0.59 = -0.50$). The two-tailed probability for this test is 0.62, so there is not sufficient evidence to reject the hypothesis that the mean actual and mean reported numbers of arrests are equal.

Figure 5.12   Self-reported vs. actual number of arrests

```
- - - - - - - - - - - - - - - - - - - - - - - - - - - - T - T E S T - - - - - - - - - - - - - - - - - - - - - - - - - - - - - - -

VARIABLE      NUMBER              STANDARD    STANDARD    *(DIFFERENCE) STANDARD    STANDARD    *      2-TAIL  *    T     DEGREES OF 2-TAIL
             OF CASES   MEAN     DEVIATION    ERROR       *    MEAN     DEVIATION    ERROR       * CORR. PROB. *  VALUE   FREEDOM   PROB.

SELF      SELF-REPORTED ARRESTS                           *                                                 *             *
                       8.9620    6.458        0.727       *                                                 *             *
              79                                          *   -0.2911   5.216        0.587       * 0.654 0.000 *  -0.50      78     0.621
                       9.2532    6.248        0.703       *                                                 *             *
TRUE      ACTUAL NUMBER OF ARRESTS                        *                                                 *             *
```

The correlation coefficient between the reported and actual number of arrests is 0.654. A positive correlation indicates that pairing has been effective in decreasing the variability of the mean difference. The larger the correlation coefficient, the greater the benefit of pairing. See Chapter 6 for further discussion of correlation.

5.13   HYPOTHESIS TESTING: A REVIEW

The purpose of hypothesis testing is to help draw conclusions about population parameters based on results observed in random samples. The procedure remains virtually the same for tests of most hypotheses.

- A hypothesis of no difference (called a null hypothesis), as well as its alternative, are formulated.
- A test statistic is chosen to evaluate the null hypothesis.
- For the sample, the test statistic is calculated.
- The probability, if the null hypothesis is true, of obtaining a test value at least as extreme as the one observed is determined.
- If the observed significance level is judged small enough, the null hypothesis is rejected.

5.14   The Importance of Assumptions

In order to perform a statistical test of any hypothesis, it is necessary to make certain assumptions about the data. The particular assumptions depend on the statistical test being used. Some procedures require stricter assumptions than others. For *parametric* tests, some knowledge about the distribution from which samples are selected is required.

The assumptions are necessary to define the sampling distribution of the test statistic. Unless the distribution is defined, correct significance levels cannot be calculated. For the pooled t test, the assumption is that the observations are random samples from normal distributions with the same variance.

For many procedures, not all assumptions are equally important. Moderate violation of some assumptions may not always be serious. Therefore, it is important to know for each procedure not only what assumptions are needed but also how severely their violation may influence results. For example the F test for equality of variances is quite sensitive to departures from normality, while the t test for equality of means is less so.

The responsibility for detecting violations of assumptions rests with the researcher. Unfortunately, unlike the experimenter in chemistry, no explosions or disintegrating terminals threaten the investigator who does not comply with good statistical practice. However, from a research viewpoint, the consequences can be just as severe.

Wherever possible, tests of assumptions—often called diagnostic checks of the model—should be incorporated as part of the hypothesis-testing procedures. Throughout SPSS, attempts have been made to provide facilities for examining assumptions. For example, in the FREQUENCIES procedure, bar charts and measures of skewness and kurtosis provide a convenient check for the normality assumption. Discussion of other such diagnostics is included with the individual procedures.

5.15 RUNNING PROCEDURE T-TEST

Procedure T-TEST computes the Student's t statistic for testing the significance of a difference in means for independent or paired samples. For independent samples, procedure T-TEST provides both separate and pooled variance estimates.

5.16 Independent Samples

Use the GROUPS= subcommand to name the variable and the criterion for dividing the sample into two independent groups and the VARIABLES= subcommand to name the variable or variables to be tested. If your grouping variable is already coded with values 1 and 2, you need only name the variable. For example, to produce the output shown in Figure 5.1, specify

```
T-TEST        GROUPS=TYPE/VARIABLES=RECALL
```

If your grouping variable is not already coded with values 1 and 2, you can divide the sample into two groups using the RECODE command. See Chapter 11 for a more complete discussion of the RECODE command. For example, to separate the sample into two age groups for a similar analysis based on age groups rather than type of commercial, specify

```
RECODE        AGE(5 THRU 7=1)(8 THRU 12=2)
T-TEST        GROUPS=AGE/VARIABLES=RECALL
```

Alternatively, you can let T-TEST divide the sample by naming a value in parentheses following the variable named in the GROUPS= subcommand. Cases equal to or greater than that value for the variable are in group one and the rest of the cases are in group two. For example, to produce the same test shown above with group one now being the older children and group two the younger ones, specify

```
T-TEST        GROUPS=AGE(8)/VARIABLES=RECALL
```

The VARIABLES= subcommand can specify a list of variables. The subcommands must be separated by a slash.

5.17   Paired Samples

To compute tests for paired samples, values for the two members of a pair must be separate variables on the same case. Use one PAIRS= subcommand to name the pair or pairs of variables to be compared. For example, to generate the test shown in Figure 5.12, specify

```
T-TEST          PAIRS=SELF,TRUE
```

If you name three or more variables, T-TEST tests all possible pairs. If you use the keyword WITH to separate variable lists, T-TEST pairs each variable to the left of the keyword with each variable to the right. For example, TIME1,TIME2 WITH TIME3,TIME4 produces four tests.

   If you are specifying both independent and paired sample tests in the same T-TEST command, the PAIRS= subcommand must follow the GROUPS= and VARIABLES= subcommands described in the previous section.

5.18   The OPTIONS Command for T-TEST

Following your T-TEST command specifications, you can enter the OPTIONS command keyword beginning in column 1 and a list of numbers beginning in column 16 or beyond. These numbers correspond to missing-value handling and format options for your tests.

OPTION 1   Include cases with missing values.
OPTION 2   Exclude missing data listwise.
OPTION 3   Do not print variable labels.

By default, pairwise deletion of cases with missing values is in effect. For independent samples, it means that a case is excluded if it has a missing value for either the grouping variable or the variable being tested. For paired samples, a case is excluded if it has a missing value for either variable being paired.

   If you choose Option 1, missing-value indicators for all variables are turned off and cases are included as if all of the values are valid. If you choose Option 2, listwise deletion of cases with missing values is in effect. For independent samples, it means that a case is excluded if it has a missing value for the grouping variable or for any variable in the VARIABLES= list. For paired samples, it means that a case is excluded if it has a missing value on any variable in the PAIRS= list.

5.19   T-TEST AND FREEFIELD INPUT

Procedure T-TEST is used frequently on small samples with very few variables. A small data file of this type can be entered into SPSS in a more convenient format than the fixed-column format described in Chapter 1. You can enter the data in *freefield* format with multiple cases on the same data line, and each value separated by one or more blanks. The values must be entered in the same sequence for each case, but not necessarily in the same columns. A value cannot be continued onto another line. However, you can leave extra blanks at the end of a line.

   To tell SPSS that you are entering freefield data, use the VARIABLE LIST and INPUT FORMAT commands rather than the DATA LIST command. On the VARIA-BLE LIST command, name the variables in the order that they are entered on the data. The variable names must be separated by a blank or comma. On the INPUT FORMAT

command, specify the keyword FREEFIELD. For example, the following SPSS job uses
freefield formatted data to produce the output shown in Figure 5.1.

```
VARIABLE LIST   TYPE RECALL
INPUT FORMAT    FREEFIELD
N OF CASES      148
VAR LABELS      TYPE TYPE OF COMMERCIAL/
                RECALL COMMERCIAL RECALL SCORE/
VALUE LABELS    TYPE (1) PREMIUM (2) HOST/
T-TEST          GROUPS=TYPE/VARIABLES=RECALL
READ INPUT DATA
1 18.05 1 11.329 1 13.508 1 19.021 1 19.265 1 18.504 1 19.373
1 19.661 1 14.893 1 17.508 1 17.598 1 19.158 1 14.429 1 17.749
  ...
  ...
  ...
2 14.988 2 16.728 2 17.8 2 18.104 2 17.32 2 13.807 2 15.293
2 16.422
FINISH
```

5.20 Listing the Data

If you are ever unsure that you have correctly entered and defined the data, use the LIST
CASES command before your first procedure to list out the data file. For example, if you
are uncertain you have correctly entered the data in freefield format—particularly since
if you omit one value, all values following it are incorrectly defined—specify

```
VARIABLE LIST   TYPE RECALL
INPUT FORMAT    FREEFIELD
N OF CASES      148
VAR LABELS      TYPE TYPE OF COMMERCIAL/
                RECALL COMMERCIAL RECALL SCORE/
VALUE LABELS    TYPE (1) PREMIUM (2) HOST/
PRINT FORMATS   RECALL(3)
LIST CASES      CASES=148/VARIABLES=TYPE RECALL
T-TEST          GROUPS=TYPE/VARIABLES=RECALL
READ INPUT DATA
1 18.05 1 11.329 1 13.508 1 19.021 1 19.265 1 18.504 1 19.373
1 19.661 1 14.893 1 17.508 1 17.598 1 19.158 1 14.429 1 17.749
  ...
  ...
  ...
2 14.988 2 16.728 2 17.8 2 18.104 2 17.32 2 13.807 2 15.293
2 16.422
FINISH
```

Enter the command keywords LIST CASES beginning in column 1 and the CASES=
and VARIABLES= subcommands beginning in column 16 or beyond. The CASES=
subcommand specifies the number of cases you want listed. If you specify a number
larger than the number of cases in your data, all of the cases are listed. If you leave off
the CASES= subcommand, SPSS lists the first 10 cases. The VARIABLES= subcommand specifies the names of the variables you want listed. You can use the keyword ALL
to specify all of the variables. If you specify eleven or fewer variables, SPSS prints the
values for each case on a separate line. (See the output from the LIST CASES in Figure
5.20). If you specify more than eleven variables, SPSS lists all the values for each case,
usually on several lines, before listing the next case. The variables are always listed in the
order that they were read.

Figure 5.20   LIST CASES output

```
CASE-N     TYPE     RECALL
     1       1.      18.050
     2       1.      11.329
     3       1.      13.508
     4       1.      19.021
     5       1.      19.265
     6       1.      18.504
     7       1.      19.373
   ...
   ...
   ...
   141       2.      14.988
   142       2.      16.728
   143       2.      17.800
   144       2.      18.104
   145       2.      17.320
   146       2.      13.807
   147       2.      15.293
   148       2.      16.422
```

The PRINT FORMATS command is included in the SPSS job above to tell SPSS to print the values for RECALL with three decimal positions. If the PRINT FORMATS command was not included, LIST CASES would truncate the values of RECALL and print them as integer numbers.

Chapter 6

Skirts and Beards:
Correlation and Scattergrams

"Fashion, though Folly's child, and guide of fools, rules e'en the wisest," claimed George Crabbe in 1781. As is well recognized, fashion dictates almost daily fluctuation of women's dress style. Patterns of male hirsute ornamentation have not received much attention until the recent study by Robinson (1976) which examined pictures of gentlemen appearing in the *Illustrated London News* from 1842 to 1972. For each year, the numbers of men with moustaches, sideburns, moustaches and sideburns, and beards were obtained. Comparing these data to women's skirt measurements obtained from international fashion magazines by Richardson and Kroeber (1940) over a 112-year period leads to some interesting coincidences.

6.1 READING A SCATTERGRAM

Figure 6.1 is a plot of the percentage of clean-shaven men for the 131 years studied by Robinson. Each point represents the values of two variables—year and percentage of clean-shaven men. For example, the circled point represents the year 1894 in which 11% of the pictures were of men without facial hair.

Since plots generated for terminals and printers have a limited number of positions in which to display points, it may not be possible to distinguish between cases with very similar values on the two variables. For example, 131 years are included in the present study, but only 101 horizontal positions are available to represent them. For some years there appear to be two values for the percentage of clean-shaven men, but these are really values for adjacent years. If the values for the percentage of clean-shaven men are sufficiently different, two separate asterisks are printed. Otherwise the overlap of several points is indicated by a number whose magnitude represents the number of superimposed points. The number 9 is used for 9 or more points. In this example, the percentages of clean-shaven men in 1943 and 1944 were 62.5% and 63.5% respectively. These two points are represented by the circled *2* in Figure 6.1.

The scale of the plot depends on the minimum and maximum values for the two variables plotted. If there are a few cases whose values on one or both of the two variables are far removed from the others, the majority of cases may appear bunched together in order to permit the outlying cases to appear on the same plot.

Figure 6.1   Percentage of clean-shaven men with time

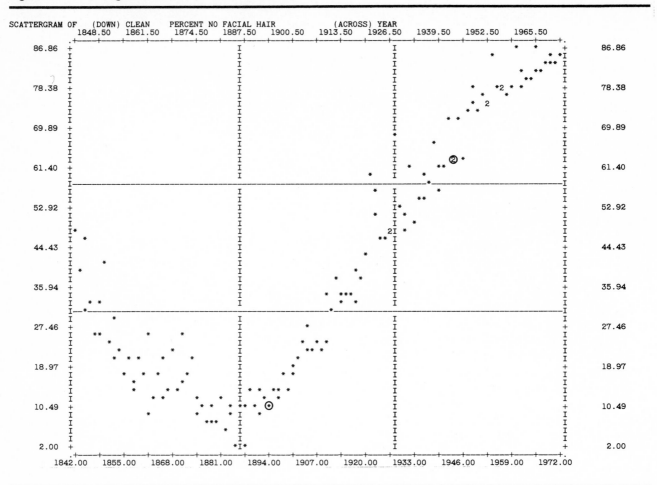

6.2   Examining Relationships Between Skirt and Beard Measurements

A scattergram can reveal various types of relationships between two variables. In Figure 6.1, the relationship of percentage of clean-shaven men to time appears to change during the study. The percentage of clean-shaven men decreases until 1886 or so, then there is a steady upward movement until the end of the study in 1972. The relationship between time and skirt width (measured as a percentage of a woman's height) from the 1940 study is even more complex, as shown in Figure 6.2a. While there is a definite upward movement until around 1860 and then a downward swing to the mid-1920's, there are several peaks and valleys during the period under study, particularly when compared to the curve for clean-shaven men.

If you compare the two plots, there seems to be little relationship between the two measures of fashion. But, curiously enough, if you shift the women's measure 21 years and compare the curve to one that measures the presence (rather than the absence) of male facial hair, there is an interesting coincidence. Figure 6.2b shows the shifted skirt data superimposed on a plot of the percentage of bearded men, so that skirt measures for 1900 are paired with 1921 beard counts, for example.

Figure 6.2a   Skirt width with time

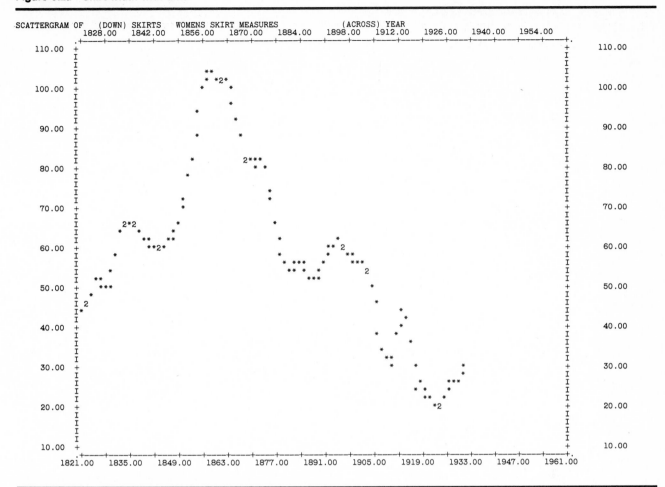

Figure 6.2b   Skirt width and percentage of bearded men with time

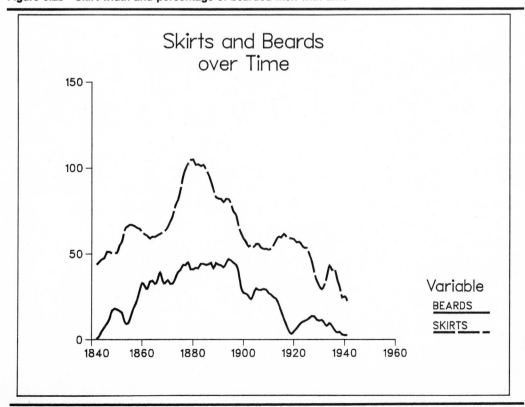

Figure 6.2c is a scattergram of skirt width against percentage of men with beards 21 years later. As noted by Robinson (1976), it appears that as skirt width increases, so does the number of beards 21 years later.

Figure 6.2c Percentage of bearded men with skirt width

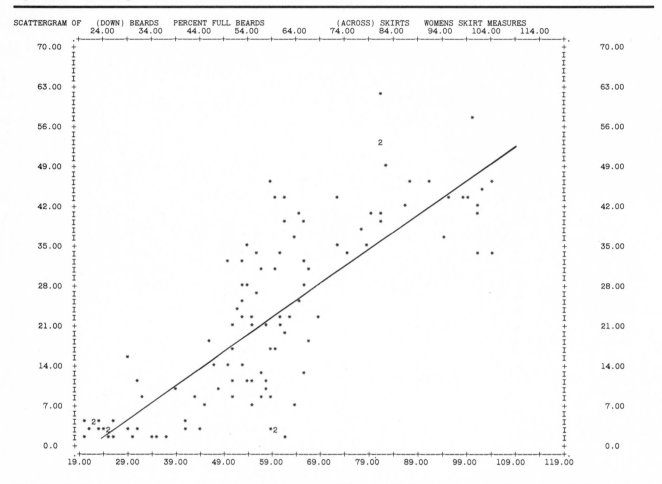

The relationship between skirt width and beard frequency in Figure 6.2c may be summarized with a straight line, although a function shaped like an elongated "S" may fit better. Since the values of both variables increase together, the association is termed positive. A negative association exists when the values of one variable tend to increase as the values of the other variable decrease.

6.3   THE CORRELATION COEFFICIENT

Although a scattergram is an essential first step in studying the association between two variables, it is often useful to quantify the strength of the association by calculating a summary index. One commonly used measure is the Pearson correlation coefficient, denoted by r. It is defined as

$$r = \frac{\sum_{i=1}^{N}(X_i - \bar{X})(Y_i - \bar{Y})}{(N-1)S_X S_Y}$$

where N is the number of cases and S_x and S_y are the standard deviations of the two variables. The absolute value of r indicates the strength of the linear relationship. The largest value possible is $+1$, which occurs when all points fall exactly on a line with positive slope. When all points are on a line with negative slope, the value of the correlation coefficient is -1 (see Figure 6.3a).

Figure 6.3a   Plots with correlation coefficients of +1 and −1

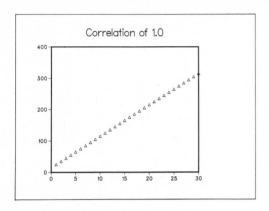 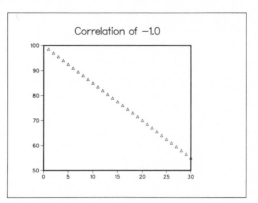

A value of zero indicates no *linear* relationship. It is very important to realize that two variables can have a strong association but a small correlation coefficient if the relationship is not linear. Figure 6.3b shows two plots with zero correlation.

Figure 6.3b   Scattergrams with correlation coefficients of zero

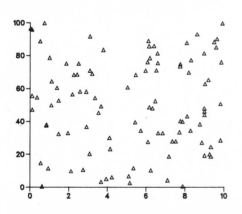 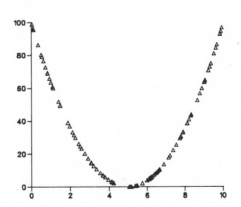

The correlation coefficient for Figure 6.1, facial hair against year, is 0.84; for Figure 6.2c, it is 0.81. But note how different the relationships are between the two sets of variables. In Figure 6.1, there is a strong positive association between year and percentage of clean-shaven men only for part of the study period. The relationship between the two variables is basically nonlinear. The correlation coefficient is large and positive because during the longer part of the study, the two variables are linearly related. The correlation coefficient is of similar magnitude for Figure 6.2c, though the scattergram is very different. The relationship between skirt width and percentage of bearded men is more linear. The points cluster more or less around a line but not as tightly as about the upswing line of Figure 6.1. It is important to examine correlation coefficients together with scattergrams since the same coefficient can result from very different underlying relationships. The correlation coefficient should be used only to summarize the strength of *linear* association.

6.4   Some Properties of the Correlation Coefficient

A common mistake in interpreting the correlation coefficient is to assume that correlation implies causation. No such conclusion is automatically justified. Although skirt width may be highly correlated with beard frequencies, any causal connection between them appears suspect. For example, both fashion trends could be caused by other phenomena.

The correlation coefficient is a symmetric measure since interchanging the two variables X and Y in the formula does not affect the results. The correlation coefficient is not expressed in any units of measure, and it is not affected by linear transformations such as adding or subtracting constants or multiplying or dividing all values of a variable by a constant.

6.5   Hypothesis Tests about the Correlation Coefficient

Although the correlation coefficient is sometimes used only as a summary index to describe the observed strength of the association, there are situations in which description and summarization are but a first step. The primary goal may be to test hypotheses about the unknown population correlation coefficient—denoted as ρ—based on its estimate, the sample correlation coefficient r. In order to test such hypotheses, certain assumptions must be made about the underlying joint distribution of the two variables. A common assumption is that independent random samples are taken from a bivariate normal distribution. If this condition is satisfied, the test that the population coefficient is 0 can be based on the statistic

$$t = r\sqrt{\frac{N - 2}{1 - r^2}}$$

which, if $\rho=0$, has a Student's t distribution with $N-2$ degrees of freedom. Either one- or two-tailed tests can be calculated. If nothing is known in advance, a two-tailed test is appropriate. That is, the hypothesis that the coefficient is zero is rejected for both extreme positive and extreme negative values of t. If the direction of the association can be specified in advance, the hypothesis is rejected only for t values that are of sufficient magnitude and in the direction specified.

Special procedures must be employed to test more general hypotheses of the form $\rho=\rho_0$—where ρ_0 is a constant. If the assumptions of bivariate normality appear unreasonable, a variety of *nonparametric* measures that make limited assumptions about the underlying distributions of the variables can be calculated. See Chapter 9 for further discussion.

6.6   CALCULATING CORRELATION COEFFICIENTS

Figure 6.6 is the matrix of coefficients generated by procedure PEARSON CORR for the variables used in this example. The first entry in the table is the correlation coefficient. The circled number, for example, is the correlation coefficient between skirt width and percentage of men with beards. The parenthesized number is the number of cases used in the computation of the correlation coefficient. For 112 years, values for the percentage of clean-shaven men and skirt width 21 years prior were available. For 19 of the years for which beard data are available, corresponding skirt data are not. A one-tailed observed significance level (the default) is printed.

Figure 6.6   Correlation matrix

```
-  -  -  -  -  -  -  -  -  -  -  -  - P E A R S O N   C O R R E L A T I O N   C O E F F I C I E N T S - -  -  -  -  -  -  -  -  -  -
           SKIRTS      BEARDS       YEAR        CLEAN       MOUST       SIDEBUR     MOUSIDE

SKIRTS     1.0000     (0.8071)    -0.5680     -0.8699     -0.2264      0.2971      0.7809
          (    0)     (   112)    (   112)    (   112)    (   112)    (   112)    (   112)
          P=*****     P=0.000     P=0.000     P=0.000     P=0.008     P=0.001     P=0.000

BEARDS     0.8071      1.0000     -0.6185     -0.8416     -0.2116      0.3277      0.6808
          (  112)     (    0)     (   131)    (   131)    (   131)    (   131)    (   131)
          P=0.000     P=*****     P=0.000     P=0.000     P=0.008     P=0.000     P=0.000

YEAR      -0.5680     -0.6185      1.0000      0.8374      0.3772     -0.8572     -0.6085
          (  112)     (   131)    (    0)     (   131)    (   131)    (   131)    (   131)
          P=0.000     P=0.000     P=*****     P=0.000     P=0.000     P=0.000     P=0.000

CLEAN     -0.8699     -0.8416      0.8374      1.0000      0.0288     -0.5439     -0.6995
          (  112)     (   131)    (   131)    (    0)     (   131)    (   131)    (   131)
          P=0.000     P=0.000     P=0.000     P=*****     P=0.372     P=0.000     P=0.000

MOUST     -0.2264     -0.2116      0.3772      0.0288      1.0000     -0.6678     -0.3536
          (  112)     (   131)    (   131)    (   131)    (    0)     (   131)    (   131)
          P=0.008     P=0.008     P=0.000     P=0.372     P=*****     P=0.000     P=0.000

SIDEBUR    0.2971      0.3277     -0.8572     -0.5439     -0.6678      1.0000      0.4590
          (  112)     (   131)    (   131)    (   131)    (   131)    (    0)     (   131)
          P=0.001     P=0.000     P=0.000     P=0.000     P=0.000     P=*****     P=0.000

MOUSIDE    0.7809      0.6808     -0.6085     -0.6995     -0.3536      0.4590      1.0000
          (  112)     (   131)    (   131)    (   131)    (   131)    (   131)    (    0)
          P=0.000     P=0.000     P=0.000     P=0.000     P=0.000     P=0.000     P=*****

(COEFFICIENT / (CASES) / SIGNIFICANCE)        (A VALUE OF 99.0000 IS PRINTED IF A COEFFICIENT CANNOT BE COMPUTED)
```

The matrix is symmetric since the correlation between X and Y is the same as the correlation between Y and X. The values on the diagonal are all 1.0 since a variable is perfectly related to itself. Care should be exercised when examining significance levels for large matrices. Even if there is no association between the variables, if enough coefficients are computed, some may be statistically significant by chance alone.

6.7   Correlation Matrices and Missing Data

For a variety of reasons, data files frequently contain incomplete observations. Respondents in surveys refuse to answer certain questions or scrawl illegible responses. Laboratory animals die before experiments are completed. Patients fail to keep scheduled clinic appointments.

Analysis of data with missing values is troublesome. Before even considering possible strategies, you should determine whether there is evidence that the missing-value pattern is not random. That is, are there reasons to believe that missing values for a variable are related to the values of that variable or other variables? For example, people with low incomes may be less willing to report their financial status than more affluent people. This may be even more pronounced for people who are poor but highly educated. One simple method of exploring such possibilities is to subdivide the data into two groups—those observations with missing data on a variable and those with complete data—and examine the distributions of the other variables in the file across these two groups. SPSS procedures CROSSTABS and T-TEST are particularly useful for this. For a discussion of more sophisticated methods for detecting nonrandomness, see Frane (1976).

If it appears that the data are not missing randomly, use great caution in attempting to analyze the data. It may be that no satisfactory analysis is possible, especially if there are few cases.

If you are satisfied that the missing data are random, several strategies are available. First, if the same few variables are missing for most cases, exclude those variables from the analysis. Since this luxury is not usually available, you can choose alternatively to keep all variables but eliminate the cases with missing values on any of them. This is termed *listwise* missing- value treatment since a case is eliminated if it has a missing value on any variable in the list. The matrix shown in Figure 6.7 is a listwise matrix in which all coefficients are based on the same number of cases. Also, the observed significance level printed here is two tailed.

Figure 6.7   Listwise correlation matrix

```
- - - - - - - - - - - - P E A R S O N   C O R R E L A T I O N   C O E F F I C I E N T S - - - - - - - - - - - -

              SKIRTS    BEARDS     YEAR      CLEAN     MOUST     SIDEBUR   MOUSIDE

SKIRTS        1.0000    0.8071    -0.5680   -0.8699   -0.2264    0.2971    0.7809
             (  112)   (  112)    (  112)   (  112)   (  112)   (  112)   (  112)
             P=*****   P=0.000    P=0.000   P=0.000   P=0.016   P=0.001   P=0.000

BEARDS        0.8071    1.0000    -0.5126   -0.8351   -0.3476    0.2332    0.6395
             (  112)   (  112)    (  112)   (  112)   (  112)   (  112)   (  112)
             P=0.000   P=*****    P=0.000   P=0.000   P=0.000   P=0.013   P=0.000

YEAR         -0.5680   -0.5126     1.0000    0.7315    0.6890   -0.8939   -0.5608
             (  112)   (  112)    (  112)   (  112)   (  112)   (  112)   (  112)
             P=0.000   P=0.000    P=*****   P=0.000   P=0.000   P=0.000   P=0.000

CLEAN        -0.8699   -0.8351     0.7315    1.0000    0.2606   -0.4820   -0.6967
             (  112)   (  112)    (  112)   (  112)   (  112)   (  112)   (  112)
             P=0.000   P=0.000    P=0.000   P=*****   P=0.006   P=0.000   P=0.000

MOUST        -0.2264   -0.3476     0.6890    0.2606    1.0000   -0.8018   -0.4628
             (  112)   (  112)    (  112)   (  112)   (  112)   (  112)   (  112)
             P=0.016   P=0.000    P=0.000   P=0.006   P=*****   P=0.000   P=0.000

SIDEBUR       0.2971    0.2332    -0.8939   -0.4820   -0.8018    1.0000    0.4037
             (  112)   (  112)    (  112)   (  112)   (  112)   (  112)   (  112)
             P=0.001   P=0.013    P=0.000   P=0.000   P=0.000   P=*****   P=0.000

MOUSIDE       0.7809    0.6395    -0.5608   -0.6967   -0.4628    0.4037    1.0000
             (  112)   (  112)    (  112)   (  112)   (  112)   (  112)   (  112)
             P=0.000   P=0.000    P=0.000   P=0.000   P=0.000   P=0.000   P=*****

(COEFFICIENT / (CASES) / SIGNIFICANCE)       (A VALUE OF 99.0000 IS PRINTED IF A COEFFICIENT CANNOT BE COMPUTED)
```

If many cases have missing data for many variables, listwise missing-value treatment could eliminate too many cases and leave you with a very small sample. One common technique is to calculate the correlation coefficient between a pair of variables based on all cases with complete information for the two variables regardless of whether the cases have missing data on any other variable. For example, if a case has information available only for variables 1, 3, and 5, it is used for computations involving variable pairs 1 and 3, 1 and 5, and 3 and 5. This is *pairwise* missing-data treatment. The matrix shown in Figure 6.6 was generated using the (default) pairwise case deletion option, which is evidenced by the different numbers of cases (112 versus 131) among the coefficients.

6.8   Choosing Pairwise Missing-Value Treatment

Several problems can arise with pairwise matrices, one of which is inconsistency. That is, there are some relationships between coefficients that are impossible but may occur when different cases are used to estimate different coefficients. For example, if age and weight and age and height have a high positive correlation, it is impossible in the same sample for height and weight to be highly negatively correlated. However, if the same cases are not used to estimate all three coefficients, such an anomaly can occur.

No such drastic difference appears between the pairwise matrix shown in Figure 6.6 and the listwise matrix shown in Figure 6.7. However, there are a few notable changes when the 19 years that are missing skirt information are included in computing the correlation coefficients for the facial hair data. When only the 112 listwise cases with valid skirt data are used to compute the correlation coefficient between the year and moustache variables, the result is 0.6890. However, when the 131 pairwise cases are used, that coefficient falls to 0.3772 indicating that the 19 years of missing information for skirt measurements were very different years with regard to the popularity of moustaches.

There is no single sample size that can be associated with a pairwise matrix since each coefficient can be based on a different number of cases. Significance levels obtained from analyses based on pairwise matrices must be viewed with caution since little is known about hypothesis testing in such situations.

It should be emphasized that missing-value problems should not be treated lightly. You should base your decision on careful examination of the data and not leave the choices up to statistical system defaults.

6.9 THE REGRESSION LINE

If there is a linear relationship between two variables, a straight line can be used to summarize the data. When the correlation coefficient is +1 or −1, little thought is needed to determine the line that best describes the data: the line passes through all of the observations. When the observations are more widely dispersed, many different lines can be drawn to represent the data.

One of the most commonly used procedures for fitting a line to the observations is the method of *least squares*. It results in the line for which the sum of squared vertical distances from the data points to the line is a minimum. For the line

$$\hat{Y} = a + bX$$

where a is the intercept (the value of $\hat{Y}$ when X is equal to 0) and b is the slope, the least squares estimators are

$$b = \frac{\sum_{i=1}^{N}(X_i - \overline{X})(Y_i - \overline{Y})}{\sum_{i=1}^{N}(X_i - \overline{X})^2}$$

$$a = \overline{Y} - b\overline{X}$$

These values are printed as part of the SPSS scattergram statistics output (Figure 6.9).

Figure 6.9   Statistics for Figure 6.2c

```
STATISTICS..
   CORRELATION (R)-       0.80710     R SQUARED      -      0.65142     SIGNIFICANCE   -     0.00000
   STD ERR OF EST -       9.65908     INTERCEPT (A)  -    -12.40825     SLOPE (B)      -     0.59542
   PLOTTED VALUES -       112         EXCLUDED VALUES-      0           MISSING VALUES -     19
```

For each pair of variables, two different regression lines can be calculated, since the values of the slope and intercept depend on which variable is dependent (the one being predicted) and which is independent (the one used for prediction). In the SPSS scattergram output, the variable plotted on the vertical axis is considered the dependent variable in the calculation of statistics.

Consider again the data shown in Figure 6.2b. When the percentage of bearded men is predicted from skirt width, the least squares equation is

Predicted % Beards = −12.408 + 0.595(Skirt Width)

Figure 6.2c shows the regression line based on these numbers.

6.10   Goodness of Fit

Although the estimated line, commonly called the *regression line*, is a useful summary of the relationship between two variables, the values of a and b alone do little to indicate how well the line actually fits the data. A *goodness of fit* index is needed.

The observed variation in the dependent variable can be subdivided into two components: that "explained" by the regression, and the residual from the regression.

TOTAL SS = REGRESSION SS + RESIDUAL SS

The *total sum of squares* is the measure of overall variation and is given by

$$\text{TOTAL SUM OF SQUARES} = \sum_{i=1}^{N}(Y_i - \overline{Y})^2$$

The *regression sum of squares*, or the sum of squares due to regression, is

$$\text{REGRESSION SUM OF SQUARES} = \sum_{i=1}^{N} (\hat{Y}_i - \overline{Y})^2$$

where $\hat{Y}_i$ is the predicted value for the *i*th case.

The *residual sum of squares*, sometimes also called the error sum of squares, is obtained by summing the squared differences between the observed values of Y and those predicted by the regression line. These differences are called *residuals*. The residual sum of squares is then

$$\text{RESIDUAL SUM OF SQUARES} = \sum_{i=1}^{N} (Y_i - \hat{Y})^2$$

The standard deviation of the residuals, often called the *standard error of the estimate*, is

$$\text{SEE} = \sqrt{\frac{\text{RESIDUAL SUM OF SQUARES}}{N-2}}$$

SPSS prints the standard error of the estimate as shown in the output in Figure 6.9

The proportion of the variation of the dependent variable that is "explained" by the linear regression is computed by comparing the total sum of squares and the regression sum of squares. That is, if two variables are linearly related, knowledge of the value of the independent variable should help predict the value of the dependent variable. If skirts and beards were perfectly linearly related, the observed variation in beard frequencies should be completely accounted for by differences in skirt width. Given a skirt width, the beard frequency should be correctly predicted by using the regression line. Of course, perfect association is rare, but the basic question remains the same. How much of the observed variation in the dependent variable can be explained by knowing the values of the independent variable? A measure of this is the square of the sample correlation coefficient (r^2), which can be expressed as

$$r^2 = \frac{\text{REGRESSION SUM OF SQUARES}}{\text{TOTAL SUM OF SQUARES}}$$

If there is no linear association in the sample, the value of r^2 is 0 since the regression sum of squares is 0. All the predicted values are just the mean of the dependent variable. If Y and X are perfectly related, the residual sum of squares is 0 and r^2 is 1.

6.11   PREDICTION

Accurate prediction is intrinsically satisfying. Tomorrow's weather, next month's interest rate, and the world's population in the year 2000 are just a few of the events that merit forecasting. Most scientific predictions are based on mathematical models derived from a combination of theory and data.

A regression line can be used to predict values of the dependent variable from values of the independent variable. For example, when skirt widths are 50% of a woman's height, the predicted percentage of men with beards 21 years later is

$$\hat{Y} = -12.408 + 0.595\,(50) = 17.342$$

Considerable caution is needed when predictions are made using values of the independent variable which are much larger or smaller than those used to derive the equation. For example, the observed skirt widths range from 19% to 110%. The regression equation may give poor results for much narrower or wider skirts since the relationship between the two variables may not be linear. Consider Figure 6.1 If the percentage of clean-shaven men in 1942 were predicted based on the data from the years 1842 to 1892, the results would be absurd. There would have to be more beards than men!

6.12 A Time-Series Perspective on Skirts and Beards

The skirts and beards data served as a lively example to introduce the SPSS regression and correlation procedures. An in-depth probe of the actual statistical connection, if any, between the two sets of data is beyond the scope of this book. Brief mention of what is entailed, however, may be of interest. Neither the skirt nor the beard measurements are random samples. They arise in a time-ordered sequence and within each series there is a strong statistical relationship between successive years. Strong relationships within each of two series can give rise to a high sample correlation between the two series, even when, over the long run, the series are independent. Preliminary analysis of the skirts and beards data using special time-series methods suggests that their relationship is of this nature. Thus, hard statistical reasoning throws cold water on entertaining speculation!

6.13 Further Topics in Regression

In these sections, only the most basic concepts of regression analysis are discussed. No attempts are made to draw inferences about the population regression line based on the results observed in samples. This topic and others only briefly mentioned in this chapter are discussed at greater length in Chapter 10 on multiple regression analysis.

6.14 RUNNING PROCEDURE SCATTERGRAM

The SCATTERGRAM procedure produces a two-dimensional plot of cases located by their values on two variables. The statistics available are those associated with simple linear regression, including the slope and intercept of the line, the Pearson product-moment correlation coefficient, and a test of significance.

6.15 The SCATTERGRAM Variable List

The only SCATTERGRAM specification following the command keyword is the variable list beginning in or beyond column 16. You name the vertical axis variable followed by the WITH keyword and the horizontal axis variable. To request the scattergram shown in Figure 6.1, specify

```
SCATTERGRAM    CLEAN WITH YEAR
```

If you want to specify your own plot limits, follow the variable name with the minimum and maximum values separated by a comma and enclosed in parentheses. For example, to produce the plot shown in Figure 6.2a, specify

```
SCATTERGRAM    SKIRTS(10,110) WITH YEAR(1828,1961)
```

Specifying a minimum greater than the actual lowest value or a maximum less than the actual highest value causes cases to be excluded from the plot (and from calculation of statistics—see Section 6.19). Keywords LOWEST and HIGHEST can be used if you want to enter only one of the limiting values, as in YEAR(LOWEST,1900). The minimum and maximum values specification applies only to the variable immediately preceding the specification.

The order in which you name the variables not only controls which variable is plotted on the vertical axis (the first one) and which is on the horizontal axis, but also directs SPSS to consider the horizontal variable as independent for the regression statistics calculated (see Section 6.19).

You can specify multiple plots in one of two ways. If you specify a list of variables without the WITH keyword, SPSS plots all possible pairs. That is, specifying the variable list RED,GREEN,BLUE,YELLOW means that SPSS plots RED with GREEN, then RED with BLUE, then RED with YELLOW, then GREEN with BLUE, etc. In the second format, multiple variables are named on either side of the WITH keyword. That is, specifying RED,GREEN WITH BLUE,YELLOW generates four plots: RED with BLUE, RED with YELLOW, GREEN with BLUE, and GREEN with YELLOW.

6.16 The OPTIONS Command for SCATTERGRAM

Following THE SCATTERGRAM variable list, you can enter the OPTIONS command keyword beginning in column 1 and a list of numbers beginning in column 16 or beyond. These numbers correspond to content and format options for plots. The following is a list of the most commonly used options; a complete list is found in Appendix B.

OPTION 1   Include cases with missing values.
OPTION 2   Exclude missing data listwise.
OPTION 3   Don't print variable labels.
OPTION 4   Don't print grid lines.
OPTION 5   Print diagonal grid lines.
OPTION 6   Calculate a two-tailed test of significance (see Section 6.19).
OPTION 7   Scale axis labels to integers.

6.17 Missing-Value Treatment Options

Unless you specify otherwise, SPSS excludes a case from the scattergram if it has a missing value on either of the variables in the plot. With multiple variables in a list, this is pairwise missing- value treatment. Option 1 tells SCATTERGRAM to ignore the missing-value status of any values and to plot the cases as if the values were valid. Option 2 tells SCATTERGRAM to exclude cases that have a missing value on any variable in the variable list even if the case has valid values on both variables being plotted. This is listwise missing-value treatment.

6.18 Plot Formatting Options

Option 3 tells SCATTERGRAM to suppress variable labels as a time-saving device. Option 4 suppresses the grid lines within the scattergram and Option 5 replaces the vertical and horizontal grid lines with diagonal ones. Finally, Option 7 forces the scales (tick marks) on the plot to integers.

For example, to produce Figure 6.2c, which has integer values for the scale of both variables and no grids, use

```
SCATTERGRAM      BEARDS WITH SKIRTS
OPTIONS          4,7
```

If you specify both a range and Option 7, the range is used.

6.19 The STATISTICS Command for SCATTERGRAM

By default, SCATTERGRAM prints only the plot. If you want statistics calculated for the plot, request them with the STATISTICS command. Enter the STATISTICS command keyword in column 1 followed by a list of numbers corresponding to the desired statistics (or the keyword ALL) beginning in column 16 or beyond.

STATISTIC 1   Pearson r
STATISTIC 2 r^2
STATISTIC 3   One-tailed significance of r unless Option 6 is selected
STATISTIC 4   Standard error of the estimate
STATISTIC 5   Intercept
STATISTIC 6   Slope
ALL   All statistics

For example, to produce the statistics shown in Figure 6.9 and the plot in Figure 6.2c, specify

```
SCATTERGRAM     BEARDS WITH SKIRTS
OPTIONS         4,7
STATISTICS      ALL
```

Statistic 3 produces a one-tailed test of significance. If you want a two-tailed test performed, you must also request Option 6.

Note that these statistics assume that the horizontal axis variable is the independent variable (Section 6.15). Therefore, the order in which you specify the variables will affect the slope and the intercept calculated.

6.20 RUNNING PROCEDURE PEARSON CORR

The PEARSON CORR procedure calculates Pearson product-moment correlations for pairs of variables. Output includes the coefficient (r), the observed significance level, and the number of cases upon which the coefficient is computed (N). Means and standard deviations as well as cross-product deviations and covariances are available.

6.21 The PEARSON CORR Variable List

The only PEARSON CORR specification following the command keywords is the variable list beginning in column 16 or after. For example, to produce the correlation matrix shown in Figure 6.6, specify

```
PEARSON CORR    SKIRTS BEARDS YEAR CLEAN TO MOUSIDE
```

The specification CLEAN TO MOUSIDE names the variables CLEAN, MOUST, SIDEBUR, and MOUSIDE—all adjacent variables on the data file. The order in which you name the variables is the order in which PEARSON CORR displays them.

6.22 The OPTIONS Command for PEARSON CORR

Following your PEARSON CORR variable list, you can enter the OPTIONS command keyword beginning in column 1 and a list of numbers beginning in column 16 or beyond. These numbers correspond to content and format options for your correlation matrices. The most commonly used options are listed below; a complete list is found in Appendix B.

OPTION 1   Include cases with missing values.
OPTION 2   Exclude missing data listwise.
OPTION 3   Calculate a two-tailed test of significance.
OPTION 5   Don't print the significance and number of cases.
OPTION 6   Print only non-redundant coefficients and statistics.

6.23 Missing-Value Treatment Options

Unless you specify otherwise, SPSS excludes a case from the calculation of a correlation coefficient if it has a missing value on either of the variables in the pair. This is pairwise missing-value treatment. Option 1 tells PEARSON CORR to ignore the missing-value status of any values and to plot the cases as if the values were valid. Option 2 tells PEARSON CORR to exclude cases that have a missing value on any variable in the list even if the case has valid values on both variables in the pair. This is listwise missing-value treatment. The choice between pairwise and listwise missing-value treatments should be made carefully; see Sections 6.7 and 6.8 for a discussion.

6.24   Matrix Formatting Options

By default, PEARSON CORR prints the coefficient, its significance, and the number of cases. Also by default, the significance test is one-tailed. Use Option 3 to request a two-tailed test. For example, the *p* values shown in Figure 6.7 are two-tailed. Figure 6.7 is produced with the specification

```
PEARSON CORR    SKIRTS BEARDS YEAR CLEAN TO MOUSIDE
OPTIONS         2,3
```

Option 5 tells PEARSON CORR to suppress printing of the test of significance and the number of cases. If you accept the default pairwise exclusion of cases with missing values, it is probably not a good idea to suppress printing of the number of cases upon which each coefficient is calculated since some might be based on few valid cases. Option 6 prints out the matrix in serial form without the diagonal or the redundant correlations that appear in the full matrix as shown in Figures 6.6 and 6.7. For example,

```
PEARSON CORR    SKIRTS BEARDS YEAR CLEAN TO MOUSIDE
OPTIONS         3,6
```

produces a shorter form of the matrix, as shown in Figure 6.24.

Figure 6.24   Nonredundant matrix—Option 6

```
- - - - - - - - - - - - - - P E A R S O N   C O R R E L A T I O N   C O E F F I C I E N T S - - - - - - - - - - - - - - 

VARIABLE              VARIABLE              VARIABLE              VARIABLE              VARIABLE              VARIABLE
PAIR                  PAIR                  PAIR                  PAIR                  PAIR                  PAIR
_____              _____              _____              _____              _____              _____

SKIRTS    0.8071      SKIRTS   -0.5680      SKIRTS   -0.8699      SKIRTS   -0.2264      SKIRTS    0.2971      SKIRTS    0.7809
WITH     N( 112)      WITH     N( 112)      WITH     N( 112)      WITH     N( 112)      WITH     N( 112)      WITH     N( 112)
BEARDS   SIG .000     YEAR     SIG .000     CLEAN    SIG .000     MOUST    SIG .016     SIDEBUR  SIG .001     MOUSIDE  SIG .000

BEARDS   -0.6185      BEARDS   -0.8416      BEARDS   -0.2116      BEARDS    0.3277      BEARDS    0.6808      YEAR      0.8374
WITH     N( 131)      WITH     N( 131)      WITH     N( 131)      WITH     N( 131)      WITH     N( 131)      WITH     N( 131)
YEAR     SIG .000     CLEAN    SIG .000     MOUST    SIG .015     SIDEBUR  SIG .000     MOUSIDE  SIG .000     CLEAN    SIG .000

YEAR      0.3772      YEAR     -0.8572      YEAR     -0.6085      CLEAN     0.0288      CLEAN    -0.5439      CLEAN    -0.6995
WITH     N( 131)      WITH     N( 131)      WITH     N( 131)      WITH     N( 131)      WITH     N( 131)      WITH     N( 131)
MOUST    SIG .000     SIDEBUR  SIG .000     MOUSIDE  SIG .000     MOUST    SIG .744     SIDEBUR  SIG .000     MOUSIDE  SIG .000

MOUST    -0.6678      MOUST    -0.3536      SIDEBUR   0.4590
WITH     N( 131)      WITH     N( 131)      WITH     N( 131)
SIDEBUR  SIG .000     MOUSIDE  SIG .000     MOUSIDE  SIG .000

          A VALUE OF 99.0000 IS PRINTED IF A COEFFICIENT CANNOT BE COMPUTED.
```

6.25   The STATISTICS Command for PEARSON CORR

Enter the STATISTICS command keyword in column 1 after your PEARSON CORR command, followed by one or both of the following numbers in column 16 or beyond.

STATISTIC 1   Univariate means and standard deviations.

STATISTIC 2   Crossproduct deviations and covariance for each pair of variables.

For example,

```
PEARSON CORR    SKIRTS BEARDS YEAR CLEAN TO MOUSIDE
OPTIONS         3
STATISTICS      1
```

produces the univariate output shown in Figure 6.25.

Figure 6.25   Univariate statistics—Statistic 1

VARIABLE	CASES	MEAN	STD DEV
SKIRTS	112	58.1955	22.0762
BEARDS	131	19.4401	16.5432
YEAR	131	1907.0000	37.9605
CLEAN	131	39.6915	26.3018
MOUST	131	23.9455	16.0678
SIDEBUR	131	13.2598	17.3953
MOUSIDE	131	3.6630	4.8341

Chapter 7

What's Your Proof?
One-Way Analysis of Variance

Rotund Italians washing down carbohydrate-laden feasts with jugs of chianti, somber Jews ritualistically sipping Sabbath wine, melancholy Irish submerging grief and frustration in a bottle—all are common ethnic stereotypes. Is there evidence to support this folk wisdom? In *Ethnic Drinking Subcultures*, Greeley (1981) examines drinking habits in a sample of five ethnic populations within four major American cities.

A total of 1107 families completed questionnaires detailing their drinking behavior and ancestral origins. Irish, Italian, Jewish, Swedish, and English families were included. Greeley investigates possible differences in drinking habits and a variety of cultural and psychological explanations for them. In this chapter, only differences in total alcohol consumption are considered.

7.1 DESCRIPTIVE STATISTICS AND CONFIDENCE INTERVALS

Figure 7.2 contains basic descriptive statistics for total yearly alcohol consumption in pints for the adult males in the study. The Italians and Irish are the biggest consumers, drinking an average of 24 pints a year. The Jewish males drink the least, an average of slightly more than 9 pints a year.

The sample mean for a group provides the single best guess for the unknown population value μ_i. It is unlikely that the value of the sample mean is exactly equal to the population parameter. Instead, it is probably not too different. Based on the sample mean, it is possible to calculate a range of values that, with a designated likelihood, include the population value. Such a range is called a *confidence interval*. For example, as shown in Figure 7.2, the 95% confidence interval for μ_{Irish} is the range 19.61 to 28.89 pints. This means that, if repeated samples are selected from a population under the same conditions and 95% confidence intervals are calculated, 95% of the intervals will contain the unknown parameter μ_{Irish}. Since the parameter value is unknown, it is not possible to determine whether a particular interval contains it.

7.2 ANALYSIS OF VARIANCE

Looking at the sample means, you might wonder whether the observed differences can be reasonably attributed to chance or whether there is reason to suspect true differences between the five groups. One of the statistical procedures commonly used to test the hypothesis that several population means are equal is *analysis of variance* or ANOVA.

Figure 7.2 Total yearly alcohol consumption for adult males (in pints)

GROUP	COUNT	MEAN	STANDARD DEVIATION	STANDARD ERROR	MINIMUM	MAXIMUM	95 PCT CONF INT FOR MEAN		
IRISH	119	24.2500	25.5620	2.3433	0.0	145.0	19.6097	TO	28.8903
ITALIAN	84	24.3120	24.1880	2.6391	0.0	128.0	19.0629	TO	29.5611
JEWISH	41	9.2500	21.6250	3.3773	0.0	87.0	2.4243	TO	16.0757
SWEDISH	74	16.5630	26.7500	3.1096	0.0	112.0	10.3655	TO	22.7605
ENGLISH	90	21.8750	21.5630	2.2729	0.0	117.0	17.3587	TO	26.3913
TOTAL	408	20.8373	24.6519	1.2204	0.0	145.0	18.4381	TO	23.2365

Certain assumptions are required for correct application of the ANOVA test. Independent samples from normally distributed populations with the same variance must be selected. In subsequent discussion, it is assumed that the populations sampled constitute the entire set of populations about which conclusions are desired. For example, the five ethnic groups are considered to be the only ones of interest. They are not viewed as a sample from all possible ethnic groups. This is called a *fixed-effects* model.

7.3 Partitioning Variation

In analysis of variance, the observed variability in the sample is subdivided into two components—variability of the observations within a group about the group mean and variability of the group means. If the amount of alcohol consumed doesn't vary much for individuals within the same ethnic group—for example, all the Swedes seem to drink about the same—but the group means differ substantially, there is evidence to suspect that the population means are not all equal.

The *within groups sum of squares* is a measure of the variability within groups. It is calculated as

$$SSW = \sum_{i=1}^{k} (N_i - 1)S_i^2$$

where S_i^2 is the variance of group i about its mean, and N_i is the number of cases in group i. For the data shown in Figure 7.2, the within groups sum of squares is

$$SSW = 25.56^2(118) + 24.19^2(83) + 21.63^2(40) + 26.75^2(73) + 21.56^2(89)$$
$$= 237,986.20$$

Variability of the group means is measured by the *between groups sum of squares*, which is

$$SSB = \sum_{i=1}^{k} N_i (\overline{X}_i - \overline{X})^2$$

The mean of the ith group is denoted $\overline{X}_i$, and the mean of the entire sample is $\overline{X}$. For the drinking study, the between groups sum of squares is

$$SSB = (24.25 - 20.84)^2(119) + (24.31 - 20.84)^2(84) + (9.25 - 20.84)^2(41)$$
$$+ (16.56 - 20.84)^2(74) + (21.88 - 20.84)^2(90)$$
$$= 9,353.89$$

The sums of squares, and other related statistics, are usually displayed in an analysis of variance table, as shown in Figure 7.3.

Figure 7.3   Analysis of variance table

```
- - - - - - - - - - - - - - - - - - - - - - - O N E W A Y - - - - - - - - - - - - - - - - - - - - - - - -

      VARIABLE   AMOUNT        AMOUNT OF ALCOHOL CONSUMED IN PINTS
   BY VARIABLE   ETHNIC        ETHNIC BACKGROUND

                                        ANALYSIS OF VARIANCE

                    SOURCE          D.F.    SUM OF SQUARES    MEAN SQUARES    F RATIO    F PROB.

          BETWEEN GROUPS             4         9353.8877       2338.4717       3.960     0.0036

          WITHIN GROUPS            403       237986.2031        590.5364

          TOTAL                    407       247340.0625
```

The mean square entries in the table shown in Figure 7.3 are obtained by dividing the sums of squares by their degrees of freedom. The between groups degrees of freedom are one less than the number of groups. There are $N-k$ degrees of freedom for the within groups sum of squares, where N is the number of cases in the entire sample and k is the number of groups.

7.4   Testing the Hypothesis

To test the hypothesis that the five ethnic groups under study consume the same average amount of alcohol—that is, that

$$\mu_{Irish} = \mu_{Italian} = \mu_{Jewish} = \mu_{Swedish} = \mu_{English}$$

the following statistic is calculated (see Figure 7.3):

$$F = \frac{\text{BETWEEN GROUPS MEAN SQUARE}}{\text{WITHIN GROUPS MEAN SQUARE}} = \frac{2338.47}{590.54} = 3.96$$

When the assumptions described in Section 7.2 are met, the observed significance level is obtained by comparing the calculated F to values of the F distribution with $k-1$ and $N-k$ degrees of freedom. The observed significance level is the probability of obtaining when all population means are equal an F statistic at least as large as the one calculated. If this probability is small enough, the hypothesis that all population means are equal is rejected. In this example, the observed significance level is approximately 0.0036 (Figure 7.3). Thus it appears unlikely that men in the five ethnic populations consume the same mean amount of alcohol.

7.5   MULTIPLE COMPARISON PROCEDURES

A significant F statistic indicates only that the population means are probably unequal. It does not pinpoint where the differences are. A variety of special techniques, termed *multiple comparison* procedures, are available for determining which population means are different from each other.

   You may question the need for special techniques—why not just calculate the t test described in Chapter 5 for all possible pairs of means? The problem is that, when many comparisons are made, some will appear to be significant even when all population means are equal. With five groups, for example, there are ten possible comparisons between pairs of means. The probability, when all population means are equal, that at least one of the ten observed significance levels would be less than 0.05 is about 0.29 (Snedecor, 1967).

Multiple comparison procedures provide protection against calling too many differences significant. These procedures set up more stringent criteria for declaring significance than does the usual t test. That is, the difference between two sample means must be larger to be identified as a true difference.

7.6   The Scheffé Test

Many multiple comparison procedures are available and they all provide protection in slightly different ways (for further discussion, see Winer (1971)). Figure 7.6a is output from the *Scheffé* multiple comparison procedure for the ethnic drinking data. The Scheffé method is conservative for pairwise comparisons of means. It requires larger differences between means for significance than most of the other methods.

Figure 7.6a   The Scheffé multiple comparison procedure

```
        VARIABLE   AMOUNT      AMOUNT OF ALCOHOL CONSUMED IN PINTS
     BY VARIABLE   ETHNIC      ETHNIC BACKGROUND


MULTIPLE RANGE TEST


SCHEFFE PROCEDURE
RANGES FOR THE 0.050 LEVEL -

        4.38   4.38   4.38   4.38

THE RANGES ABOVE ARE TABLE RANGES.   THE VALUE ACTUALLY COMPARED WITH MEAN(J)-MEAN(I) IS..
       17.1834 * RANGE * SQRT(1/N(I) + 1/N(J))

    (*) DENOTES PAIRS OF GROUPS SIGNIFICANTLY DIFFERENT AT THE 0.050 LEVEL


                         J  S  E  I  I
                         E  W  N  R  T
                         W  E  G  I  A
                         I  D  L  S  L
                         S  I  I  H  I
                         H  S  S     A
                            H  H     N

        MEAN       GROUP

       9.2500      JEWISH
      16.5630      SWEDISH
      21.8750      ENGLISH
      24.2500      IRISH      *
      24.3120      ITALIAN    *
```

The means are ordered and printed from smallest to largest, thus giving the groups the order shown in Figure 7.6a. Pairs of means that are significantly different at the 0.05 level in this case are indicated with an asterisk in the matrix at the bottom of the output. In this example, Jews are significantly different from the Irish and the Italians. No other pair is found to be significantly different.

The output above this table indicates how large an observed difference must be to attain significance using the particular multiple comparison procedure.

If the sample sizes in all groups are equal, or an average sample size is used in the computations, a somewhat modified table is printed (Figure 7.6b). Instead of indicating which groups are significantly different, means that are not different are grouped. Subset 1 shows that Jews, Swedes, and English are not different. Subset 2 groups Swedes, English, Irish, and Italians. Jews do not appear in the same subset as Irish and Italians since they are significantly different from these two.

Figure 7.6b   Homogeneous subsets

```
        VARIABLE  AMOUNT      AMOUNT OF ALCOHOL CONSUMED IN PINTS
      BY VARIABLE  ETHNIC      ETHNIC BACKGROUND


  MULTIPLE RANGE TEST


  SCHEFFE PROCEDURE

     HOMOGENEOUS SUBSETS     (SUBSETS OF GROUPS, WHOSE HIGHEST AND LOWEST MEANS DO NOT DIFFER BY MORE THAN THE SHORTEST
                              SIGNIFICANT RANGE FOR A SUBSET OF THAT SIZE)


  SUBSET  1

  GROUP       JEWISH       SWEDISH       ENGLISH
  MEAN        9.2500       16.5630       21.8750
  - - - - - - - - - - - - - - - - - - - - - - - -

  SUBSET  2

  GROUP       SWEDISH      ENGLISH       IRISH        ITALIAN
  MEAN        16.5630      21.8750       24.2500      24.3120
```

7.7   EXPLANATIONS

Both cultural and psychological explanations for differences in drinking habits among ethnic groups have been suggested (Greeley, 1981). In Jewish culture, the religious symbolism associated with drinking, as well as strong cultural norms against drunkenness, seem to discourage abuse of alcohol. For the Irish, alcohol is a vehicle for promotion of fun and pleasure, as well as a potent tranquilizer for dissipating grief and tension. Such high expectations of alcohol make it a convenient escape and foster dependency. Italians have accepted drinking as a natural part of daily life. Alcohol is treated almost as a food and not singled out for its special pleasures.

7.8   Tests for Equality of Variance

As previously discussed, one of the assumptions needed for applying analysis of variance properly is that of equality of variances. That is, all of the populations from which random samples are taken must not only be normal but must also have the same variance σ^2. Several procedures are available for testing this assumption of *homogeneity of variance*. Unfortunately, they are not very useful since they are influenced by characteristics of the data other than the variance.

Figure 7.8   Tests for homogeneity of variance

```
  TESTS FOR HOMOGENEITY OF VARIANCES

        COCHRANS C = MAX. VARIANCE/SUM(VARIANCES) = 0.2479, P = 0.248 (APPROX.)
        BARTLETT-BOX F =                            1.349, P = 0.249
        MAXIMUM VARIANCE / MINIMUM VARIANCE =       1.539
```

Figure 7.8 contains the three tests for homogeneity of variance available in SPSS. If the significance levels are not small, there is no reason to worry. Also, even if the variances appear different but the sample sizes in all groups are similar, there is no cause for alarm since the ANOVA test is not particularly sensitive to violations of equality of variance under such conditions. However, if the sample sizes are quite dissimilar and the variances unequal, you should consider transforming the data or using a statistical procedure that requires less stringent assumptions (Chapter 9).

7.9   RUNNING PROCEDURE ONEWAY

Procedure ONEWAY produces a one-way analysis of variance. Output includes sums of squares, degrees of freedom, mean squares, and the *F* ratio and its significance.

7.10   The Variable List

The only required specification for procedure ONEWAY is the name of at least one dependent variable, the keyword BY, and the independent variable name followed by the minimum and maximum values separated by a comma and enclosed in parentheses. For example, to produce the analysis shown in Figure 7.3, specify

```
ONEWAY        AMOUNT BY ETHNIC(1,5)/
```

The minimum and maximum values are the lowest and highest values of the independent variable to be used in the analysis.

You can name more than one dependent variable, but only one independent variable. If you name more than one dependent variable, a separate one-way analysis of variance is produced for each one named.

7.11   The RANGES= Subcommand

Use the RANGES= subcommand to request one of the seven multiple comparison procedures. Each keyword specifies a type of multiple comparison and can be followed by a desired level of significance in parentheses. If you don't specify a level of significance, procedure ONEWAY uses the significance value of 0.05. The available keywords are

LSD   *Least significant difference.*
DUNCAN   *Duncan's multiple range test.* Available significance values are 0.1, 0.05, and 0.01.
SNK   *Student—Newman—Keuls test.* Only significance value 0.05 (the default) is available.
TUKEYB   *Tukey's alternate procedure.* Only significance value 0.05 (the default) is available.
TUKEY   *Honestly significant difference.* Only significance value 0.05 (the default) is available.
LSDMOD   *Modified LSD.*
SCHEFFE *Scheffé's test.*

For example, to produce the multiple comparison output shown in Figure 7.6a, specify

```
ONEWAY        AMOUNT BY ETHNIC(1,5)/
              RANGES=SCHEFFE/
```

7.12   The OPTIONS Command for ONEWAY

Following the ONEWAY specifications, you can enter the OPTIONS command keyword beginning in column 1 and a list of numbers beginning in column 16 or beyond. These numbers correspond to missing-data and format options. The most commonly used options are listed below; a complete list can be found in Appendix B.

OPTION 1   Include cases with missing values.
OPTION 2   Delete from the analysis any case with a missing value for any dependent variable in the list.
OPTION 3   Do not print variable labels.
OPTION 6   Print the first eight characters of the value label.

For example, to label the output using the first eight characters of the value labels, specify

```
ONEWAY        AMOUNT BY ETHNIC(1,5)/
              RANGES=SCHEFFE/
OPTIONS       6
```

7.13 The STATISTICS Command for ONEWAY

Enter the STATISTICS command keyword in column 1 after your ONEWAY command, followed by a list of numbers (or the keyword ALL) beginning column 16 or beyond. There are three optional statistics available.

STATISTIC 1 Print group means, standard deviations, standard errors, minimum, maximum, and 95% confidence interval for the mean.

STATISTIC 2 Print both fixed- and random-effects measures.

STATISTIC 3 Print homogeneity of variance statistics.

Output from Statistic 1 is shown in Figure 7.2 and the output from Statistic 3 is shown in Figure 7.8.

7.14 ONEWAY and Other SPSS Commands

The SPSS command file used to produce the output in this chapter is

```
RUN NAME        DRINKING STUDY
DATA LIST       FIXED/1 ETHNIC 1 AMOUNT 2-6 (2)
VAR LABELS      AMOUNT AMOUNT OF ALCOHOL CONSUMED IN PINTS/
                ETHNIC ETHNIC BACKGROUND/
VALUE LABELS    ETHNIC (1)IRISH (2)ITALIAN (3)JEWISH (4)SWEDISH
                (5)ENGLISH/
ONEWAY          AMOUNT BY ETHNIC(1,5)/
                RANGES=SCHEFFE/
OPTIONS         6
STATISTICS      1,3
READ INPUT DATA
[data records]
END INPUT DATA
FINISH
```

DATA LIST. The DATA LIST command reads the variable named ETHNIC from column 1 and the variable AMOUNT from columns 2 through 6. The variable AMOUNT is measured in pints with two decimal positions. However, the decimal point has not been recorded on the data file so that an amount of 24.45 has been recorded as 2445. To define the variable AMOUNT with two decimal places, specify the number two enclosed in parentheses following the column specification, as shown in the DATA LIST command.

Chapter 8

Beauty and the Writer: Analysis of Variance

Despite constitutional guarantees, any mirror will testify that all citizens are not created equal. The consequences of this inequity are pervasive. Physically attractive persons are perceived as more desirable social partners, more persuasive communicators, and generally more likeable and competent. Even cute children and attractive burglars are disciplined more leniently than their homely counterparts (Sigall and Ostrove, 1975).

Much research on physical attractiveness focuses on its impact on heterosexual relationships and evaluations. Its effect on same-sex evaluations has received less attention. Anderson and Nida (1978) examined the influence of attractiveness on the evaluation of writings by college students. In the study, 144 male and 144 female students were asked to appraise essays purportedly written by college freshmen. A slide of the "author" was projected during the rating as part of "supplemental information." Half of the slides were of authors of the same sex as the rater, the other half of authors of the opposite sex. The slides had previously been determined to be of high, medium, and low attractiveness. Each participant evaluated one essay for creativity, ideas, and style. The three scales were combined to form a composite measure of performance.

8.1 DESCRIPTIVE STATISTICS

Figure 8.1 contains average composite scores for the essays subdivided by the three categories of physical attractiveness and the two categories of sex similarity. The table is similar to the summary table shown for the one-way analysis of variance in Chapter 7. The difference here is that there are two independent (or grouping) variables, attractiveness and sex similarity. The first mean printed (25.1) is for the entire sample. The number of cases (288) is shown in parentheses. Then for each of the independent variables, mean scores are displayed for each of the categories. The attractiveness categories are ordered from low (coded 1) to high (coded 3). Evaluations in which the rater and author are of the same sex are coded as 1, while opposite-sex evaluations are coded as 2. Finally, a table of means is printed for cases classified by both grouping variables. Attractiveness is the row variable, sex is the column variable. Each mean is based on the response of 48 subjects.

Figure 8.1   Table of group means

```
*x* * * * * * * * * * * *   C E L L   M E A N S   * * * * * * * * * * * * * *
            SCORE
         BY ATTRACT
            SEX
* * * * * * * * * * * * * * * * * * * * * * * * * * * * * * * * * * * * * *
TOTAL POPULATION

     25.11
   (   288)


ATTRACT
        1           2           3

     22.98       25.78       26.59
   (    96)    (    96)    (    96)


SEX
        1           2

     25.52       24.71
   (   144)    (   144)



        SEX
                  .1          2
ATTRACT  1       22.79       23.17
               (    48)    (    48)

         2       28.63       22.92
               (    48)    (    48)

         3       25.13       28.04
               (    48)    (    48)
```

The overall average score is 25.11. Highly attractive individuals received the highest average score (26.59) while those rated low in physical appeal had the lowest score (22.98). There doesn't appear to be much difference between the average scores assigned to same (25.52) and opposite-sex (24.71) individuals. Highly attractive persons received an average rating of 25.13 when evaluated by individuals of the same sex, 28.04 when evaluated by students of the opposite sex.

8.2   ANALYSIS OF VARIANCE

Three hypotheses are of interest in the study: Does attractiveness relate to the composite scores? Does the sex similarity relate to the scores? And is there an interaction between the effects of attractiveness and sex? The statistical technique used to evaluate these hypotheses is an extension of the one-way analysis of variance outlined in Chapter 7. The same assumptions as before are needed for correct application: the observations should be independently selected from normal populations with equal variances. Again, discussion here is limited to the situation in which both grouping variables are considered fixed. That is, they constitute the populations of interest.

The total observed variation in the scores is subdivided into four components: the sum of squares due to attractiveness, sex, their interaction, and the residual. That is

TOTAL SS = ATTRACTIVENESS SS + SEX SS + INTERACTION SS + RESIDUAL SS

Figure 8.2 is the analysis of variance table for this study. The first column lists the sources of variation. The sums of squares attributable to each of the components are given in the second column. The sum of squares for each independent variable alone are sometimes termed the "main effect" sum of squares. The "explained" sum of squares is the total sum of squares for the main effect and interaction terms in the model.

The degrees of freedom for sex and attractiveness, listed in the third column, are one fewer than the number of categories. For example, since there are three levels of attractiveness, there are two degrees of freedom. Similarly, sex has one degree of freedom. Two degrees of freedom are associated with the interaction term (the product of the degrees of freedom of each of the individual variables).

Figure 8.2   Analysis of variance table

```
* * * * * * * * * *A N A L Y S I S   O F   V A R I A N C E* * * * * * * * * *
              SCORE
         BY ATTRACT
            SEX
* * * * * * * * * * * * * * * * * * * * * * * * * * * * * * * * * * * *
                         SUM OF              MEAN           SIGNIF
SOURCE OF VARIATION      SQUARES    DF       SQUARE     F     OF F

MAIN EFFECTS             733.700     3      244.567   3.276  0.022
    ATTRACT              686.850     2      343.425   4.600  0.011
    SEX                   46.850     1       46.850   0.628  0.429

2-WAY INTERACTIONS       942.350     2      471.175   6.311  0.002
    ATTRACT   SEX        942.350     2      471.175   6.311  0.002

EXPLAINED               1676.050     5      335.210   4.490  0.000

RESIDUAL               21053.140   282       74.656

TOTAL                  22729.190   287       79.196
```

The mean square entries in Figure 8.2 are obtained by dividing each sum of squares by its degrees of freedom. Hypothesis tests are based on the ratios of the mean squares of each of the sources of variation to the mean square for the residual. When the assumptions are met, and the true means are in fact equal, the distribution of the ratio is an *F* with the degrees of freedom for the numerator and denominator terms.

8.3   Testing for Interaction

The *F* value associated with the attractiveness and sex interaction is 6.311. The observed significance level is approximately 0.002. Therefore, it appears that there is an interaction between the two variables. What does this mean?

Figure 8.3a   Cell means
(Plot from SPSS Graphics)

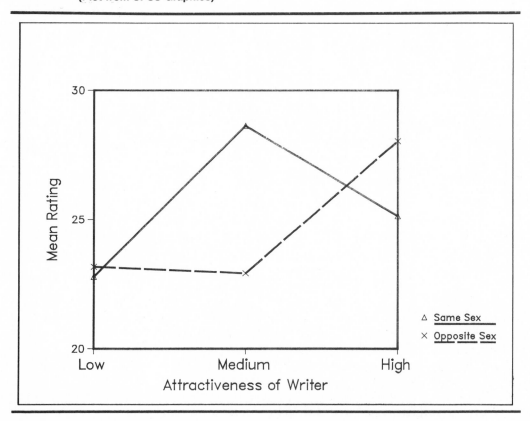

Consider Figure 8.3a, which is a plot of the cell means in Figure 8.1. Notice how the mean scores relate not only to the attractiveness of the individual and to the sex of the rater, but also to the particular combination of the values of the variables. Opposite-sex raters assign the highest scores to highly attractive individuals. Same-sex raters assign the highest scores to medium attractive individuals. Thus, the ratings for each level of attractiveness depend on the sex variable. If there were not interaction between the two variables, a plot like that shown in Figure 8.3b might result, where the difference between the two types of raters is the same for the three levels of attractiveness.

**Figure 8.3b   Cell means with no interaction
(Plot from SPSS Graphics)**

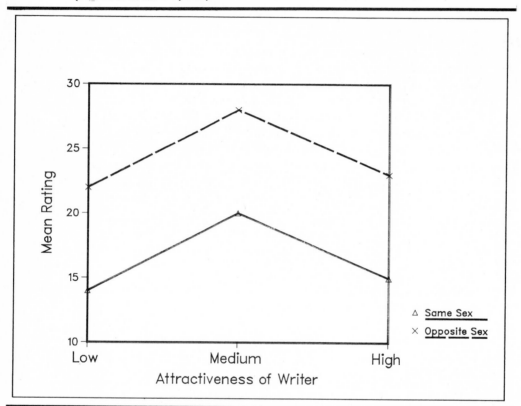

8.4   Tests for Sex and Attractiveness

Once the presence of interaction has been established, it is not particularly useful to continue hypothesis testing since the two variables *jointly* affect the dependent variable. If there is no significant interaction, the grouping variables can be tested individually. The *F*- value associated with attractiveness would provide a test of the hypothesis that attractiveness does not affect the rating. Similarly, the *F*-value associated with sex would test the hypothesis that sex has no main effect on evaluation.

Note that the small *F*-value associated with sex does not indicate that response is unaffected by sex since sex is included in the significant interaction term. Instead, it shows that when response is averaged over attractiveness levels, the two sex category means are not significantly different.

8.5   EXPLANATIONS

Several explanations are consistent with the results of this study. Since most people consider themselves moderately attractive, the highest degree of identification should be with same-sex individuals of moderate attractiveness. The higher empathy may result in the higher scores. An alternative theory is that moderately attractive individuals are generally perceived as more desirable same-sex friends: they have more favorable personality profiles and don't encourage unfavorable comparisons. Their writing scores may benefit from their perceived popularity.

Although we don't want friends who outshine us, handsome (and beautiful) dates provide a favorable reflection and enhance our status. Physical beauty is advantageous for heterosexual relationships, but not same-sex friendships. This prejudice may affect all evaluations of highly attractive members of the opposite sex. Regardless of the explanation, certain practical conclusions are apparent. Students, choose your instructors carefully! Authors, think twice before including your photo on the book jacket!

8.6 EXTENSIONS

Analysis of variance techniques can be used with any number of grouping variables. For example, the data in Table 8.1 originated from a more complicated experiment than described here. There were four factors—essay quality, physical attractiveness, sex of writer, and sex of subject. The original data were analyzed with a 3 x 3 x 2 x 2 ANOVA table. (The numbers indicate how many categories each grouping variable has.) The conclusions from our simplified analysis are the same as those from the more elaborate analysis.

Each of the cells in this experiment has the same number of subjects. This greatly simplifies the analysis and its interpretation. When unequal sample sizes occur in the cells, the total sum of squares cannot be partitioned into nice components which sum to the total. A variety of different techniques are available for calculating sums of squares in such "non-orthogonal" designs. The methods differ in the way they adjust the sums of squares to account for other effects in the model. Each method results in different sums of squares and tests different hypotheses. However, when all cell frequencies are equal, the methods yield the same results. For discussion of various procedures for analyzing designs with unequal cell frequencies, see Kleinbaum and Kupper (1978) and Overall and Klett (1972).

8.7 RUNNING PROCEDURE ANOVA

Procedure ANOVA produces an n-way analysis of variance. Up to five factors or independent variables can be used in one design and several dependent variables can be analyzed in one ANOVA procedure. In addition to the analysis of variance table, ANOVA also prints cell means and sample sizes.

The only required specification for procedure ANOVA is the name of at least one dependent variable, the keyword BY, and one to five independent variables followed by their minimum and maximum values separated by a comma and enclosed in parentheses. To produce the analysis of variance table in Figure 8.2, specify

```
ANOVA          SCORE BY ATTRACT(1,3) SEX (1,2)
```

The minimum and maximum values are the lowest and highest values to be used in the analysis. Recall that attractiveness had three levels in our example. They are coded 1=low, 2=medium, and 3=high. Since the independent variables are simply categories, the numbers you use to represent the categories are arbitrary from a statistical point of view. However, they are not arbitrary from a computational point of view since these values are used to define the dimensions of the table of means and variances from which the analysis of variance is computed. If we had coded ATTRACT as 1, 5, and 10, SPSS would build a table more than three times as large as required for codes 1, 2, and 3. If your categorical variables do not have contiguous values, RECODE them (see Section

8.10) before running ANOVA or you may find out that SPSS does not have enough computer resources to complete your job.

 If you name more than one dependent variable, a separate set of output is produced for each one named.

8.8 The OPTIONS Command for ANOVA

To select one or more of the following options, enter the OPTIONS command keyword in column 1 following your ANOVA specifications with the available option numbers beginning in or beyond column 16. The following list includes the most commonly used options; a complete list is found in Appendix B.

OPTION 1   Include cases with missing values.
OPTION 2   Do not print variable labels.
OPTION 11 Print all output with an 80 character width.

8.9 The STATISTICS Command for ANOVA

Three optional statistics are available. The most commonly used one is listed below; the complete list is found in Appendix B.

STATISTIC 3 Print the means and counts table.

To produce the table of group means shown in Figure 8.1, specify

```
ANOVA          SCORE BY ATTRACT(1,3) SEX (1,2)
STATISTICS     3
```

Note that no special STATISTICS command is required to print the analysis of variance table.

8.10 ANOVA and Other SPSS Commands

To obtain the results in Figures 8.1 and 8.2, the following SPSS commands can be used.

```
RUN NAME          ANALYSIS OF VARIANCE
DATA LIST         FIXED/1 ATTRACT 1-2 SEX 3 SCORE 4-5
RECODE            ATTRACT (1=1) (5=2) (10=3)
VAR LABELS        ATTRACT, ATTRACTIVENESS LEVEL/
                  SEX, SEX SIMILARITY/
                  SCORE, COMPOSITE SCORE/
VALUE LABELS      ATTRACT (1) LOW (2) MEDIUM (3) HIGH/
                  SEX (1) SAME (2) OPPOSITE/
ANOVA             SCORE BY ATTRACT (1,3) SEX (1,2)
STATISTICS        3
READ INPUT DATA
 1118
 1224
 5115
 5213
 ...
 ...
 ...
 10127
 10225
END INPUT DATA
FINISH
```

This SPSS job assumes that the variable ATTRACT is originally coded 1=low, 5=medium, and 10=high.

RECODE. The RECODE command is used to change the values of ATTRACT to consecutive values of 1, 2, and 3 so that the ANOVA procedure will be more efficient. The recode specification (1=1), although unnecessary, is included to give a complete description of the values of ATTRACT. All values not mentioned on the RECODE command will remain unchanged. See Chapter 11 for a discussion of the RECODE specifications.

Chapter 9

Fats and Rats:
Distribution-Free or Nonparametric Tests

Coffee and carrots have recently joined saccharin, tobacco, laetrile, and interferon on the ever- expanding list of rumoured causes of and cures for cancer. This list is necessarily tentative and complicated. The two major sources of evidence—experiments on animals and examination of the histories of afflicted persons—are fraught with problems. It is difficult to predict, based on large dosages of suspect substances given to small animals, the consequences of small amounts consumed by humans over a long time span.

In studies of people, life style components tend to cluster, and it is challenging, if not impossible, to unravel the contribution of a single factor. For example, what is the role of caffein based on a sample of overweight, sedentary, coffee- and alcohol-drinking, cigarette- smoking, urban dwellers?

Nutrition is also thought to be an important component in cancer development and progression. For example, the per capita consumption of dietary fats is positively correlated with the incidence of mammary and colon cancer in humans (Wynder, 1976). In a recent study, King *et al.* (1979) examined the relationship between diet and tumor development in rats. Three groups of animals of the same age, species, and physical condition were injected with tumor cells. The rats were divided into three groups and fed either low fat, saturated fat, or unsaturated fat diets.

One of the hypotheses of interest is whether the length of time until a tumor develops differs for rats fed saturated and unsaturated diets. If it is tenable to assume that tumor-free time is normally distributed, the two-sample *t* test described in Chapter 5 can be used to test the hypothesis that the population means are equal. However, if the distribution of times does not appear to be normal, and especially if the sample sizes are small, statistical procedures that do not require assumptions about the shapes of the underlying distributions should be considered.

9.1 THE MANN-WHITNEY TEST

The *Mann-Whitney test*, sometimes also known as the Wilcoxon test, does not require assumptions about the shape of the underlying distributions. It tests the hypothesis that two independent samples come from populations having the same distribution. The form of the distribution need not be specified. The test does not require that the variable be measured on an interval scale; an ordinal scale is sufficient.

9.2 Ranking the Data

To compute the test, the observations from both samples are first combined and ranked from smallest to largest. Consider the data in Table 9.2, which are a sample of the King data reported by Lee (1979). Case 4 has the shortest elapsed time to development of a tumor, 68 days. It is assigned a rank of 1. The next shortest time is for case 3, so it is assigned a rank of 2. Cases 5 and 6 both exhibited tumors on the same day. They are both assigned a rank of 3.5, the average of ranks 3 and 4 for which they are tied. Case 2, the next largest, is given a rank of 5, and case 1 is given a rank of 6.

Table 9.2 Ranking the data

	Saturated			Unsaturated	
Case	Time	Rank	Case	Time	Rank
1	199	6	4	68	1
2	126	5	5	112	3.5
3	81	2	6	112	3.5

9.3 Calculating the Test

The statistic for testing the hypothesis that the two distributions are equal is the sum of the ranks for each of the two groups. If the groups have the same distribution, their sample distribution of ranks should be similar. If one of the groups has more than its share of small or large ranks there is reason to suspect that the two underlying distributions are different.

Figure 9.3 shows the output from the Mann-Whitney test for the complete King data. For each of the two groups, the mean rank and number of cases is given. (The mean rank is the sum of the ranks divided by the number of cases.) Note that the unsaturated-diet group has only 29 cases since one rat died of causes unrelated to the experiment. The entry printed under W is the sum of the ranks for the group with the smaller number of observations. If both groups have the same number of observations, W is the rank sum for the group named first in the NPAR TESTS command (see Section 9.13). For this example, it is 963, the sum for the saturated-diet group.

Figure 9.3 Mann-Whitney output

```
- - - - MANN-WHITNEY U - WILCOXON RANK SUM W TEST

    TUMOR
BY DIET

       DIET    =        0     DIET    =        1
     MEAN RANK       NUMBER   MEAN RANK       NUMBER
       26.90           30      33.21           29

                              CORRECTED FOR TIES
            U           W         Z      2-TAILED P
          342.0       963.0     -1.4112    0.1582
```

The number identified on the output as U is the number of times a value in the unsaturated-diet group precedes a value in the saturated-diet group. To understand what this means, consider the data in Table 9.2 again. All three cases in the unsaturated-diet group have smaller ranks than the first case in the saturated-diet group, so they all precede case 1 in the rankings. Similarly, all three unsaturated-diet group cases precede case 2. Only one of the unsaturated-diet cases (case 4) is smaller in value than case 3. Thus, the number of times an unsaturated-diet case's value precedes a saturated-diet case's value is 3+3+1=7. The number of times a saturated-diet case's value precedes an unsaturated-diet case's value is 2, since case 3 has a smaller rank than both cases 5 and 6.

The smaller of these two numbers is printed on the output as U. If the two distributions are equal, values from one group should not consistently precede values in the other.

The significance levels associated with U and W are the same. They can be obtained by transforming the score to a standard normal deviate (Z). If the total sample size is less than 30, an exact probability level based on the distribution of the score is also printed. From Figure 9.3, the observed significance level for this example is 0.158. Since the significance level is large, there is no reason to reject the hypothesis that tumor-free time has the same distribution for the two diet groups.

9.4   Which Diet?

You should not conclude from these findings that it doesn't matter—as far as tumors are concerned—what kind of fat you (or rats) eat. King *et al.* found that rats fed the unsaturated diet had a total of 96 tumors at the end of the experiment, while rats fed the saturated diet had only 55 tumors. They also found that large tumors were more common in the unsaturated-diet group than in the saturated-diet group. Thus, unsaturated fats may be more hazardous than saturated fats.

9.5   Assumptions

The Mann-Whitney test requires only that the observations be a random sample and that ordering of the values be possible. These assumptions, especially randomness, are not to be made lightly, but they are less restrictive than those for the two-sample t test for means. The t test further requires that the observations be selected from normally distributed populations with equal variances. (Note that an approximate test for the case of unequal variances is presented in Chapter 5).

Since the Mann-Whitney test can always be calculated instead of the t test, what determines which should be used? If the assumptions needed for the t test are met, the t test is more powerful than the Mann-Whitney test. That is, the t test will detect true differences between the two populations more often than will the Mann-Whitney test since the t test uses more information from the data. Substitution of ranks for the actual values loses potentially useful information. On the other hand, using the t test when its assumptions are substantially violated may result in an observed significance level that is in error.

In general, if the assumptions of the t test appear reasonable, it should be used. When the data are ordinal—or interval from a markedly nonnormal distribution—the Mann-Whitney test is the procedure of choice.

9.6   NONPARAMETRIC TESTS

Many statistical procedures, like the Mann-Whitney test, require limited distributional assumptions about the data. Collectively they are termed *distribution-free* or *nonparametric* tests. Like the Mann-Whitney test, these distribution-free tests are generally less powerful than their parametric counterparts. They are most useful in situations where parametric procedures are not appropriate: nominal or ordinal data, or interval data from markedly nonnormal distributions. Significance levels for certain nonparametric tests can be determined regardless of the shape of the population distribution, since they are based on ranks.

In the following sections, various nonparametric tests will be used to reanalyze some of the data described in previous chapters. Since the data were chosen to illustrate the parametric procedures, they satisfy assumptions that are more restrictive than those for nonparametric procedures. However, they provide the opportunity for learning new procedures with familiar data, and for comparing results from different types of analyses.

9.7 The Sign Test

In Chapter 5, the paired t-test for means is used to test the hypothesis that the mean numbers of actual and reported arrests are equal. Remember that the assumption that the differences are normally distributed is required for this test.

The *sign test* is a nonparametric procedure used in two related samples to test the hypothesis that the distributions of two variables are the same. It needs no assumption about the shape of these distributions.

To compute the sign test, the difference between the number of observed and reported arrests is calculated for each case. (The distribution of these differences is shown in Figure 2.1a). Next, the numbers of positive and negative differences are obtained. If the distributions of the two variables are the same, the numbers of positive and negative differences should be similar.

Figure 9.7 Sign test output

```
- - - - SIGN TEST

       SELF
WITH TRUE
        CASES   -DIFFERENCES   +DIFFERENCES        Z       2-TAILED P
         79          31             38           0.722       0.470
```

From the output shown in Figure 9.7, the number of negative differences is 31, while the number of positive differences is 38. The total number of cases is 79, including 10 with 0 differences. The observed significance level is 0.47. Since this value is large, the hypothesis that the distributions are the same is not rejected.

9.8 The Wilcoxon Signed Rank Test

The sign test makes use of only the direction of the differences of the pairs and ignores the magnitude. A discrepancy of 15 between observed and reported arrests is treated in the same way as a discrepancy of 1. The *Wilcoxon signed rank test* incorporates information about the magnitude of the differences and is therefore more powerful than the sign test.

To compute the Wilcoxon signed rank test, the differences are ranked ignoring the signs. In the case of ties, average ranks are assigned. The sums of the ranks for positive and negative differences are then calculated.

Figure 9.8 Wilcoxon signed rank test output

```
- - - - WILCOXON MATCHED-PAIRS SIGNED-RANKS TEST

      SELF
WITH TRUE

                        31 -RANKS      38 +RANKS
      CASES    TIES       MEAN           MEAN          Z       2-TAILED P
       79       10        35.90          34.26       -0.565      0.572
```

From Figure 9.8, the average rank of the 31 negative differences is 35.90. The average positive rank is 34.26. There are 10 cases with the same value for both variables; this is the entry under TIES in Figure 9.8. The observed significance level associated with the test is 0.572. Again, it is large and the hypothesis of no difference is not rejected.

9.9 The Kruskal-Wallis Test

The experiment described in the first sections of this chapter investigates the effects of three diets on tumor development. The Mann-Whitney signed rank test was calculated to examine possible differences between saturated and unsaturated diets. To test for differences between all three diets, an extension of the Mann-Whitney test can be used. This test is known as the *Kruskal- Wallis one-way analysis of variance.*

The procedure for computing the Kruskal-Wallis test is similar to that used in the Mann-Whitney test. All cases from the groups are combined and ranked. Average ranks are assigned in the case of ties. For each of the groups, the ranks are summed, and the Kruskal-Wallis H statistic is computed from these sums. The H statistic has approximately a chi-square distribution under the hypothesis that the three groups have the same distribution.

Figure 9.9   Kruskal-Wallis oneway analysis of variance output

```
- - - - KRUSKAL-WALLIS 1-WAY ANOVA

     TUMOR
  BY DIET

      DIET         0          1          2
    NUMBER        30         29         29
MEAN RANKS     34.12      43.50      56.24
                                         CORRECTED FOR TIES
        CASES    CHI-SQUARE  SIGNIFICANCE   CHI-SQUARE  SIGNIFICANCE
         88        11.126       0.004        11.261        0.004
```

From the output in Figure 9.9, notice that the third group, the low-fat-diet group, has the largest average rank. The value of the Kruskal-Wallis statistic (labeled CHI-SQUARE) is 11.126. When the statistic is adjusted for the presence of ties, the value changes to 11.261 (labeled CORRECTED CHI- SQUARE). The small observed significance level suggests that the time until development of tumor is not the same for all three groups.

9.10   The One-Sample Chi-Square Test

In Chapter 1, frequencies of cardiac arrests for the days of the week are examined. The FREQUENCIES output suggests that the days of the week are not equally hazardous with regard to heart attacks. To test this, the *one-sample chi-square test* can be used. This nonparametric test requires only that the data be a random sample.

To calculate the one-sample chi-square statistic, the data are first classified into mutually exclusive categories of interest—days of the week in this example—and then expected frequencies for these categories are computed. Expected frequencies are the frequencies that would be expected if a given hypothesis is true. For the cardiac-arrest data, the hypothesis to be tested is that the probability of having a heart attack is the same for each day of the week. There are 152 patients for whom the day of death is known. The hypothesis to be tested implies that the expected frequency of cardiac arrests for each weekday is 152 divided by 7, or 21.71. Once the expected frequencies are obtained, the chi-square statistic is computed as

$$\chi^2 = \sum_{i=1}^{k} (O_i - E_i)^2 \big/ E_i$$

where O_i is the observed frequency for the ith category, E_i is the expected frequency for the ith category, and k is the number of categories.

Figure 9.10   One-sample chi-square output

```
- - - - CHI-SQUARE TEST

     DAY

    VALUE      1.       2.       3.       4.       5.       6.       7.
    COUNT     38.      17.      16.      29.      15.      17.      20.
  EXPECTED  21.71    21.71    21.71    21.71    21.71    21.71    21.71

        CHI-SQUARE              D.F.          SIGNIFICANCE
          20.421                 6               0.002
```

If the hypothesis from which the expected frequencies are obtained is true, then the chi-square statistic has approximately a chi-square distribution with $k-1$ degrees of freedom. This statistic will be large if the observed and expected frequencies are substantially different. Figure 9.10 is the output from the one-sample chi-square test for the cardiac arrest data. The codes associated with the days of the week are listed in the row labeled VALUE. The observed frequencies are in the next row, labeled COUNT. The observed significance level is only 0.002, so it appears that the day of the week does affect the chance of having a heart attack.

9.11   The Rank Correlation Coefficient

The Pearson product-moment correlation discussed in Chapter 6 is appropriate only for data that attain at least an interval level of measurement, such as the skirts and beards data used as examples in that chapter. Normality is also assumed when testing hypotheses about this correlation coefficient. However, another measure of the linear relationship between two variables is available for ordinal data or for interval data that do not satisfy the normality assumption. This is *Spearman's rank correlation coefficient.*

The rank correlation coefficient is the Pearson correlation coefficient based on the ranks of the data if there are no ties (adjustments are made if some of the data are tied). That is, if the original data for each variable have no ties, the data for each variable are ranked and the Pearson correlation coefficient between the ranks for the two variables is computed. Like the Pearson correlation coefficient, the rank correlation ranges between -1 and 1, where -1 and 1 indicate a perfect linear relationship between the ranks for the two variables. The interpretation is therefore the same except that the relationship between *ranks* is examined.

Figure 9.11   The rank correlation coefficient

```
- - - - - - - - - - - S P E A R M A N   C O R R E L A T I O N   C O E F F I C I E N T S - - - - - - - - - - - -

VARIABLE              VARIABLE              VARIABLE              VARIABLE              VARIABLE              VARIABLE
PAIR                  PAIR                  PAIR                  PAIR                  PAIR                  PAIR
--------              --------              --------              --------              --------              --------

SKIRTS      0.8023    SKIRTS     -0.5815    SKIRTS     -0.9108    SKIRTS     -0.2382    SKIRTS      0.5512    SKIRTS      0.8121
WITH      N( 112)     WITH      N( 112)     WITH      N( 112)     WITH      N( 112)     WITH      N( 112)     WITH      N( 112)
BEARDS    SIG .001     YEAR     SIG .001     CLEAN    SIG .001     MOUST    SIG .006     SIDEBUR   SIG .001     MOUSIDE   SIG .001

BEARDS     -0.6663    BEARDS     -0.8796    BEARDS     -0.1937    BEARDS      0.6621    BEARDS      0.8027    YEAR        0.7861
WITH      N( 131)     WITH      N( 131)     WITH      N( 131)     WITH      N( 131)     WITH      N( 131)     WITH      N( 131)
YEAR      SIG .001     CLEAN    SIG .001     MOUST    SIG .013     SIDEBUR   SIG .001     MOUSIDE   SIG .001     CLEAN    SIG .001

YEAR        0.4376    YEAR       -0.9145    YEAR       -0.7645    CLEAN       0.0989    CLEAN      -0.7202    CLEAN      -0.8569
WITH      N( 131)     WITH      N( 131)     WITH      N( 131)     WITH      N( 131)     WITH      N( 131)     WITH      N( 131)
MOUST     SIG .001     SIDEBUR  SIG .001     MOUSIDE  SIG .001     MOUST    SIG .130     SIDEBUR   SIG .001     MOUSIDE   SIG .001

MOUST      -0.6241    MOUST      -0.3836    SIDEBUR     0.8081
WITH      N( 131)     WITH      N( 131)     WITH      N( 131)
SIDEBUR   SIG .001     MOUSIDE  SIG .001     MOUSIDE  SIG .001

          A VALUE OF 99.0000 IS PRINTED IF A COEFFICIENT CANNOT BE COMPUTED.
```

Figure 9.11 shows the matrix of rank correlation coefficients for the skirts and beards data. As expected, these coefficients are similar in sign and magnitude to the Pearson coefficients obtained in Chapter 6 (Figure 6.6).

9.12   RUNNING PROCEDURE NPAR TESTS

All of the nonparametric tests described in Sections 9.1 through 9.10, and several more, are available in the NPAR TESTS procedure. Enter the NPAR TESTS command keyword in column one followed by one or more of the test subcommands beginning in column 16 or beyond. A complete list of the nonparametric tests available in the NPAR TESTS procedure can be found in Appendix B. See Section 9.16 for a discussion of the NONPAR CORR procedure used for the rank correlations.

9.13   The Mann-Whitney and Kruskal-Wallis Tests

Use the subcommand M-W= to specify the Mann-Whitney test or the subcommand K-W= for the Kruskal Wallis test. The subcommand specification for either is the name of the variable to be analyzed followed by the keyword BY, the name of the grouping variable, and the values defining the groups in parentheses. The grouping variable indicates which group each case belongs to. For example, the command used to produce the output shown in Figure 9.3 is

```
NPAR TESTS     M-W=TUMOR BY DIET(0,1)
```

where TUMOR is the time until development of a tumor and the value 0 of variable DIET indicates that a case is from the unsaturated-diet group and the value 1 indicates a case is from the saturated- diet group. The Kruskal-Wallis test in Figure 9.9 is obtained with

```
NPAR TESTS     K-W=TUMOR BY DIET(0,2)
```

9.14   The Sign and Wilcoxon Tests

Use the SIGN= subcommand for the sign test and the WILCOXON= subcommand for the Wilcoxon test. For either test, you specify one variable name, the keyword WITH, and the other variable name. For example, to produce the output shown in Figure 9.8, specify

```
NPAR TESTS     WILCOXON = SELF WITH TRUE
```

where variable SELF records the self-reported number of arrests and TRUE records the actual arrests. The sign test output in Figure 9.7 is produced by

```
NPAR TESTS     SIGN=SELF WITH TRUE
```

9.15   The One-Sample Chi-Square Test

The NPAR TESTS command for the one-sample chi-square test is the subcommand CHI-SQUARE= followed by the variable name. The following SPSS job will produce the output shown in Figure 9.10.

```
VARIABLE LIST     DAY, DAYFREQ
INPUT FORMAT      FREEFIELD
N OF CASES        7
VAR LABELS        DAYFREQ   FREQ OF CARDIAC ARR BY DAYS OF WEEK
WEIGHT            DAYFREQ
NPAR TESTS        CHI-SQUARE = DAY
READ INPUT DATA
1 38   2 17   3 16   4 29   5 15   6 17   7 20
FINISH
```

In this SPSS job, the data are entered as aggregated data in freefield format. Each day of the week represents one case in the aggregated file—a total of seven cases. Variable DAY is entered with the same coding scheme used in Chapter 1, and the total number of cardiac arrests, variable DAYFREQ, is entered for each day. The first case in the aggregated data represents Monday with the value 1 for DAY and 38, the frequency of cardiac arrests on Monday, for DAYFREQ. Likewise, for the second case (Tuesday), the value 2 is recorded for DAY and 17, the frequency of cardiac arrests on Tuesday, for DAYFREQ, and so forth for each day of the week. Then variable DAYFREQ is used on the WEIGHT command to replicate cases for the analysis (see Chapter 3).

The data are entered in freefield format with multiple cases on the same line, and each value separated by one or more blanks. The keyword FREEFIELD is specified on the INPUT FORMAT command, and the names of the variables in the order that they are entered on the data are declared on the VARIABLE LIST command. The N OF CASES command tells SPSS how many cases to read. See Chapter 5 for another example of using freefield formatted data.

9.16   RUNNING PROCEDURE NONPAR CORR

The NONPAR CORR procedure produces Spearman rank correlations for pairs of variables. Output includes the coefficient, the test of significance, and the number of cases upon which the coefficient is based.

9.17   The NONPAR CORR Variable List

The only NONPAR CORR specification following the command keywords is the variable list beginning in column 16 or after. For example, to produce the output shown in Figure 9.11, specify

```
NONPAR CORR    SKIRTS BEARDS YEAR CLEAN TO MOUSIDE
```

The order in which you name the variables is the order in which NONPAR CORR displays them.

You can use the keyword WITH to specify rank correlations for specific pairs of variables. For example, to request rank correlations for SKIRTS with BEARDS, and SKIRTS with YEAR, specify

```
NONPAR CORR    SKIRTS WITH BEARDS YEAR
```

9.18   The OPTIONS Command for NONPAR CORR

Following your NONPAR CORR variable list, you can enter the OPTIONS command keyword beginning in column 1 and a list of numbers beginning in column 16 or beyond. The most commonly used options are listed below; a complete list is found Appendix B.

OPTION 1   Include cases with missing values.
OPTION 2   Exclude missing data listwise.
OPTION 3   Calculate a two-tailed test of significance.

Unless you specify otherwise, SPSS excludes a case from the calculation of a correlation coefficient if it has a missing value on either of the variables in the pair. This is pairwise missing-value treatment. Option 1 tells NONPAR CORR to ignore the missing-value status of any values and to treat the cases as if the values were valid. Option 2 tells NONPAR CORR to exclude cases that have a missing value on any variable in the list even if the case has valid values on both variables in the pair. This is listwise missing-value treatment. The choice between pairwise and listwise missing-value treatments should be made carefully; see Sections 6.7 and 6.8 for a discussion.

Chapter 10

Statistical Models for Salary: Multiple Linear Regression Analysis

In Chapter 4, procedure BREAKDOWN is used to describe beginning salary levels for groups of bank employees based on race and sex. In this chapter, both beginning salary and salary progression are examined for the same employees hired between 1969 and 1971. A mathematical model is developed that relates beginning salary to various employee characteristics such as seniority, education, and previous work experience. One important objective is to determine whether the sex and race variables are important predictors of salary.

The technique used to build the model is linear regression analysis, one of the most versatile procedures for data analysis. Regression can be used to summarize data as well as to quantify relations among variables. Another frequent application of regression analysis is predicting values of new observations based on a previously derived model.

10.1 INTRODUCTION TO REGRESSION STATISTICS

Before building a model that relates beginning salary to several other variables, consider the relationship between beginning salary and "current" (March 1977) salary. For employees hired during a similar time period, beginning salary should serve as a reasonably good predictor of salary at a later date. Although superstars and underachievers might progress differently from the group as a whole, salary progression should be similar for the others. The scattergram of beginning salary and current salary in Figure 10.1 supports this hypothesis.

A scattergram may suggest what type of mathematical functions may be appropriate for summarizing the data. A variety of functions have been found to be useful in fitting models to data. Parabolas, hyperbolas, polynomials, trigonometric functions, and many more are potential candidates. For the scattergram in Figure 10.1, current salaries tend to increase linearly with increases in beginning salary. If the plot indicates that a straight line is not a good summary measure of the relationship, you should consider other possibilities, including attempts to transform the data to linearity (see Section 10.27).

91

Figure 10.1 Scatterplot of beginning and current salaries

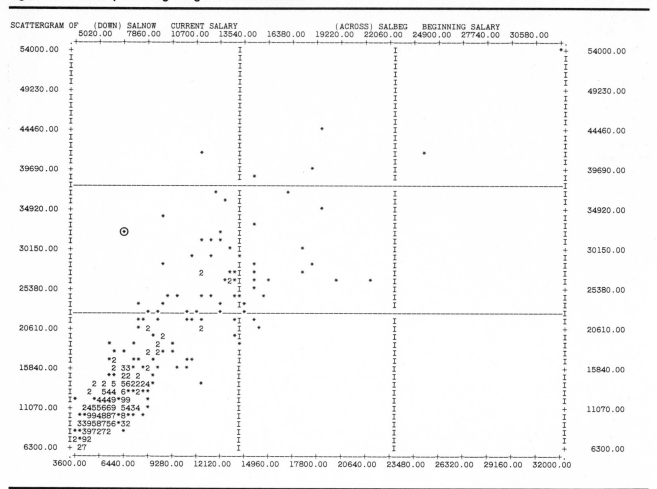

10.2 Outliers

A plot may also indicate the presence of points suspiciously different from the others. Examine carefully such observations, termed *outliers*, to see if they came from errors in data gathering, coding, or entry. The circled point in Figure 10.1 appears to be an outlier. Though neither the value of beginning salary ($6300) nor the value of current salary ($32,000) is very different, jointly they are unusual.

The treatment of outliers can be difficult. If the point is really incorrect, due to coding or entry problems, one should correct it and rerun the analysis. If there is no apparent explanation for the outlier, consider interactions with other variables as a possible explanation. For example, it may be that the circled employee was hired as a low-paid clerical worker while pursuing an MBA degree. After graduation, a rapid rise in position was possible, making education the variable that explains the unusual salary characteristics of the employee.

10.3 Choosing a Regression Line

Since current salary tends to increase linearly with beginning salary, a straight line can be used to summarize the relationship. The equation for the line is

predicted current salary $= B_0 + B_1$(beginning salary)

The *slope* (B_1) is the change in the fitted current salary for a dollar change in the beginning salary. The *intercept* (B_0) is the theoretical estimate of current salary if there were a beginning salary of 0.

The observed data points do not all fall on a straight line but cluster about it. Many lines can be drawn through the data points and the problem is to select among them. The method of *least squares* results in a line that minimizes the sum of squared vertical distances from the observed data points to the line. Any other line has a larger sum. Figure 10.3a shows the least squares line superimposed on the salary scattergram. Some vertical distances from points to the line are also shown.

Figure 10.3a   Regression line for beginning and current salaries

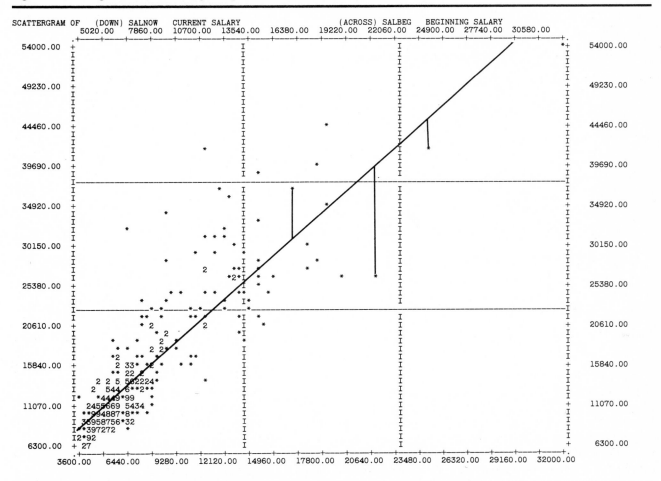

You can use SPSS procedure NEW REGRESSION to calculate the least squares line. For the data in Figure 10.1, that line is

predicted current salary = 771.28 + 1.91(beginning salary)

The slope and intercept values are shown in the column labeled B in the output shown in Figure 10.3b.

Figure 10.3b   Regression equation statistics

```
----------------- VARIABLES IN THE EQUATION -------------------

VARIABLE            B          SE B       BETA         T    SIG T

SALBEG          1.90945      0.04741    0.88012     40.276  0.0000
(CONSTANT)    771.28230    355.47194                 2.170  0.0305
```

10.4   From Samples to Populations

Generally, more is required from regression analysis than a description of observed data. One wishes to draw inferences about the relationship of the variables in the population from which the sample was taken. How are beginning and current salaries related for all employees, not just those included in the sample? To draw inferences about population values based on sample results, the following assumptions are needed:

Normality and Equality of Variance.   For any fixed value of the independent variable X, the distribution of the dependent variable Y is normal with mean $\mu_{Y/X}$ (the mean of Y for a given X), and a constant variance of σ^2. Figure 10.4 illustrates this assumption. This assumption specifies that not all employees with the same beginning salary have the same current salary. Instead, there is a normal distribution of current salaries for each beginning salary. Though the distributions have different means, they have the same variance σ^2.

Figure 10.4   Regression assumptions

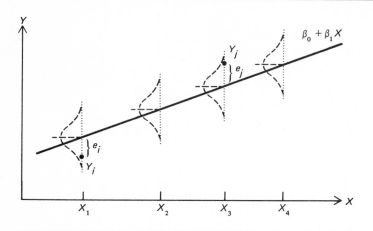

Independence.   The Ys are statistically independent of each other. That is, observations are in no way influenced by other observations. For example, if repeated measurements are obtained from the same experimental unit, the observations are not independent. If three observations are taken from each of four families, the twelve observations are not independent.

Linearity.   The mean values $\mu_{Y/X}$ all lie on a straight line which is the population regression line. This line is drawn in Figure 10.4. An alternative way of stating this assumption is that the linear model is correct.

When there is a single independent variable, the model can be summarized by

$$Y_i = \beta_0 + \beta_1 X_i + e_i$$

The population values for the slope and intercept are denoted by β_1 and β_0. An e_i, often called an error or disturbance, is the difference between the observed value of Y_i and the subpopulation mean at the point X_i. The e_i are normally distributed, independent random variables with a mean 0 and variance of σ^2 (see Figure 10.4).

10.5   Estimating Population Parameters

Since β_0 and β_1 are unknown population parameters, they must be estimated from the sample. The least squares estimators B_0 and B_1 discussed in Section 10.3 are used to estimate the population parameters.

However, the slope and intercept estimated from a single sample typically differ from the population values and vary from sample to sample. To use these estimates for inference about the population values, the sampling distributions of the two statistics are needed. (See Chapter 5 for further discussion of sampling distributions and hypothesis testing.) When the assumptions of linear regression are met, the sampling distributions of B_0 and B_1 are normal with means of β_0 and β_1. The standard error of B_0 is

$$\sigma_{B_0} = \sigma \sqrt{\frac{1}{N} + \frac{\overline{X}^2}{(N-1)S_X{}^2}}$$

where $S_X{}^2$ is the sample variance of the independent variable. The standard error of B_1 is

$$\sigma_{B_1} = \frac{\sigma}{\sqrt{(N-1)S_X{}^2}}$$

Since the population variance of the errors, σ^2, is not known, it, along with the variance of the slope and intercept, must be estimated. The usual estimate of σ^2 is

$$S^2 = \frac{\sum\limits_{i=1}^{N}(Y_i - B_0 - B_1 X_i)^2}{N-2}$$

The positive square root of this quantity is termed the *standard error of the estimate*, or the standard deviation of the residuals. (The reason for this name is discussed in Section 10.15.) The estimated standard errors of the slope and intercept are printed in the third column (labeled SE B) in Figure 10.3b.

10.6 Testing Hypotheses

A frequently tested hypothesis is that there is no linear association between X and Y—that the slope of the population regression line is 0. One statistic used to test this hypothesis is

$$t = \frac{B_1}{S_{B_1}}$$

The distribution of the statistic, when the assumptions are met and the hypothesis of no linear association is true, is the Student's t distribution with $N-2$ degrees of freedom. To test the hypothesis that the intercept is 0, the test statistic is

$$t = \frac{B_0}{S_{B_0}}$$

Its distribution is also the Student's t with $N-2$ degrees of freedom.

These t statistics and their two-tailed observed significance levels are printed in the last two columns of Figure 10.3b. The small observed significance level (less than 0.00005) associated with the slope for the salary data supports the hypothesis that beginning and current salary are linearly related.

10.7 The Standardized Regression Coefficient

The *standardized regression coefficient*, labeled BETA in Figure 10.3b, is defined as

$$BETA = B_1 \frac{S_X}{S_Y}$$

Multiplication of the regression coefficient by the ratio of the standard deviation of the independent variable to the standard deviation of the dependent variable results in a dimensionless coefficient. In fact, the BETA coefficient is the slope of the least squares line when both Y and X are expressed as Z-scores. The BETA coefficient is further discussed in Section 10.37.

10.8 Confidence Intervals

A statistic calculated from a sample provides a point estimate of the unknown parameter. A point estimate can be thought of as the single best guess for the population value. The estimated value from the sample is typically different from the value of the unknown population parameter. Hopefully, it isn't too far away. Based on the sample estimate, it is possible to calculate a range of values that, with a designated likelihood, includes the population value. Such a range is called a *confidence interval*. For example, as shown in Figure 10.8, the 95% confidence interval for β_1, the population slope, is 1.816 to 2.003.

Figure 10.8 Confidence intervals

```
VARIABLE        95% CONFDNCE INTRVL B

SALBEG           1.81629      2.00261
(CONSTANT)      72.77921   1469.78540
```

Ninety-five percent confidence means that, if repeated samples are drawn from a population under the same conditions and 95% confidence intervals are calculated, 95% of the intervals contain the unknown parameter β_1. Since the parameter value is unknown, it is not possible to determine whether or not a particular interval contains the population parameter.

10.9 Goodness of Fit

An important part of any statistical procedure that builds models from data is establishing how well the model actually fits. This topic encompasses the detection of possible violations of the required assumptions in the data being analyzed. The present discussion is limited to the question of how close to the fitted line the observed points fall. Subsequent sections discuss other assumptions and tests for their violation.

10.10 The R^2 Coefficient

A commonly used measure of the goodness of fit of a linear model is R^2, sometimes also called the *coefficient of determination*. It can be thought of in a variety of ways. Besides being the square of the correlation coefficient between variables X and Y, it is the square of the correlation coefficient between Y, the observed value of the dependent variable, and $\hat{Y}$, the predicted value of Y from the fitted line. If for each employee one computes (based on the coefficients in the output in Figure 10.3b) the predicted salary

predicted current salary = 771.28 + 1.91(beginning salary)

and then calculates the square of the Pearson correlation coefficent between the predicted current salary and that actually observed, R^2 is obtained. If all the observations fall on the regression line, R^2 is 1. If there is no linear relationship between the dependent and independent variables, R^2 is 0.

Note that R^2 is a measure of the goodness of fit of a particular model and that an R^2 of 0 does not necessarily mean that there is no association between the variables. Instead, it indicates that there is no *linear association* (see Chapter 6 for further discussion).

Figure 10.10   Summary statistics for the equation

```
MULTIPLE R         0.88012
R SQUARE           0.77461
ADJUSTED R SQUARE  0.77413
STANDARD ERROR  3246.14226
```

In the output shown in Figure 10.10, R^2 is labeled R-SQUARE; its square root is called MULTIPLE R. The sample R^2 tends to be an optimistic estimate of how well the model fits in the population. The model usually does not fit the population as well as it fits the sample from which it is derived. *Adjusted R^2* is a statistic that attempts to correct R^2 to more closely reflect the goodness of fit of the model in the population. Adjusted R^2 is given by

$$R_a{}^2 = R^2 - \frac{p(1 - R^2)}{N - p - 1}$$

where p is the number of independent variables in the equation (1 in the salary example).

10.11   Analysis of Variance

To test the hypothesis of no linear relationship between X and Y, several equivalent statistics can be computed. The hypotheses that the population R^2 and the population slope are 0 are identical when there is a single independent variable. The test for $R^2_{pop}=0$ is usually obtained from the *analysis of variance* (ANOVA) table shown in Figure 10.11a.

Figure 10.11a   Analysis of variance table

```
ANALYSIS OF VARIANCE
                     DF      SUM OF SQUARES         MEAN SQUARE
REGRESSION            1   17092967800.01931      0.17093D 11
RESIDUAL            472    4973671469.79483   10537439.55465

F =     1622.11776       SIGNIF F = 0.0000
```

The total observed variability in the dependent variable is subdivided into two components—that which is attributable to the regression (REGRESSION) and that which is not (RESIDUAL). Consider Figure 10.11b. For a particular point, the distance from Y_i to the mean of the Ys, $\overline{Y}$, can be subdivided into two parts.

$$Y_i - \overline{Y} = (Y_i - \hat{Y}_i) + (\hat{Y}_i - \overline{Y})$$

Figure 10.11b   Components of variability

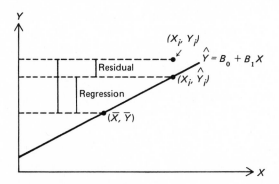

The distance from Y_i, the observed value, to $\hat{Y}_i$, the value predicted by the regression line, is $(Y_i - \hat{Y}_i)$. This distance is 0 if the regression line passes through the point. It is called the *residual from the regression*. The second component $(\hat{Y}_i - \overline{Y})$ is the distance from the regression line to the mean of the Ys. This distance is "explained" by the regression, in that it represents the change in the estimate of the dependent variable achieved by the regression. Without the regression, the mean of the dependent variable $(\overline{Y})$ is used as the estimate. It can be shown that

$$\sum_{i=1}^{N} (Y_i - \overline{Y})^2 = \sum_{i=1}^{N} (Y_i - \hat{Y}_i)^2 + \sum_{i=1}^{N} (\hat{Y}_i - \overline{Y})^2$$

The first quantity following the equals sign is called the *residual sum of squares* and the second quantity is the *regression sum of squares*. The sum of these is called the *total sum of squares*.

The ANOVA table displays these two sums of squares under the heading SUM OF SQUARES (Figure 10.11a). The MEAN SQUARE for each entry is the SUM OF SQUARES divided by the degrees of freedom. If the regression assumptions are met, the ratio of the mean square regression to mean square residual is distributed as an F statistic with p and $N-p-1$ degrees of freedom. F serves to test how well the regression model fits the data. If the probability associated with the F statistic is small, the hypothesis that $R^2_{pop}=0$ is rejected. For the present example, the F statistic is

$$F = \frac{\text{MEAN SQUARE REGRESSION}}{\text{MEAN SQUARE RESIDUAL}} = 1622$$

The observed significance level (SIGNIF F) is less than 0.00005.

The square root of the F value, 40.28, is the value of the t statistic for the slope in Figure 10.3b. The square of a t value with k degrees of freedom is an F value with 1 and k degrees of freedom. Therefore, either t or F values can be computed to test that $\beta_i=0$.

10.12   Another Interpretation of R^2

Partitioning the sum of squares of the dependent variable allows another interpretation of R^2. It is the proportion of the variation in the dependent variable "explained" by the model.

$$R^2 = 1 - \frac{\text{RESIDUAL SUM OF SQUARES}}{\text{TOTAL SUM OF SQUARES}} = 0.775$$

Similarly, adjusted R^2 is

$$R^2_a = 1 - \frac{\text{RESIDUAL SUM OF SQUARES}/(N - p - 1)}{\text{TOTAL SUM OF SQUARES}/(N - 1)}$$

where p is the number of independent variables in the equation (1 in the salary example).

10.13   Predicted Values and Their Standard Errors

By comparing the observed dependent variable values to the values predicted by the regression equation, much can be learned about how well a model and the various assumptions fit the data (see the discussion beginning with Section 10.17). Predicted values are also of interest when the results are applied to prediction of new data. You may wish to predict the mean Y at a given value of X, denoted X_0, or to predict the value of Y for a single case. For example, you can predict either the mean salary for all employees with a beginning salary of \$10,000 or the salary for a particular employee with a beginning salary of \$10,000. In both situations, the predicted value

$$\hat{Y}_0 = B_0 + B_1X_0 = 771 + 1.91 \times 10,000 = 19,871$$

is the same. What differs is the standard error.

10.14　Predicting Mean Response

The estimated standard error for the predicted mean Y at X_0 is

$$S_{\hat{Y}} = S\sqrt{\frac{1}{N} + \frac{(X_0 - \overline{X})^2}{(N-1)S_X{}^2}}$$

The formula for the standard error shows that the smallest value occurs when X_0 is equal to $\overline{X}$, the mean of X. The larger the distance from the mean, the greater the standard error. Thus the mean of Y for a given X is better estimated for central values of the observed Xs than for outlying values. Figure 10.14a is a plot of the standard errors of predicted mean salaries for different values of beginning salary.

Figure 10.14a　Standard errors for predicted mean responses

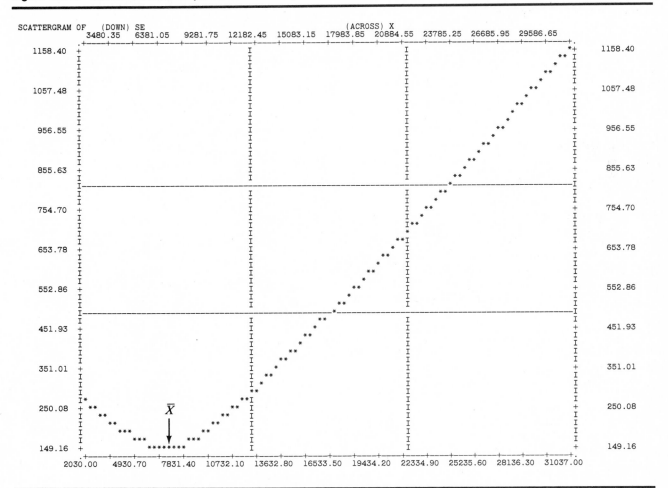

Confidence intervals for the mean predicted salary are calculated in the standard way. The $1-\alpha$ confidence interval at X_0 is

$$\hat{Y} \pm t_{\left(1-\frac{\alpha}{2}, N-2\right)} S_{\hat{Y}}$$

Figure 10.14b shows a typical 95% confidence band for predicted mean responses. It is narrowest at the mean of X and increases as the squared distance from the mean, $(X_0 - \bar{X})^2$, increases.

Figure 10.14b 95% confidence band for mean prediction

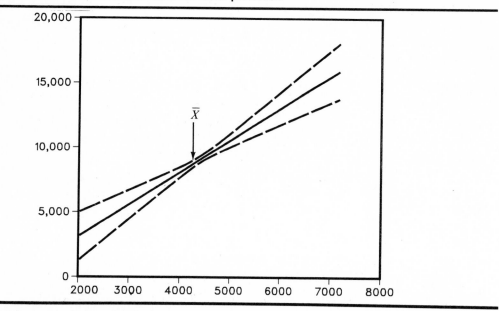

10.15 Predicting a New Value

Although the predicted value for a single new observation at X_0 is the same as the predicted value for the mean at X_0, the standard error is not. The two sources of error when predicting an individual observation are illustrated in Figure 10.15. They are the following:

1 The individual value may differ from the population mean of Y for X_0.

2 The estimate of the population mean at X_0 may differ from the population mean.

Figure 10.15 Sources of error in predicting individual observations

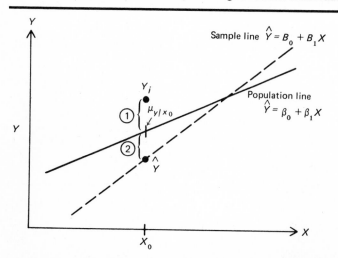

When estimating the mean response, only the second error component must be considered. The variance of the individual prediction is the variance of the mean prediction plus the variance of Y_i for a given X. This can be written as

$$S^2{}_{ind\hat{Y}} = S^2{}_{\hat{Y}} + S^2 = S^2\left(1 + \frac{1}{N} + \frac{(X_0 - \overline{X})^2}{(N-1)S_X{}^2}\right)$$

Prediction intervals for the new observation are obtained by substituting $S_{ind\hat{Y}}$ for $S_{\hat{Y}}$ in the equation for the confidence intervals for the mean given in Section 10.14. If the sample size is large, the terms $1/N$ and

$$\frac{(X_0 - \overline{X})^2}{(N-1)S_X{}^2}$$

are negligible. In that case, the standard error is simply S, which explains the name *standard error of the estimate* for S (see Section 10.5).

10.16 Reading the Casewise Plot

Figure 10.16 shows the output from the beginning and end of a plot of the salary data. The sequence number of the case and an optional labeling variable (SEXRACE) are listed first; then the plot of standardized residuals; then the observed (SALNOW), predicted (PRED), and residual (RESID) values; and finally the standard error of the mean prediction (SEPRED). The variance of an individual prediction can be obtained by adding S^2 to the square of each of the standard error values. You can generate and save predicted values and the standard errors of the mean responses in the NEW REGRESSION procedure. Both can be printed for all cases or for a subset of cases along with a casewise plot.

Figure 10.16   Casewise plot with predicted values and standard errors

```
CASEWISE PLOT OF STANDARDIZED RESIDUAL

                -3.0        0.0        3.0
SEQNUM  SEXRACE  0:.........:.........:0     SALNOW      *PRED       *RESID      *SEPRED
   1    1.0000   .          .  *.    .     16080.0000  16810.6600   -730.6600   167.1489
   2    1.0000   .     *     .         .    41400.0000  46598.0758  -5198.0758   828.6655
   3    1.0000   .          .   *       .   21960.0000  20247.6695   1712.3305   219.3531
   4    1.0000   .          .   *       .   19200.0000  17383.4949   1816.5051   174.0406
   5    1.0000   .     *     .         .    28350.0000  33995.7076  -5645.7076   523.9021
   6    1.0000   .          .    *       .  27250.0000  25586.4910   1663.5090   329.1520
   7    1.0000   .          .   *       .   16080.0000  13946.4854   2133.5146   149.1662
   8    1.0000   .          .     *      .  14100.0000  11082.3108   3017.6892   163.3307
   9    1.0000   .          .    *       .  12420.0000  10394.9089   2025.0911   171.0096
  10    1.0000   .         *. .         .   12300.0000  12800.8156   -500.8156   151.0211
  11    1.0000   .          .   *       .   15720.0000  12800.8156   2919.1844   151.0211
  12    1.0000   .       *  .         .      8880.0000  12227.9807  -3347.9807   153.9241
 ...
 ...
 ...
 470    4.0000   .          *        .      9420.0000   9592.9401   -172.9401   181.5927
 471    4.0000   .          .*       .      9780.0000   9134.6721    645.3279   188.3196
 472    4.0000   .        *  .       .      7680.0000   9249.2391  -1569.2391   186.5956
 473    4.0000   .         *. .      .      7380.0000   8561.8372  -1181.8372   197.3294
 474    4.0000   .        *  .       .      8340.0000  10738.6099  -2398.6099   166.9964
SEQNUM  SEXRACE  0:.........:.........:0     SALNOW      *PRED       *RESID      *SEPRED
                -3.0        0.0        3.0
```

10.17   Searching for Violations of Assumptions

You usually don't know in advance the appropriateness of a model such as linear regression. Instead, a search, focused on residuals, is conducted to look for evidence that the necessary assumptions are violated.

10.18   Residuals

In model building, a *residual* is what is left after the model is fit. It is the difference between an observed value and the value predicted by the model.

$$E_i = Y_i - B_0 - B_1 X_i = Y_i - \hat{Y}_i$$

In regression analysis, the true errors e_i are assumed to be independent normal values with a mean of 0 and a constant variance of σ^2. If the model is appropriate for the data, the observed residuals E_i, which are estimates of the true errors e_i, should have similar characteristics.

If B_0 is included in the equation, the mean of the residuals is always 0, so it provides no information about the true mean of the errors. Since the sum of the residuals is constrained to be 0, they are *not* strictly independent. However, if the number of residuals is large when compared to the number of independent variables, the dependency among the residuals can be ignored for practical purposes.

The relative magnitude of residuals is easier to judge when they are divided by estimates of their standard deviations. The resulting standardized residuals are expressed in standard deviation units above or below the mean. That is, the fact that a particular residual is -5198.1 provides little information. If you know that its standardized form is -3.1, you know not only that the observed value is less than the predicted value but also that the residual is in absolute value larger than most.

Residuals are usually adjusted in one of two ways. The *standardized residual* for case i is the residual divided by the sample standard deviation of the residuals. Standardized residuals have a mean of 0 and a standard deviation of 1. The *Studentized residual* is the residual divided by an estimate of its standard deviation that varies from point to point, depending on the distance of X_i from the mean of X. Usually standardized and Studentized residuals are close in value, but not always. The Studentized residual reflects more precisely differences in the error variances from point to point.

10.19 Linearity

For the bivariate situation, a scattergram is a good means for judging how well a straight line fits the data. Another convenient way is to plot the residuals against the predicted values. If the assumptions of linearity and homogeneity of variance are met, there should be no relationship between the value of the residual and the predicted value. You should be suspicious of any observable pattern. For example, fitting a least squares line to the data in the two left-hand plots in Figure 10.19a would yield the residual plots shown on the right.

Figure 10.19a   Standardized residuals scattergrams

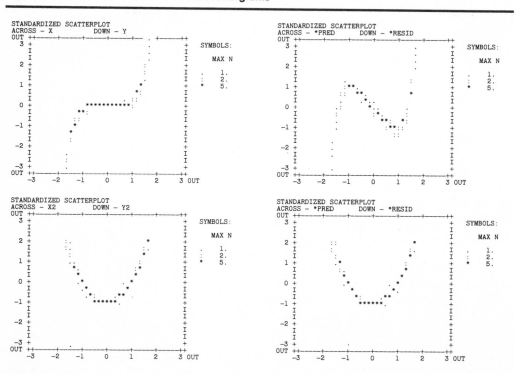

Patterns of residuals can be seen in the residual plots in Figure 10.19a since straight lines do not fit the data well. The associations between the predicted values and the residuals suggest a possible violation of the linearity assumption. If the assumption is met, the residuals should be randomly distributed in a band about the horizontal straight line through 0 as shown in Figure 10.19b.

Figure 10.19b   Randomly distributed residuals

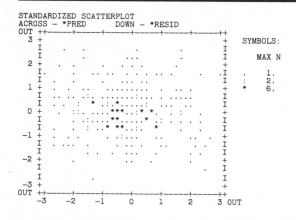

Residuals can also be plotted against individual independent variables. Again, if the assumptions are met, you should see a horizontal band of residuals. Consider plotting the residuals against independent variables not in the equation as well. If the residuals are not randomly distributed, you may want to include the variable in the equation using multiple regression techniques as described in the sections beginning with 10.32.

10.20   Equality of Variance

The previously described plots can be used to check for violations of the constancy of variance assumption. If the spread of the residuals increases or decreases with values of the independent variables or with predicted values, you should question the assumption of constant variance of Y for all values of X.

Figure 10.20   Unequal variance

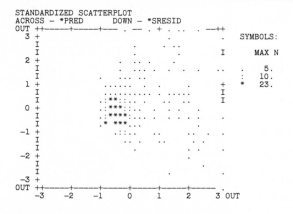

Figure 10.20 is a plot of the Studentized residuals against the predicted values for the salary data. The spread of the residuals increases with the magnitude of the predicted values, suggesting that the variability of current salaries increases with salary level, which seems reasonable.

10.21 Independence of Error

Whenever the data are collected and recorded sequentially, you should plot residuals against the sequence variable. Even if time is not considered a variable in the model, it could influence the residuals. For example, if you were studying survival time after surgery as a function of length of surgery, amount of blood transfused, dosage of medication, etc., it is possible that the surgeon's skills increased with each operation and that the patients' survival times are influenced by the number of prior patients treated. The plot of residuals in time sequence (Figure 10.21) shows a shorter survival time for earlier patients than for later patients. If sequence and the residual are independent, you should not see a discernible pattern in the sequence.

Figure 10.21 Casewise serial plot

```
CASEWISE PLOT OF STUDENTIZED RESIDUAL

                       -3.0      0.0      3.0      LIFE     *PRED    *RESID   *SRESID
        SEQNUM   TIME   0:.............:.........:0
             1   78012      .  *       .          15.0000   19.5624  -4.5624  -2.2598
             2   78055      .  *       .          13.5000   17.8974  -4.3974  -2.1856
             3   78122      .   *      .           9.9000   13.8390  -3.9390  -1.9871
             4   78134      .    *     .          15.5000   18.5218  -3.0218  -1.4997
             5   78233      .    *     .          35.0000   38.2933  -3.2933  -1.7466
             6   78298      .     *    .          14.7000   16.6487  -1.9487   -.9720
             7   78344      .     *    .          34.8000   36.0040  -1.2040   -.6258
             8   79002      .      *   .          20.8000   20.8111   -.0111   -.0055
             9   79008      .      *   .          15.9000   14.8796   1.0204    .5123
            10   79039      .      *   .          22.0000   21.6436    .3564    .1762
            11   79101      .        * .          13.7000   11.7578   1.9422    .9910
            12   79129      .        * .          14.2000   11.4456   2.7544   1.4082
            13   79178      .         *.          33.2000   30.3847   2.8153   1.4144
            14   79188      .         *.          26.2000   22.4761   3.7239   1.8401
            15   79189      .          *          37.4000   33.2984   4.1016   2.0920
           ...
```

The *Durbin-Watson* statistic, a test for correlation of error terms, is defined as

$$D = \frac{\sum_{t=2}^{N} (E_t - E_{t-1})^2}{\sum_{t=1}^{N} E_t^2}$$

The differences between successive residuals tend to be small when error terms are positively correlated, and the differences tend to be large when error terms are negatively correlated. Thus, small values of D indicate positive correlation and large values of D indicate negative correlation. Consult tables of the D statistic for bounds upon which significance tests can be based (Neter and Wasserman, 1974).

10.22 Normality

The distribution of residuals may not appear to be normal for reasons other than actual nonnormality: misspecification of the model, nonconstant variance, a small number of residuals actually available for analysis, etc. Therefore, you should pursue several lines of investigation. One of the simplest is to construct a histogram of the standardized or Studentized residuals as shown in Figure 10.22a for the salary data.

The NEW REGRESSION histogram contains a tally of the observed number of residuals (cases) in each interval (labeled N) and the number expected in a normal distribution with the same mean and variance as the residuals (EXP N). The first and last intervals (OUT) contain residuals more than 3.16 standard deviations from the mean. Such residuals deserve examination. A histogram of expected Ns is superimposed on that of the observed Ns. A period is used to identify expected frequencies. When observed and expected frequencies overlap, a colon is printed. It is unreasonable to expect the observed residuals to be exactly normal—some deviation is expected because of sampling variation. Even if the errors are normally distributed in the population, sample

Figure 10.22a   Histogram of Studentized residuals

```
HISTOGRAM
STUDENTIZED RESIDUAL
   N   EXP N     ( * = 2 CASES,    . : = NORMAL CURVE)
   7    0.37   OUT ****
   2    0.73  3.00 *
   4    1.85  2.66 :*
   2    4.23  2.33 *.
   6    8.65  2.00 ***.
  12   15.85  1.66 ****** .
   7   26.01  1.33 ****     .
  18   38.23  1.00 ********* .
  35   50.34  0.66 ***************** .
  63   59.38  0.33 *****************************:**
  87   62.74  0.00 *********************************:*************
 114   59.38 -0.33 ********************************:*******************************
  64   50.34 -0.66 **************************:*******
  32   38.23 -1.00 ****************  .
   9   26.01 -1.33 ****     .
   6   15.85 -1.66 ***    .
   1    8.65 -2.00 *  .
   1    4.23 -2.33 *.
   2    1.85 -2.66 :
   0    0.73 -3.00
   2    0.37   OUT *
```

residuals are only approximately normal. In the histogram in Figure 10.22a, the distribution does not seem normal since there is an exaggerated clustering of residuals toward the center and a straggling tail toward large positive values.

Another way to compare the observed distribution of residuals to that expected under the assumption of normality is to plot the two cumulative distributions against each other for a series of points. If the two distributions are identical, a straight line results. By observing how points scatter about the expected straight line, you can compare the two distributions.

Figure 10.22b   A normal probability (P-P) plot

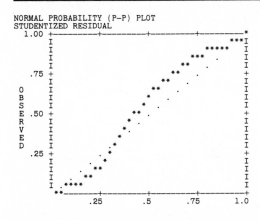

Figure 10.22b is a cumulative probability plot of the salary residuals. Initially, the observed residuals are below the straight line since there is a smaller number of residuals than expected. However, once the greatest concentration of residuals is reached, the observed points are above the line since the observed cumulative proportion exceeds the expected.

10.23   Locating Outliers

You can spot outliers readily on residual plots since they are cases with very large positive or negative residuals. In the histogram, cases with values greater than 3.16 or less than −3.16 appear in the OUT interval. In the scattergrams, they appear on the borders of the plot, labelled OUT. Since you usually want more information about outliers, use the casewise plotting facility to print identification numbers and a variety of other statistics for cases having residuals greater than a specified cutoff point.

Figure 10.23   Casewise plot of residuals outliers

```
CASEWISE PLOT OF STUDENTIZED RESIDUAL

OUTLIERS = 3

                    -6.            -3  3            6.
    SEQNUM  SEXRACE  0:.............:  :.............:0      SALNOW       *PRED       *RESID
        24   1.0000  .               ..  *          .     28000.0000   17383.4949   10616.5051
        60   1.0000  .               ..            *.     32000.0000   12800.8156   19199.1844
        67   1.0000  .            *  ..             .     26400.0000   37043.1894  -10643.1894
       114   1.0000  .               ..  *          .     38800.0000   27511.2163   11288.7837
       122   1.0000  .         *     ..             .     26700.0000   40869.7266  -14169.7266
       123   1.0000  .               ..  *          .     36250.0000   24639.4039   11610.5961
       129   1.0000  .               ..        *    .     33500.0000   17383.4949   16116.5051
       149   1.0000  .               ..            *.     41500.0000   21782.8671   19717.1329
       177   1.0000  .               ..       *     .     36500.0000   23295.1513   13204.8487

        9 OUTLIERS FOUND.
```

Figure 10.23 lists information for the nine cases with Studentized residuals greater than 3 in absolute value. Only two of these nine employees have current salaries less than those predicted by the model (cases 67 and 122), while the others have larger salaries. The second column contains identifier information that indicates that all outliers are white males (SEXRACE = 1). They all have large salaries, an average of $33,294, while the average for the sample is only $13,767. Thus there is some evidence to suspect that the model may not fit well for the highly paid cases.

10.24   Other Unusual Observations: Mahalanobis Distance

The employee (case 60) discussed in Section 10.2 is identified as an outlier since the combination of values for beginning and current salaries is untypical. There is another unusual employee—case 56 has a beginning salary of $31,992. Since the average beginning salary for the entire sample is only $6806 and the standard deviation is 3148, the case is 8 standard deviations above the mean. Cases that are unusual in the values of the independent variables can have a substantial impact on the results of analysis and should be identified. One measure of the distance of cases from the average values of the independent variables is the *Mahalanobis distance*. In the case of a regression equation with a single independent variable, it is the square of the standardized value of X.

$$D_i = \left(\frac{X_i - \overline{X}}{S_X}\right)^2$$

When there is more than one independent variable—when the Mahalanobis distance is most valuable—the computations are more complex. Figure 10.24 contains information for the ten cases with the largest Mahalanobis distances.

Figure 10.24   Mahalanobis distances

```
OUTLIERS - MAHALANOBIS' DISTANCE

    SEQNUM  SUBFILE    SEXRACE      *MAHAL
        56   BANK      1.00000     63.99757
         2   BANK      1.00000     29.82579
       122   BANK      1.00000     20.32558
        67   BANK      1.00000     14.99121
       132   BANK      1.00000     12.64145
        55   BANK      1.00000     12.64145
       415   BANK      2.00000     11.84140
         5   BANK      1.00000     11.32255
       172   BANK      1.00000     10.49187
        23   BANK      1.00000     10.46720
```

10.25   Influential Cases:
Deleted Residuals and Cook's Distance

Certain observations in a set of data can have a large influence on estimates of the parameters. Figure 10.25a shows such a point, with and without which quite different regression lines are obtained. The residual for the circled point is not particularly large when the case (number 8) is included in the computations and does not therefore arouse suspicion (see the plot in Figure 10.25b).

Figure 10.25a   Influential observation

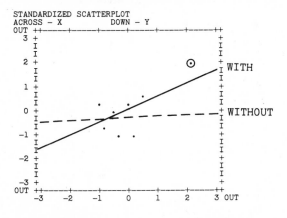

One way to identify an influential case is to compare the residuals for a case when the suspected case is included in the equation and when it is not. The *adjusted predicted value* (ADJPRED) for case *i* when it is not included in the computation of the regression line is

$$\hat{Y}_i^{(i)} = B_0^{(i)} + B_1^{(i)}X_i$$

where the superscript (*i*) indicates that the *i*th case is excluded. The residual calculated for a case when it is not included is called the *deleted residual* (DRESID), computed as

$$Y_i - \hat{Y}_i^{(i)}$$

The deleted residual can be divided by its standard error to produce the *Studentized deleted residual* (SDRESID).

Although the difference between the deleted and ordinary residual for a case is useful as an index of the influence of that case, this measure does not reflect changes in residuals of other observations when the *i*th case is deleted. *Cook's distance* does consider changes in all residuals when case *i* is omitted (Cook, 1977). It is defined as

$$C_i = \frac{\sum_{j=1}^{N} (\hat{Y}_j^{(i)} - \hat{Y}_j)^2}{(p + 1)S^2}$$

The casewise plot for the data in Figure 10.25a is shown in Figure 10.25b. The line for case 8 describes the circled point. It has neither a very large Studentized residual nor a very large Studentized deleted residual. However, the deleted residual is 5.86 (*Y*−ADJPRED=12−6.14), which is somewhat larger than the ordinary residual (1.24). The large Mahalanobis distance identifies the case as having an *X* value far from the mean, while the large Cook's *D* identifies the case as an influential point.

Figure 10.25b   Casewise plot to study influential observation

```
CASEWISE PLOT OF STANDARDIZED RESIDUAL
           -3.0     0.0      3.0
  SEQNUM   0:........:........:0        Y     *RESID  *SRESID  *SDRESID  *ADJPRED   *MAHAL   *COOK D
     1     .     .      . *    .     7.0000    2.9394   1.4819    1.6990   2.9096    1.0947   0.4300
     2     .     *.     .       .    4.0000   -0.5758  -0.2780   -0.2554   4.7349    0.6401   0.0107
     3     .     . *    .       .    6.0000    0.9091   0.4262    0.3951   4.9062    0.3068   0.0184
     4     .   * .      .       .    3.0000   -2.6061  -1.2000   -1.2566   6.0252    0.0947   0.1158
     5     .     . *    .       .    7.0000    0.8788   0.4016    0.3717   5.9950    0.0038   0.0116
     6     .  *  .      .       .    3.0000   -3.6364  -1.6661   -2.0747   7.1791    0.0341   0.2071
     7     .     .*     .       .    8.0000    0.8485   0.3937    0.3641   7.0000    0.1856   0.0138
     8     .     . *    .       .   12.0000    1.2425   1.1529    1.1929   6.1426    4.6402   2.4687
  SEQNUM   0:........:........:0        Y     *RESID  *SRESID  *SDRESID  *ADJPRED   *MAHAL   *COOK D
           -3.0     0.0      3.0
```

The regression coefficients with and without case 8 are as shown in Figures 10.25c and 10.25d. Both $B_0^{(8)}$ and $B_1^{(8)}$ are far removed from B_0 and B_1 since case 8 is an influential point.

Figure 10.25c   Regression results from all cases

```
------------------------- VARIABLES IN THE EQUATION -------------------------

VARIABLE          B         SE B      95% CONFDNCE INTRVL B     BETA        T   SIG T

X              0.51514    0.21772     -0.01759     1.04788    0.69476     2.366 0.0558
(CONSTANT)     3.54547    1.41098      0.09294     6.99799                2.513 0.0457
```

Figure 10.25d   Regression coefficients without case 8

```
----------------- VARIABLES IN THE EQUATION -----------------

VARIABLE          B         SE B       BETA        T   SIG T

X              0.07141    0.42738     0.07451     0.167 0.8739
(CONSTANT)     5.14294    1.91132                 2.691 0.0433
```

10.26   When Assumptions Appear to be Violated

When evidence of violation of assumptions appears, there are are two strategies. One can formulate an alternative model, such as weighted least squares, or one can transform the variables so that the current model will be more adequate. For example, taking logs, square roots, or reciprocals can stabilize the variance, achieve normality, or linearize a relationship.

10.27   Coaxing a Nonlinear Relationship to Linearity

To try to achieve linearity, you can transform either the dependent or independent variables or both. If you alter the scale of independent variables, linearity can be improved without any effect on the distribution of the dependent variable. That is, if the dependent variable is normally distributed with constant variance, it remains so.

When you transform the dependent variable, its distribution is changed. It is this new distribution that must satisfy the assumptions of the analysis. For example, if logs of the dependent variable values are taken, log Y—not the original Y—must be normally distributed with constant variance.

The choice of transformations depends on several considerations. If the form of the true model governing the relationship is known, it should dictate the choice. For instance, if it is known that $\hat{Y} = AC^X$ is an adequate model, taking logs of both sides of the equation results in

$$\log \hat{Y}_i = \underset{[B_0]}{(\log A)} + \underset{[B_1]}{(\log C)} \, X_i$$

Thus log Y is linearly related to X.

Figure 10.27   A transformed relationship

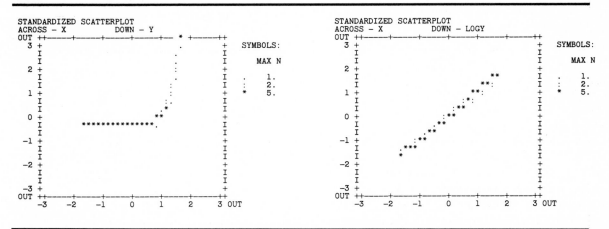

If the true model is not known, you should choose the transformation by examining the plotted data. Frequently, a relationship appears nearly linear for part of the data, but is curved for the rest. The first plot in Figure 10.27 is an example. Taking the log of the dependent variable results in the second plot—an improved linear fit.

Other transformations that may diminish curvature are the square root of Y and $-1/Y$. The choice depends, to a certain extent, on the severity of the problem.

10.28   Coping with Skewness

When the distribution of residuals is positively skewed, the log transformation is often helpful. For negatively skewed distributions, the square transformation is common. It should be noted that the F tests used in regression hypothesis testing are usually quite insensitive to moderate departures from normality.

10.29   Stabilizing the Variance

If the variance of the residuals is not constant, you can try a variety of remedial measures:

- When the variance is proportional to the mean of Y for a given X, use the square root of Y if all Y_i are positive.
- When the standard deviation is proportional to the mean, try the logarithmic transformation.
- When the standard deviation is proportional to the square of the mean, use the reciprocal of Y.
- When Y is a proportion or rate, the arcsin transformation may stabilize the variance.

10.30   Transforming the Salary Data

The assumptions of constant variance and normality appear to be violated with the salary data (see Figures 10.20 and 10.22a). A regression equation using logs of beginning and current salary was developed in hope of obtaining a better fit to the assumptions. Figure 10.30a is a scattergram of Studentized residuals against predicted values when logs of both variables are used in constructing the regression equation.

Figure 10.30a   Scatterplot of transformed salary data

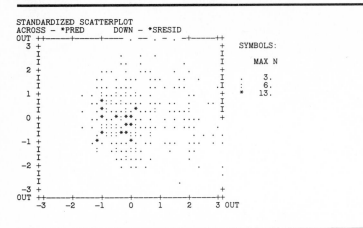

```
STANDARDIZED SCATTERPLOT
ACROSS - *PRED      DOWN - *SRESID
OUT ++----+----+----- . — . - . -+----++
  3 +                           .            +      SYMBOLS:
    I                        .        .       I
    I                     .  .    .       .   I        MAX N
  2 +             ...  .. .                    +
    I          .. . .    ... ...  .   .        I      .    3.
    I          ...  ...   ...  ...  .     .I        :    6.
  1 +       .  . . :..::. :.  .        ..  I      *   13.
    I         .*::::::.*   .          ..  I
    I      .  .*.::*::.*.: .:          I
  0 +        .. *.* .**   . .  . .  .     +
    I      .  .  .**: .    .  .          I
    I         .*.::.**::. :       . . .   .
 -1 +        .*..*.* .   . .   ..        .
    I         :  .:.::. ..   ..  ...
    I            .:::..  .   . .
 -2 +            . . . .          .
    I
    I
 -3 +                   .                  +
OUT ++----+----+----+----+----+----++
    -3   -2   -1    0    1    2    3 OUT
```

Compare Figures 10.20 and 10.30a and note the improvement in the behavior of the residuals. The spread no longer increases with increasing salary level. Also compare Figures 10.22a and 10.30b and note that the second distribution is nearly normal.

Figure 10.30b   Histogram of transformed salary data

```
HISTOGRAM
STUDENTIZED RESIDUAL
 N  EXP N     ( * = 2 CASES,    . : = NORMAL CURVE)
 3  0.37   OUT **
 1  0.73  3.00 *
 3  1.85  2.66 :*
 4  4.23  2.33 *:
10  8.65  2.00 ***:*
14 15.85  1.66 *******.
21 26.01  1.33 **********  .
31 38.23  1.00 ***************
48 50.34  0.66 ************************.
55 59.38  0.33 ***************************  .
63 62.74  0.00 *******************************:.*
64 59.38 -0.33 *******************************:**
62 50.34 -0.66 *************************:******
44 38.23 -1.00 ******************:***
28 26.01 -1.33 *************:*
14 15.85 -1.66 *******.
 7  8.65 -2.00 ***:
 1  4.23 -2.33 *.
 1  1.85 -2.66 :
 0  0.73 -3.00
 0  0.37   OUT
```

For the transformed data, the multiple R increases slightly to 0.8864 and the outlier plot contains only 4 cases (compare with Figures 10.10 and 10.23). Thus the transformation appears to have resulted in a better model.

10.31   A Final Comment on Assumptions

Rarely are assumptions not in one way or another violated in regression analysis as well as in many other statistical procedures. However, this is not a justification for ignoring them. Regressions can be cranked out with little thought to possible departures from the necessary assumptions, leading to problems in interpreting and applying results. Significance levels, confidence intervals, and other results are sensitive to certain types of violations and cannot be interpreted in the usual fashion if serious departures exist.

By carefully examining residuals, and using transformations or other methods of analysis if need be, you are in a much better position to pursue analyses that solve the problems you are investigating. Even if everything isn't perfect, you can at least knowledgeably gauge the possible extent of difficulties.

10.32   MULTIPLE REGRESSION MODELS

Beginning salary seems to be a good predictor of current salary, given the evidence shown above. Nearly 80% ($R^2 = 0.77$ from Figure 10.10) of the observed variability in current salaries can be explained by beginning salary levels. Given the importance of one's beginning salary, then, how do variables such as education level, years of experience, race, and sex contribute to the prediction of the salary level at which one enters the company?

10.33   Predictors of Beginning Salary

Multiple linear regression extends bivariate regression by incorporating multiple independent variables. The model can be written as

$$Y_i = \beta_0 + \beta_1 X_{1i} + \beta_2 X_{2i} + \ldots + \beta_p X_{pi} + e_i$$

The notation X_{ki} indicates the value of the kth independent variable for case i. Again, the β_k terms are unknown parameters and the e_i terms are independent random variables that are normally distributed with mean 0 and constant variance σ^2. The model assumes that there is a normal distribution of the dependent variable for every combination of the values of the independent variables in the model. For example, if child's height is the dependent variable and age and maternal height are the independent variables, it is assumed that for every combination of age and maternal height there is a normal distribution of children's heights and that, though the means of these distributions may differ, all have the same variance.

10.34   The Correlation Matrix

One of the first steps in developing an equation with several independent variables is to calculate a correlation matrix for all variables, as shown in Figure 10.34. The variables are the log of beginning salary, years of education, sex, years of work experience, race, and age in years. Variables sex and race are represented by *indicator variables*. That is, SEX is coded 1 for female and 0 for male and MINORITY is coded 1 for nonwhite and 0 for white.

Figure 10.34   The correlation matrix

	LOGBEG	EDLEVEL	SEX	WORK	MINORITY	AGE
LOGBEG	1.000	0.686	-0.548	0.040	-0.173	-0.048
EDLEVEL	0.686	1.000	-0.356	-0.252	-0.133	-0.281
SEX	-0.548	-0.356	1.000	-0.165	-0.076	0.052
WORK	0.040	-0.252	-0.165	1.000	0.145	0.804
MINORITY	-0.173	-0.133	-0.076	0.145	1.000	0.111
AGE	-0.048	-0.281	0.052	0.804	0.111	1.000

The matrix shows the correlations between the dependent variable and the independent variable and the correlations between the independent variables. Particularly note any large intercorrelations between the independent variables since they can substantially affect the results of multiple regression analysis.

10.35   Partial Regression Coefficients

The summary output for the multiple regression equation when all independent variables are entered is given in Figure 10.35a. The F test associated with the analysis of variance table is a test of the hypothesis that $\beta_1=\beta_2=\beta_3=\beta_4=\beta_5=0$. That is, it is a test of whether there is a linear relationship between the dependent variable and the set of independent variables.

Figure 10.35a   Statistics for the equation

```
MULTIPLE R           0.78420      ANALYSIS OF VARIANCE
R SQUARE             0.61497                        DF      SUM OF SQUARES    MEAN SQUARE
ADJUSTED R SQUARE    0.61086      REGRESSION          5           6.83036        1.36607
STANDARD ERROR       0.09559      RESIDUAL          468           4.27641        0.00914

                                  F =     149.49952      SIGNIF F = 0.0000
```

The statistics for the independent variables in Figure 10.35b parallel those obtained in regression with a single independent variable. The coefficients labeled B are called the *partial regression coefficients* since the coefficient for a particular variable is adjusted for other independent variables in the equation. The equation that relates the predicted log of beginning salary to the independent variables is

LOGBEG = 3.3853+0.00102(AGE)−0.10358(SEX)−0.05237(MINORITY)
         + 0.03144(EDLEVEL)+0.00161(WORK)

Figure 10.35b   Statistics for variables in the equation

```
------------------- VARIABLES IN THE EQUATION -------------------

VARIABLE           B          SE B         BETA          T   SIG T

AGE           0.00102   0.6613D-03      0.07811      1.535  0.1254
SEX          -0.10358      0.01032     -0.33699    -10.038  0.0000
MINORITY     -0.05237      0.01084     -0.14157     -4.832  0.0000
EDLEVEL       0.03144      0.00175      0.59195     17.988  0.0000
WORK          0.00161   0.9241D-03      0.09143      1.740  0.0826
(CONSTANT)    3.38530      0.03323               101.866  0.0000
```

Since the dependent variable is in log units, the coefficients can be approximately interpreted in percentage terms. For example, the coefficient of −0.104 for the SEX variable indicates that female salaries are estimated to be about 10 percent less than male salaries, after statistical adjustment for age, education, work history, and minority status.

10.36   Determining Important Variables

In multiple regression, one frequently wants to assign relative importance to each independent variable. For example, one might want to know whether education is more influential in predicting beginning salary than previous work experience. There are two possibly different answers depending on which of the following questions is being asked:

- How important are education and work experience when each of them alone is used to predict beginning salary?
- How important are education and work experience when, along with other independent variables in the regression equation, they are used to predict beginning salary?

The first question is answered by looking at the correlation coeffients between salary and the independent variables. The larger the correlation coefficient is in absolute value, the stronger the linear association. From Figure 10.34, education correlates more highly with log of salary than does previous work experience (0.686 and 0.040 respectively). Thus you would assign more importance to education as a predictor of salary.

The answer to the second question is considerably more complicated. When the independent variables are correlated among themselves, the unique contribution of each is difficult to assess. Any statement about an independent variable is contingent upon the other variables in the equation. For example, the regression coefficient (B) for work experience is 0.0007 when it is the sole independent variable in the equation, compared to 0.00161 when the other four independent variables are also in the equation. The second coefficient is more than twice the size of the first.

10.37   BETA Coefficients

It is sometimes tempting to interpret the Bs as indicators of the relative importance of variables. Variables with large coefficients are thought to contribute more to the overall regression equation. If all independent variables are measured in the same units—years for example—this approach may be reasonable. However, when variables differ substantially in units of measurement, the magnitude of the coefficients is not a good index of relative importance.

One way to make regression coefficients somewhat more comparable is to calculate *BETA* weights, which are the multipliers of the independent variables when the variables are expressed in standardized (Z score) form. The BETA coefficients can be calculated directly from the regression coefficients using

$$BETA_k = B_k \left(\frac{S_k}{S_Y} \right)$$

where S_k is the standard deviation of the kth independent variable.

The values of the BETA coefficients, like the usual regression coefficients, are contingent on the other independent variables in the equation. They are also affected by the correlations of the independent variables and do not in any absolute sense reflect the importance of the various independent variables.

10.38   Part and Partial Coefficients

Another way of assessing the relative importance of independent variables is to consider the increase in R^2 when a variable is entered into the equation that already contains the other independent variables. This increase is

$$R^2_{change} = R^2 - R^2_{(i)}$$

where $R^2_{(i)}$ is the square of the multiple correlation coefficent when all independent variables except the ith are in the equation. A large change in R^2 indicates that a variable provides unique information about the dependent variable that is not available from the other independent variables in the equation. The signed square root of the increase is called the *part correlation coefficient*. It is the correlation between Y and X_i when the linear effects of the other independent variables have been removed from X_i. (If all independent variables are uncorrelated, the change in R^2 as a variable is entered into the equation is simply the square of the correlation coefficient between that variable and the dependent variable.)

Figure 10.38   Zero-order, part, and partial correlation coefficients

```
VARIABLE(S) ENTERED ON STEP NUMBER  5..    EDLEVEL      EDUCATIONAL LEVEL

MULTIPLE R            0.78420
R SQUARE             0.61498          R SQUARE CHANGE   0.26619
ADJUSTED R SQUARE    0.61086          F CHANGE         323.55430
STANDARD ERROR       0.09559          SIGNIF F CHANGE    0.0000

------------ VARIABLES IN THE EQUATION --------------

VARIABLE      CORREL PART COR  PARTIAL       F   SIG F

AGE          -0.04780  0.04404  0.07080      2.357 0.1254
SEX          -0.54802 -0.28792 -0.42090    100.761 0.0000
MINORITY     -0.17284 -0.13860 -0.21799     23.349 0.0000
WORK          0.03994  0.04990  0.08015      3.026 0.0826
EDLEVEL       0.68572  0.51593  0.63934    323.554 0.0000
(CONSTANT)                               10376.612 0.0000
```

From the output shown in Figure 10.38, it can be seen that the addition of years of education to an equation that contains the other four independent variables results in a change in R^2 of 0.266 (0.51593^2). The square of the part coefficient tells only how much R^2 increases when a variable is added to the regression equation. It does not indicate what proportion of the unexplained variation this increase constitutes. If most of the variation has been explained by the other variables, a small part correlation is all that is possible for the remaining variable. It may therefore be difficult to compare part coefficients.

A coefficient that measures the proportional reduction in variation is

$$Pr_i^2 = \frac{R^2 - R_{(i)}^2}{1 - R_{(i)}^2}$$

The numerator is the square of the part coefficient; the denominator is the proportion of unexplained variation when all but the ith variable are in the equation. The signed square root is the *partial correlation coefficient*. It can be interpreted as the correlation between the ith independent variable and the dependent variable when the linear effects of the other independent variables have been removed from both X_i and Y. Since the denominator of Pr_i^2 is always less than or equal to 1, the part correlation coefficient is never larger in absolute value than the partial correlation coefficient.

10.39   Variance of the Estimators

The variability of the estimated regression coefficients must also be considered in evaluating the relative importance of the independent variables. Coefficients with large standard errors are unreliable and may differ markedly from sample to sample. It is a dangerous practice to identify variables as important for prediction based only on their significant individual t values.

When the independent variables are correlated among themselves, the parameter estimates are correlated as well. High intercorrelations among the variables can affect the regression estimates in several ways. The estimated variance of the regression coefficient for the ith independent variable is

$$S_{B_i}^2 = \frac{S^2}{(1 - R_i^2)(N - 1)S_i^2}$$

Here, R_i^2 is the squared multiple correlation when the ith independent variable is considered the dependent variable and the regression equation between it and the other independent variables is calculated. A large value of R_i^2 indicates that the ith independent variable is almost a linear function or combination of the other independent variables. The proportion of variability not explained by the other variables is, as before, $1-R_i^2$. This quantity is usually called the *tolerance* of the variable. As can be seen from the equation above, for a fixed sample size and standard error S, the smaller the tolerance the larger the standard error of the coefficient. Small tolerance values can also cause computational problems for regression solutions. SPSS prints the tolerances as shown in Figure 10.39a.

Figure 10.39a   Tolerances

```
VARIABLE        TOLERANCE

AGE             0.31792
SEX             0.72998
MINORITY        0.95839
EDLEVEL         0.75966
WORK            0.29784
```

The variance-covariance matrix and the correlation matrix of the parameter estimates are shown in Figure 10.39b. The entries on the diagonal are the variances of the coefficients. The correlations are printed above the diagonal and the covariances are printed below. Note the high correlations between the coefficients for work experience and age (-0.80753). Very small and very large values are printed in scientific notation. The exponent follows the letter "D". For example, $0.117D-03$ is 0.000117.

Figure 10.39b   Variance-covariance output

```
VAR-COVAR MATRIX OF REGRESSION COEFFICIENTS (B)
BELOW DIAGONAL:  COVARIANCE    ABOVE:  CORRELATION

                  AGE         SEX     MINORITY     EDLEVEL        WORK
AGE        0.437D-06    -0.28621    -0.00722     0.00388    -0.80753
SEX       -0.195D-05     0.106D-03   0.10271     0.40581     0.38399
MINORITY  -0.517D-07     0.115D-04   0.117D-03   0.13519    -0.04290
EDLEVEL    0.448D-08     0.732D-05   0.256D-05   0.306D-05   0.18683
WORK      -0.493D-06     0.366D-05  -0.430D-06   0.302D-06   0.854D-06
```

10.40   Building a Model

Selection of the five variables to predict beginning salary has been arbitrary to some extent. It is unlikely that all relevant variables have been identified and measured. Doubtless, some good variables have been excluded, while some of those included may not be very good predictors. This is not unusual; one frequently must try to build a model from available data, as voluminous or scanty as they may be. Before considering several formal procedures for model building, some of the consequences of adding and deleting variables from regression equations are described. The SPSS statistics for variables not in the equation are also described.

10.41   Adding and Deleting Variables

The equation and summary statistics with years of education as the sole independent variable and log of beginning salary as the dependent variable are shown in the first step in Figure 10.41. Consider the second step in the same figure when another variable, sex, is added. The value printed as R SQUARE CHANGE in the second step is the change in R^2 when sex is added. R^2 for education alone is 0.47021, so R^2_{change} is $0.57598-0.47021$ or 0.10577.

Figure 10.41   Adding a variable to the equation

```
VARIABLE(S) ENTERED ON STEP NUMBER
      1..   EDLEVEL       EDUCATIONAL LEVEL

MULTIPLE R          0.68572
R SQUARE            0.47021      R SQUARE CHANGE   0.47021
ADJUSTED R SQUARE   0.46909      F CHANGE          418.92032
STANDARD ERROR      0.11165      SIGNIF F CHANGE   0.0000

----------------- VARIABLES IN THE EQUATION -------------------

VARIABLE            B         SE B      BETA        T   SIG T

EDLEVEL        0.03642    0.00178    0.68572    20.468  0.0000
(CONSTANT)     3.31001    0.02455               134.821 0.0000


BEGINNING BLOCK NUMBER  2.   METHOD:   ENTER      SEX

VARIABLE(S) ENTERED ON STEP NUMBER
      2..   SEX          SEX OF EMPLOYEE

MULTIPLE R          0.75893
R SQUARE            0.57598      R SQUARE CHANGE   0.10577
ADJUSTED R SQUARE   0.57418      F CHANGE          117.48557
STANDARD ERROR      0.09999      SIGNIF F CHANGE   0.0000

----------------- VARIABLES IN THE EQUATION -------------------

VARIABLE            B         SE B      BETA        T   SIG T

EDLEVEL        0.02984    0.00171    0.56183    17.498  0.0000
SEX           -0.10697    0.00987   -0.34802   -10.839  0.0000
(CONSTANT)     3.44754    0.02539               135.806 0.0000
```

The null hypothesis that the true population value for the change in R^2 is 0 can be tested using

$$F_{change} = \frac{R^2_{change}(N - p - 1)}{q(1 - R^2)} = \frac{(0.1058)\,(474\text{-}2\text{-}1)}{1(1\text{-}0.5760)} = 117.48$$

where N is the number of cases in the equation, p is the total number of independent variables in the equation, and q is the number of variables entered at this step. Under the hypothesis that the true change is 0, the significance of the value labeled F CHANGE in SPSS can be obtained from the F distribution with q and $N-p-1$ degrees of freedom.

The hypothesis that the real change in R^2 is 0 can also be formulated in terms of the β parameters. When only the ith variable is added in a step, the hypothesis that the change is 0 is equivalent to the hypothesis that β_i is 0. The F value printed for the change in R^2 is the square of the t value printed for the test of the coefficient as shown in Figure 10.41.

When q independent variables are entered in a single step, the test that R^2 is 0 is equivalent to the simultaneous test that the coefficients of all q variables are 0. That is, if sex and age were added in the same step to the regression equation that contains education, the test for R^2 change is the same as the test of the hypothesis that $\beta_{sex} = \beta_{age} = 0$.

Entering sex into the equation with education has had other effects besides changing R^2. If you compare the output from the first and second steps in Figure 10.41, you will note the decrease in the magnitude of the regression coefficient for education (from 0.03642 to 0.02984). This is attributable to the correlation between sex and level of education.

When highly intercorrelated independent variables are included in a regression equation, apparently anomalous results are possible. The overall regression may be significant while none of the individual coefficients are significant. The signs of the regression coefficients may be counterintuitive. High correlations inflate the variances of the estimates, making them quite unreliable without adding much to the overall fit of the model. The problem of linear relationships between independent variables is discussed further in Sections 10.51 to 10.53.

10.42 Statistics for Variables Not in the Equation

When some independent variables have not been entered into the equation, you can examine what would happen if they were entered at the next step. Statistics describing these variables are shown in Figure 10.42. The column labeled BETA IN is the standardized regression coefficient that would result if the variable were entered into the equation at the next step. The F test and level of significance are for the hypothesis that the coefficient is 0. (Remember that the F test and t test for the hypothesis that a coefficient is zero are equivalent.) The partial correlation coefficient with the dependent variable adjusts for the variables already in the equation. The column labeled MIN TOLER gives the smallest tolerance that would be obtained for the independent variables—including the variable being listed—in the equation if the variable were entered.

Figure 10.42 Coefficients for variables not in the equation

```
-------------- VARIABLES NOT IN THE EQUATION --------------

VARIABLE     BETA IN  PARTIAL  MIN TOLER      F  SIG F

WORK         0.14425  0.20567   0.77382   20.759 0.0000
MINORITY    -0.12902 -0.19464   0.84758   18.507 0.0000
AGE          0.13942  0.20519   0.80425   20.659 0.0000
```

From statistics calculated for variables not in the equation, you can decide what variable should be entered next. This process is detailed in Section 10.44.

10.43 The "Optimal" Number of Independent Variables

Having witnessed what happens when sex is added to the equation containing education (Figure 10.41), consider now what happens when the remaining three independent variables are entered in no particular order. Summary output is shown in Figure 10.43. The line labeled step 5 shows the statistics for the equation with all independent variables entered. Step 3 describes the model with education, sex, and work experience as the independent variables.

Figure 10.43 All independent variables in the equation

STEP	MULTR	RSQ	ADJRSQ	F(EQU)	SIGF	RSQCH	FCH	SIGCH		VARIABLE	BETAIN	CORREL	LABEL
1	0.6857	0.4702	0.4691	418.920	0.000	0.4702	418.920	0.000	IN:	EDLEVEL	0.6857	0.6857	EDUCATIONAL LEVEL
2	0.7589	0.5760	0.5742	319.896	0.000	0.1058	117.486	0.000	IN:	SEX	-0.3480	-0.5480	SEX OF EMPLOYEE
3	0.7707	0.5939	0.5913	229.130	0.000	0.0179	20.759	0.000	IN:	WORK	0.1442	0.0399	WORK EXPERIENCE
4	0.7719	0.5958	0.5923	172.805	0.000	0.0019	2.149	0.143	IN:	AGE	0.0763	-0.0478	AGE OF EMPLOYEE
5	0.7842	0.6150	0.6109	149.501	0.000	0.0192	23.349	0.000	IN:	MINORITY	-0.1416	-0.1728	MINORITY CLASSIFICATION

Examination of the output in Figure 10.43 shows that R^2 never decreases as independent variables are included. This is always true in regression analysis. However, this does not necessarily mean that the equation with more variables better fits the population. As the number of parameters estimated from the sample increases, so does the goodness of fit to the sample as measured by R-squared. For example, if a sample contains six cases, a regression equation with six parameters fits the sample exactly, even though there may be no true statistical relationship at all between the dependent variable and the independent variables.

As indicated in Section 10.10, the sample R^2 in general tends to be too large as an estimate of the population value of R^2. Adjusted R^2 attempts to correct the optimistic bias of the sample R^2. Adjusted R^2 does not necessarily increase as additional variables are added to an equation and is the preferred measure of goodness of fit because it is not subject to the inflationary bias of unadjusted R^2. This statistic is shown in the column labeled ADJRSQ in the output.

Although adding independent variables increases R^2, it does not necessarily decrease the standard error of the estimate. The standard error may increase when the decrease in the residual sum of squares is very slight and not sufficient to make up for the loss of a degree of freedom for the residual sum of squares. The F value for the test of the overall regression decreases when the regression sum of squares does not increase as fast as the degrees of freedom for the regression. Each time a variable is added to the equation, a degree of freedom is lost from the residual sum of squares and one is gained for the regression sum of squares.

The arbitrary inclusion of large numbers of independent variables in a regression model is not necessarily a good strategy, unless there are strong previous indications to suggest that all should be included. The observed increase in R^2 need not reflect a better fit of the model in the population. Including irrelevant variables increases the standard errors of all estimates without improving prediction. A model with many variables is often difficult to interpret. Of course, it is important not to exclude potentially good predictors.

The following section presents various procedures for selecting variables to be included in a regression model. The goal is to build a concise model that makes good prediction possible.

10.44   Procedures for Selecting Variables

You can construct a variety of regression models from the same set of variables. For instance, you can build seven different equations from three independent variables: three with only one independent variable, three with two independent variables, and one with all three. As the number of variables increases, so does the number of potential models (ten independent variables yield 1023 models).

Although there are procedures for computing all possible regression equations, several other methods do not require as much computation and are more frequently used. Among these procedures are forward selection, backward elimination, and stepwise reqression. None of these variable selection procedures is "best" in any absolute sense; they merely identify subsets of variables that, at least for the sample, are good predictors of the dependent variable.

10.45   Forward Selection

In *forward selection*, the first variable entered into the equation is the one with the largest positive or negative correlation with the dependent variable. The F test for the hypothesis that the coefficient of the entered variable is 0 is then calculated. In order to judge whether this variable (and each succeeding variable) is important, a criterion must be established. There are two possible criteria in SPSS. You can specify the actual value of the F statistic that a variable must achieve in order to enter, called *F-to-enter* (keyword FIN), with a default value of 3.84. The other criterion you can specify is the probability associated with the F statistic, called *probability of F-to-enter* (keyword PIN), with a default of 0.05. That is, a variable enters into the equation only if the probability associated with the F test is less than or equal to the default 0.05 or the value you specify.

These two criteria are not necessarily equivalent. As variables are added to the equation, the degrees of freedom associated with the residual sum of squares decrease while the regression degrees of freedom increase. Thus, a fixed F value has different significance levels depending on the number of variables currently in the equation. For large samples, the differences are negligible. By default, the probability of F-to-enter is the criterion used.

The actual significance level associated with the F-to-enter statistic is not the one usually obtained from the F distribution, since many variables are being examined and the largest F value selected. The problems encountered are similar to the multiple comparison problems described for procedures ONEWAY and PEARSON CORR. Unfortunately, the true significance level is difficult to compute since it depends not only on the numbers of cases and variables, but also on the correlations between the independent variables.

If the first variable selected for entry meets the criterion for inclusion, forward selection continues. Otherwise, the procedure terminates with no variables in the equation. Once one variable is entered, the statistics for variables not in the equation are used to select the next one. The partial correlations between the dependent variable and each of the independent variables not in the equation, adjusted for the independent variables in the equation, are examined. The variable with the largest partial correlation is the next candidate. Choosing the variable with the largest partial correlation in absolute value is equivalent to selecting the variable with the largest F value.

If the criterion is met, the variable is entered into the equation and the procedure is repeated. If not, the procedure stops when there are no other variables that meet the entry criterion.

If you want an equation with a specific number of independent variables, you can specify the number of steps and SPSS selects only the first n variables that meet entry requirements. Another criterion that is always checked before a variable is entered is the tolerance, which is discussed in Section 10.39.

Figure 10.45a   Summary statistics for forward selection

```
STEP   MULTR    RSQ  ADJRSQ    F(EQU)  SIGF   RSQCH     FCH SIGCH      VARIABLE  BETAIN  CORREL   LABEL
  1   0.6857  0.4702  0.4691   418.920 0.000  0.4702  418.920 0.000  IN: EDLEVEL   0.6857  0.6857  EDUCATIONAL LEVEL
  2   0.7589  0.5760  0.5742   319.896 0.000  0.1058  117.486 0.000  IN: SEX      -0.3480 -0.5480  SEX OF EMPLOYEE
  3   0.7707  0.5939  0.5913   229.130 0.000  0.0179   20.759 0.000  IN: WORK      0.1442  0.0399  WORK EXPERIENCE
  4   0.7830  0.6130  0.6097   185.750 0.000  0.0191   23.176 0.000  IN: MINORITY -0.1412 -0.1728  MINORITY CLASSIFICATION
```

Figure 10.45a shows output generated from a forward inclusion procedure using the salary data. The default entry criterion is PIN=0.05. At the first step, education is entered since it has the highest correlation with beginning salary. The significance level associated with it is less than 0.0005 so it certainly meets the criterion for entry.

Figure 10.45b   Status of the variables at the first step

```
------------------ VARIABLES IN THE EQUATION --------------------          ------------- VARIABLES NOT IN THE EQUATION --------------

VARIABLE            B        SE B      BETA       F  SIG F          VARIABLE    BETA IN  PARTIAL  MIN TOLER       F  SIG F

EDLEVEL          0.03642   0.00178   0.68572   418.920 0.0000       SEX        -0.34802 -0.44681   0.87327  117.486 0.0000
(CONSTANT)       3.31001   0.02455           18176.766 0.0000       WORK        0.22747  0.30241   0.93632   47.408 0.0000
                                                                    MINORITY   -0.08318 -0.11327   0.98234    6.121 0.0137
                                                                    AGE         0.15718  0.20726   0.92113   21.140 0.0000
```

To see how the sex variable was selected next, look at the statistics shown in Figure 10.45b for variables not in the equation (when only education is in the equation). The variable with the largest partial correlation is SEX. If entered at the next step, it would have an F value of approximately 120 for the test that its coefficient is 0. Since the probability associated with the F is less than 0.05, it is included in the second step.

Figure 10.45c   The last step

```
-------------- VARIABLES NOT IN THE EQUATION --------------

VARIABLE    BETA IN  PARTIAL  MIN TOLER       F  SIG F

AGE         0.07811  0.07080   0.29784     2.357 0.1254
```

Once variable SEX enters at step 2, the statistics for variables not in the equation must be examined (see Figure 10.42). The variable with the largest absolute value of the partial correlation coefficient is now years of work experience. Its F value is 20.759 with a probability less than 0.05, so variable WORK is included in the next step. The same process takes place with variable MINORITY and it is entered, leaving AGE as the only variable out of the equation. However, as shown in Figure 10.45c, the significance level associated with the age coefficient F value is 0.1254, which is too large for entry. Thus, forward selection yields the summary table for the four steps shown in Figure 10.45a.

10.46   Backward Elimination

While forward selection starts with no independent variables in the equation and enters variables sequentially, *backward elimination* starts with all variables in the equation and sequentially removes them. Instead of entry criteria, removal criteria are specified.

Two removal criteria are available in SPSS. The first is the F value that a variable must have in order to remain in the equation, with variables having F values less than this *F-to- remove* being eligible for removal. You can specify either the actual F value (keyword FOUT) or its probability (POUT) as the criterion. The default FOUT value is 2.71 and the default POUT value is 0.10. The default criterion is POUT.

Figure 10.46a Backward elimination at the first step

```
------------------------------ VARIABLES IN THE EQUATION ------------------------------

VARIABLE          B         SE B      BETA    CORREL PART COR  PARTIAL       F    SIG F

AGE           0.00102  0.6613D-03   0.07811 -0.04780  0.04404  0.07080     2.357 0.1254
SEX          -0.10358    0.01032   -0.33699 -0.54802 -0.28792 -0.42090   100.761 0.0000
MINORITY     -0.05237    0.01084   -0.14157 -0.17284 -0.13860 -0.21799    23.349 0.0000
EDLEVEL       0.03144    0.00175    0.59195  0.68572  0.51593  0.63934   323.554 0.0000
WORK          0.00161  0.9241D-03   0.09143  0.03994  0.04990  0.08015     3.026 0.0826
(CONSTANT)    3.38530    0.03323                                        10376.612 0.0000
```

Look at the salary example again, this time constructing the model with backward elimination. The output in Figure 10.46a is from the first step, at which all variables are entered into the equation. The variable with the smallest partial correlation coefficient is AGE. Since the probability of its F is 0.1254 which is greater than the default POUT criterion value of 0.10, variable AGE is removed. The equation is recalculated without AGE and the statistics shown in Figure 10.46b are obtained.

Figure 10.46b Backward elimination at the last step

```
------------------------------ VARIABLES IN THE EQUATION ------------------------------

VARIABLE          B         SE B      BETA    CORREL PART COR  PARTIAL       F    SIG F

SEX          -0.09904    0.00990   -0.32223 -0.54802 -0.28733 -0.41933   100.063 0.0000
MINORITY     -0.05225    0.01085   -0.14125 -0.17284 -0.13828 -0.21700    23.176 0.0000
EDLEVEL       0.03143    0.00175    0.59176  0.68572  0.51577  0.63827   322.412 0.0000
WORK          0.00275  0.5458D-03   0.15659  0.03994  0.14489  0.22685    25.444 0.0000
(CONSTANT)    3.41195    0.02838                                        14454.042 0.0000
```

The variable with the smallest partial correlation is MINORITY. However, its significance is less than the 0.10 criterion, so backward elimination stops. The equation resulting from backward elimination is the same as that obtained from forward selection. This is not always the case, however. Forward and backward selection procedures can give different results even with comparable entry and removal criteria.

10.47 Stepwise Selection

Stepwise selection of independent variables is probably the most commonly used procedure in regression. It is really a combination of backward and forward procedures. The first variable is selected in the same manner as in forward selection. If the variable fails to meet entry requirements (either FIN or PIN), the procedure terminates with no independent variables in the equation. If it passes the criterion, the second variable is selected based on the highest partial correlation and, if it also passes entry criteria, it enters the equation. From this point, stepwise selection differs from forward selection since the F value of the first variable is examined to see whether it is small enough for the variable to be removed according to the removal criterion (FOUT or POUT) as in backward elimination.

The next step is to examine the variables not in the equation for entry, followed by examination of the variables in the equation for removal. Variables are removed until none remain that meet the removal criterion. To prevent the same variable from being repeatedly entered and removed, PIN must be less than POUT (or FIN greater than FOUT). Variable selection terminates when no more variables meet entry and removal criteria.

In the salary example, stepwise selection with the default criteria results in the same equation produced by both forward selection and backward elimination. In general, the three procedures need not result in the same equation, though you should be encouraged when they do. The model selected by any of the methods should be carefully studied for violations of the assumptions. It is often a good idea to develop several acceptable models and then choose among them based on interpretability, ease of variable acquisition, parsimony, etc.

10.48   Checking for Violation of Assumptions

Procedures discussed in Section 10.17 for checking on violations of assumptions for bivariate regression can also be applied in the multivariate case. Residuals should be plotted against predicted values as well as against each of the independent variables. The distribution of residuals should be examined for normality. Plots of Studentized residuals against deleted residuals will show outliers. The Mahalanobis distance and Cook's distance are particularly important, since they convey information not readily available otherwise.

10.49   Interpreting the Equation

The multiple regression equation obtained from the previous analyses suggests several findings. Education appears to be the best predictor of beginning salary, at least among the variables included in this study (Figure 10.46a). The sex of the employee also appears to be important. Women are paid less than men since the sign of the regression coefficient is negative (men are coded 0 and women are coded 1). Years of prior work experience and race are also related to salary, but when education and sex are included in the equation, the effect of experience and race is less striking.

Do these results indicate that there is discrimination? Not necessarily. It is well recognized that all education is not equally profitable. Master's degrees in business administration and political science are treated quite differently in the marketplace. Thus, a possible explanation of the observed results is that women enter fields that are just not very well paid. Although this may suggest inequities in societal evaluation of skills, it need not imply discrimination at the bank being examined. Further, many other potential job-related skills or qualifications are not included in the model. Also, some of the existing variables, such as age, may make nonlinear as well as linear contributions to the fit. Such contributions can often be approximated by including new variables that are simple functions of the existing one. For example, the age values squared may improve the fit obtained above.

10.50   Statistics for Unselected Cases

As previously noted, a model usually fits the sample from which it is derived better than it fits the population. A sometimes useful strategy for obtaining an estimate of how well the model fits the population is randomly to split the sample into two parts. One part is then used to develop the model, while the remaining cases are reserved for testing its goodness of fit.

It is also sometimes interesting to split the data on some characteristics of the sample. For example, you can develop the salary equation for males alone and then apply it to females to see how well it fits. For example, Figure 10.50 shows histograms of residuals for males (denoted as selected cases) and females (unselected cases). Note that the females' salaries are too large when predicted from the male equation since most of the residuals are negative. The multiple R for the females is 0.45596, smaller than the 0.73882 for males (stepwise selection was used).

Figure 10.50 Histograms for males (selected) and females (unselected)

```
HISTOGRAM                      - SELECTED CASES
STUDENTIZED RESIDUAL
 N  EXP N       ( * = 1 CASES,    . : = NORMAL CURVE)
 3   0.20   OUT ***
 3   0.40   3.00 ***
 0   1.01   2.66 .
 1   2.30   2.33 *.
 2   4.71   2.00 ** .
 7   8.63   1.66 ******* .
10  14.16   1.33 ********** .
18  20.81   1.00 ****************** .
28  27.40   0.66 ************************.*
33  32.32   0.33 ****************************:*
31  34.15   0.00 ******************************* .
30  32.32  -0.33 ****************************** .
42  27.40  -0.66 **************************:****************
30  20.81  -1.00 ******************:********
11  14.16  -1.33 ********** .
 5   8.63  -1.66 ***** .
 3   4.71  -2.00 *** .
 0   2.30  -2.33 .
 1   1.01  -2.66 :
 0   0.40  -3.00
 0   0.20   OUT


HISTOGRAM                      - UNSELECTED CASES
STUDENTIZED RESIDUAL
 N  EXP N       ( X = 1 CASES,    . : = NORMAL CURVE)
 0   0.17   OUT
 0   0.33   3.00
 0   0.84   2.66 .
 0   1.93   2.33 .
 0   3.94   2.00 .
 1   7.22   1.66 X .
 1  11.85   1.33 X .
 2  17.42   1.00 XX .
 5  22.94   0.66 XXXXX .
10  27.06   0.33 XXXXXXXXXX .
14  28.59   0.00 XXXXXXXXXXXXXX .
32  27.06  -0.33 XXXXXXXXXXXXXXXXXXXXXXXXXX :XXXXX
35  22.94  -0.66 XXXXXXXXXXXXXXXXXXXXXXX:XXXXXXXXXXX
49  17.42  -1.00 XXXXXXXXXXXXXXX:XXXXXXXXXXXXXXXXXXXXXXXXXXXXXXXX
22  11.85  -1.33 XXXXXXXXXX:XXXXXXXXXX
13   7.22  -1.66 XXXXX:XXXXX
13   3.94  -2.00 XXX:XXXXXXXXX
 7   1.93  -2.33 X:XXXXX
 7   0.84  -2.66 :XXXXXX
 1   0.33  -3.00 X
 4   0.17   OUT XXXX
```

10.51 Problems of Multicollinearity

Preceding sections deal with the consequences of correlated independent variables in regression analysis. The estimates of the β and the sum of squares attributable to each variable are dependent on the other variables in the equation. Variances of the estimators also increase when independent variables are interrelated. This may result in a regression equation with a significant R^2, although virtually none of the coefficients is significantly different from 0. If any independent variable is a perfect linear combination of other independent variables, the correlation matrix is *singular* and a unique unbiased least squares solution does not exist.

Although situations involving singularities do occur, they are not as commonly encountered as those involving near-singularities—variables that are almost linear combinations of other independent variables. These variables are often called *multicollinear*.

10.52 Methods of Detection

There are several ways in which multicollinearities can be detected. Large coefficients in the correlation matrix always signal the presence of multicollinearity. However, it is possible for multicollinearity to exist without any of the correlation coefficients being very large. A determinant of a correlation matrix close to 0 is another indicator of near-singularity. However, this does not indicate which variables are causing the problem.

One of the most frequently used indicators of interdependency between variables is the tolerance (see Section 10.39). If the variable has a large R^2—or equivalently a small tolerance—when it is predicted from the other independent variables, a potentially troublesome situation exists. Not only are the variances of the estimators inflated, but computational problems can occur.

10.53 SPSS and Multicollinearity

In the SPSS REGRESSION procedure, various steps are taken to warn you of, and protect you from, potentially serious multicollinearity. Before an independent variable is entered into the equation, its tolerance with other independent variables already in the equation is calculated.

Since it is possible for a variable not in the equation to have an acceptable tolerance level, yet when entered to cause the tolerance of other variables already in the equation to become unacceptably small (Berk, 1977; Frane, 1977), the tolerances of all the variables in the equation are recomputed. If either the tolerance of the variable or the tolerance of any variable already in the equation is less than 0.01, a warning is issued and the variable is not entered unless the default TOLERANCE criterion has been altered (see Section 10.68).

Both the tolerance of a variable and the minimum tolerance of all independent variables in the equation if the variable were to be entered can be printed in SPSS.

10.54 RUNNING PROCEDURE NEW REGRESSION

The NEW REGRESSION procedure provides five equation-building methods: forward selection, backward elimination, stepwise selection, forced entry, and forced removal. The residuals analysis subcommands provide aid in detecting influential data points, outliers, and violations of the regression model assumptions.

10.55 Building the Equation

To build a simple regression model, specify three required subcommands: a VARIA-BLES subcommand to name the variables to be analyzed, a DEPENDENT subcommand to indicate which variable is dependent, and a subcommand that names the method to be used. For example, to build the simple bivariate model of beginning salary and current salary used in introducing the statistics in this chapter, you would specify

```
NEW REGRESSION VARIABLES=SALBEG,SALNOW/
               DEPENDENT=SALNOW/
               ENTER SALBEG/
```

The beginning (SALBEG) and current (SALNOW) salaries are named, with the latter specified as the dependent variable. Then the ENTER subcommand is used to enter beginning salary into the equation. The output produced from this command is shown in Figures 10.3b, 10.10, and 10.11a.

Subcommands and specifications begin in column 16 or beyond and are separated from each other with slashes. Subcommands and keyword specifications in NEW REGRESSION can be truncated to at least three characters, and the equals sign following the subcommand is optional. The above specification could read

```
NEW REGRESSION VARS SALBEG,SALNOW/DEP SALNOW/ENT SALBEG/
```

However, the examples that follow use no abbreviations and include the optional equals signs.

10.56 Subcommands VARIABLES and DEPENDENT

All variables needed for regression analysis are named on the VARIABLES subcommand, including the dependent variable named on the subsequent DEPENDENT subcommand. If you want to analyze several equations in the same NEW REGRES-SION command, you can include more than one VARIABLES subcommand, each with its own DEPENDENT subcommand or subcommands. For example, to run both the bivariate and multivariate examples developed in the preceding discussions of regression analysis, specify

```
NEW REGRESSION VARIABLES=SALBEG,SALNOW/
                DEPENDENT=SALNOW/
                ENTER SALBEG/
                VARIABLES=LOGBEG,EDLEVEL,SEX,WORK,MINORITY,AGE/
                DEPENDENT=LOGBEG/
                ENTER EDLEVEL TO AGE/
```

The TO convention for naming consecutive variables used in the second ENTER subcommand refers to the order in which the variables are named on the previous VARIABLES subcommand. See Figures 10.35a and 10.35b for the default output from the second equation.

Usually only one variable is named as a dependent variable in a single DEPENDENT subcommand. If you name more than one dependent variable, SPSS develops an equation for the first variable, then for the second, etc.

10.57   The Method Subcommands

The method used in developing the regression equation is specified by one (or more) of the method subcommand keywords optionally followed by a list of variables.

FORWARD   *Forward variable selection.* Variables are entered one at a time based on entry criteria (Section 10.45).

BACKWARD   *Backward variable elimination.* All variables are entered and then removed one at a time based on removal criteria. (Section 10.46).

STEPWISE   *Stepwise variable entry and removal.* Variables are examined at each step for entry or removal (Section 10.47).

ENTER   *Forced entry.* The variables named are entered. The default variable list is all independent variables.

REMOVE varlist *Forced removal.* The variables named are removed.

The *varlist* following the REMOVE subcommand is required. It is optional for all other subcommands. Generally, the FORWARD, BACKWARD, and STEPWISE subcommands are used without specifying a variable list. For example, to request the backward elimination method discussed in Section 10.46, specify

```
NEW REGRESSION VARIABLES=LOGBEG,EDLEVEL,SEX,WORK,MINORITY,AGE/
                DEPENDENT=LOGBEG/
                BACKWARD/
```

The method subcommand keywords can be combined as shown in Section 10.58 where the ENTER keyword is used twice to enter two variables separately into an equation. You might also want to force education into the equation first and then enter the remaining variables in a forward selection fashion, as in

```
NEW REGRESSION VARIABLES=LOGBEG,EDLEVEL,SEX,WORK,MINORITY,AGE/
                DEPENDENT=LOGBEG/
                ENTER EDLEVEL/FORWARD=SEX TO AGE/
```

10.58   The STATISTICS Subcommand

By default, NEW REGRESSION prints four sets of statistics corresponding to keywords R, ANOVA, COEFF, and OUTS explained below and shown in Figures 10.3b, 10.10, and 10.11a for the bivariate equation, and in Figures 10.35a and 10.35b for the multivariate equation. You can specify exactly what you want printed by using combinations of the following keywords for the STATISTICS subcommand.

DEFAULTS*   *Implies statistics keywords R, ANOVA, COEFF, and OUTS.* Note that the asterisk (*) indicates the default; these keywords do not have to be specified if default output is desired.

R   *Statistics for the equation:* R, R^2, adjusted R^2, and standard error.

ANOVA   *Analysis of variance table:* degrees of freedom, sums of squares, mean squares, F value for multiple R, and the observed significance level of F.

COEFF	*Statistics for variables in the equation:* regression coefficient B, standard error of B, standardized coefficient BETA, t value for B, and two-tailed significance level of t.
OUTS	*Statistics for variables not in the equation:* BETA if the variable entered, t value for BETA, significance level of t, partial correlation with the dependent variable controlling for variables in the equation, and minimum tolerance.
CHANGE	*Change in R^2:* change in R^2 between steps, F value for change in R^2, and significance of F. See the output in Figure 10.41.
BCOV	*Variance-covariance matrix.* See the description of Figure 10.39b.
ZPP	*Zero-order, part, and partial correlation.* See Figure 10.38.
CI	*Confidence intervals.* See Figure 10.8.
F	*F value for B and significance of F.* Displayed instead of t for COEFF and OUTS. See, for example, Figures 10.45b, 10.45c, 10.46a, and 10.46b.
TOLERANCE	*Tolerance.* See Figure 10.39a.
HISTORY	*Step history.* See the output in Figures 10.43 and 10.45a.
ALL	*All regression statistics.*

The STATISTICS subcommand must appear before the DEPENDENT subcommand that initiates the equation. For example, to produce the output shown in Figure 10.8, specify

```
NEW REGRESSION VARIABLES=SALBEG,SALNOW/
                STATISTICS=CI/
                DEPENDENT=SALNOW/
                ENTER SALBEG/
```

To obtain the STATISTICS subcommand defaults as well as the confidence intervals, specify

```
                STATISTICS=DEFAULTS,CI/
```

Or to produce the output shown in Figure 10.41 for the multivariate example, specify

```
NEW REGRESSION VARIABLES=LOGBEG,EDLEVEL,SEX,WORK,MINORITY,AGE/
                STATISTICS=R,CHANGE,COEFF/
                DEPENDENT=LOGBEG/
                ENTER EDLEVEL/ENTER SEX/
```

10.59   Residual Analysis

Once you have built an equation, NEW REGRESSION can calculate eleven temporary variables containing several types of residuals, predicted values, and related measures for detecting outliers and influential data points and for examining regression assumptions as described in Sections 10.13 through 10.25. Use the following keyword variable names in any of the residuals-related subcommands.

PRED	*Unstandardized predicted values* (Section 10.13).
ZPRED	*Standardized predicted values* (Section 10.13).
SEPRED	*Standard error of the predicted values* (Section 10.15).
RESID	*Unstandardized residuals* (Section 10.18).
ZRESID	*Standardized residuals* (Section 10.18).
SRESID	*Studentized residuals* (Section 10.18).
MAHAL	*Mahalanobis distance* (Section 10.24).
ADJPRED	*Adjusted predicted values* (Section 10.25).
DRESID	*Deleted residuals* (Section 10.25).
SDRESID	*Studentized deleted residuals* (Section 10.25).
COOK	*Cook's distance* (Section 10.25).

Residual analysis is specified with three subcommands RESIDUALS, CASEWISE, and SCATTERPLOT. There is no order to these subcommands, but you cannot specify more than one of each per equation and they must immediately follow the last method subcommand that completes the equation.

10.60 The RESIDUALS Subcommand

Unless you specify the RESIDUALS subcommand keyword, you get none of the following statistics and plots. If you specify the keyword RESIDUALS only, you get DEFAULTS.

DEFAULTS	*Includes default HISTOGRAM, NORMPROB, and OUTLIERS plots, and DURBIN test.*
HISTOGRAM(varlist)	*Histogram of standardized temporary variables named.* Default is ZRESID; not available for MAHAL, COOK, or SEPRED. See Figure 10.22a.
NORMPROB(varlist)	*Normal probability (P-P) plot of standardized temporary variables named.* Default is ZRESID; not available for MAHAL, COOK, or SEPRED. See Figure 10.22b.
SMALL	*Print small plots.* The default is LARGE plots which try to use most of the output page.
OUTLIERS(varlist)	*Ten largest values for the temporary variables named.* Default is ZRESID; variables can be RESID, DRESID, SRESID, SDRESID, MAHAL, and COOK. See Figure 10.24.
DURBIN	*Durbin-Watson test.* See Section 10.21.
ID(varname)	*Label casewise and outlier plots with values of this variable.* See Figures 10.23 and 10.24.

For example, to produce the output shown in Figures 10.24, 10.22a, and 10.22b, specify

```
NEW REGRESSION VARIABLES=SALBEG,SALNOW/
               DEPENDENT=SALNOW/
               ENTER SALBEG/
               RESIDUALS=SMALL HISTOGRAM(SRESID) NORMPROB
                         OUTLIERS(MAHAL) ID(SEXRACE)/
```

10.61 The CASEWISE Subcommand

You can display a casewise plot of one of the temporary variables accompanied by a listing of the values of the dependent and the temporary variables. The plot can be requested for all cases or limited to outliers. If you specify the CASEWISE subcommand keyword alone, you get DEFAULTS.

DEFAULTS	*Includes OUTLIERS(3), PLOT(ZRESID), DEPENDENT, PRED, and RESID.*
OUTLIERS(value)	*Limit plot to outliers defined by this value.* The default is greater than or equal in absolute value to 3. See Figure 10.23.
PLOT(varname)	*Plot the values of this temporary variable.* The default is ZRESID. See Figure 10.23.
varlist	*List values of DEPENDENT and the temporary variables named.* See Figures 10.16, 10.23, etc.
ALL	*Plot all cases,* not just outliers.

For example, to produce the casewise plot shown in Figure 10.16, specify

```
NEW REGRESSION VARIABLES=SALBEG,SALNOW/
               DEPENDENT=SALNOW/
               ENTER SALBEG/
               RESIDUALS=SMALL HISTOGRAM(SRESID) NORMPROB
                         OUTLIERS(MAHAL) ID(SEXRACE)/
               CASEWISE=ALL DEPENDENT PRED RESID SEPRED/
```

If you want a plot of outliers whose absolute values are equal to or greater than 3 based on ZRESID, you need only specify the CASEWISE subcommand. Or if you want the plot based on Studentized residuals as shown in Figure 10.23, specify

```
NEW REGRESSION VARIABLES=SALBEG,SALNOW/
               DEPENDENT=SALNOW/
               ENTER SALBEG/
               CASEWISE=PLOT(SRESID)/
```

10.62 The SCATTERPLOT Subcommand

You can generate any number of scattergrams of the temporary variables and any of the variables in the equation by specifying the SCATTERPLOT subcommand followed by pairs of variable names separated by commas, with each pair enclosed in parentheses. For example, to generate the scattergram shown in Figure 10.20, specify

```
NEW REGRESSION VARIABLES=SALBEG,SALNOW/
                DEPENDENT=SALNOW/
                ENTER SALBEG/
                RESIDUALS=SMALL HISTOGRAM(SRESID) NORMPROB
                        OUTLIERS(MAHAL) ID(SEXRACE)/
                CASEWISE=ALL DEPENDENT PRED RESID SEPRED/
                SCATTERPLOT=(*SRESID,*PRED)/
```

Whenever you name a temporary variable in a SCATTERPLOT subcommand, preface the keyword with an asterisk to identify it as a temporary variable.

To produce the scattergram of the same two temporary variables shown above (SRESID and PRED) based on the logarithmic transformation of both the dependent and independent variables as shown in Figure 10.30a, the SCATTERPLOT subcommand does not change, but you need some transformation commands.

```
COMPUTE         LOGBEG=LG10(SALBEG)
COMPUTE         LOGNOW=LG10(SALNOW)
NEW REGRESSION VARIABLES=LOGBEG,LOGNOW/
                DEPENDENT=LOGNOW/
                ENTER LOGBEG/
                SCATTERPLOT=(*SRESID,*PRED)/
```

The first variable you name inside the parentheses becomes the vertical-axis (Y) variable and the second becomes the horizontal-axis (X) variable. All scattergrams are standardized in NEW REGRESSION, which is illustrated in Figure 10.25a where the specification SCATTERPLOT=(Y,X) generated a scattergram of the standardized values of variables X and Y.

If you want more than one scattergram, simply add pairs of variable names in parentheses, as in

```
SCATTERPLOT=(*SRESID,*PRED)(SALBEG,*PRED)/
```

10.63 Additional Subcommands for the Equation

In addition to the subcommands described in Sections 10.54 through 10.58, you control your output with the WIDTH subcommand, list additional statistics with the DESCRIPTIVES subcommand, select cases within the NEW REGRESSION procedure with the SELECT subcommand, and control missing-value treatment with the MISSING subcommand. All of these should appear before the VARIABLES subcommand.

Use the CRITERIA subcommand to control the criteria by which variable selection takes place. The CRITERIA subcommand must appear after the VARIABLES subcommand and before the DEPENDENT subcommand.

10.64 The WIDTH Subcommand

Output from NEW REGRESSION is flexible for available page width. If possible, it will use all available page width, but you can limit it to as few as 65 columns. For example, to make certain that the equation statistics shown in Figure 10.10 are displayed separately from the ANOVA statistics shown in Figure 10.11a rather than side-by-side, specify a smaller page width, as in

```
NEW REGRESSION WIDTH=90/
                VARIABLES=SALBEG,SALNOW/
                DEPENDENT=SALNOW/
                ENTER SALBEG/
```

A smaller page width limits the number of statistics that can be printed in output from STATISTICS=HISTORY. Also, casewise, scatter, and normal probability plots are affected in residuals output.

10.65   The DESCRIPTIVES Subcommand

You can request a number of statistics based on your variable list. These are displayed before the equation is developed. If you specify the DESCRIPTIVES subcommand keyword alone, you get DEFAULTS.

DEFAULTS	*Includes MEAN, STDDEV, CORR. These are the defaults if you specify the DESCRIPTIVE subcommand alone.*
MEAN	*Variable means.*
STDDEV	*Variable standard deviations.*
VARIANCE	*Variable variances.*
CORR	*Correlation matrix.*
SIG	*One-tailed significance levels of the correlation coefficients.*
BADCORR	*Correlation matrix only if some coefficients cannot be computed.*
COVARIANCE	*Covariance matrix.*
XPROD	*Cross-product deviations from the mean.*
N	*Number of cases used to compute the correlation coefficients (see the MISSING subcommand).*

For example, to produce the correlation matrix shown in Figure 10.34, specify

```
NEW REGRESSION WIDTH=90/
               DESCRIPTIVES=CORR/
               VARIABLES=LOGBEG,EDLEVEL,SEX,WORK,MINORITY,AGE/
               DEPENDENT=LOGBEG/
               ENTER EDLEVEL TO AGE/
```

10.66   The SELECT Subcommand

Within NEW REGRESSION, you can select a subset of your data for constructing the equation. Then you can observe residuals and predicted values both for the cases used in computing the coefficients and for cases not used. Specify

SELECT *varname relation value*

where *relation* is EQ, NE, LT, LE, GT, or GE. For example, to generate the separate residuals histograms shown in Figure 10.50 for males and females, based on the equation developed for males alone (SEX = 0), specify

```
NEW REGRESSION WIDTH=90/
               SELECT SEX EQ 0/
               VARIABLES=LOGBEG,EDLEVEL,SEX,WORK,MINORITY,AGE/
               DEPENDENT=LOGBEG/
               STEPWISE/
               RESIDUALS=HISTOGRAM/
```

10.67   The MISSING Subcommand

To specify how NEW REGRESSION is to treat cases with missing values, specify one of the following keywords.

LISTWISE*	*Listwise deletion of cases with missing values.* By default, cases are excluded from the analysis if they have a missing value for any variable in the VARIABLES subcommand.
PAIRWISE	*Pairwise deletion of cases with missing values.* Each correlation coefficient is computed using cases with complete data on the pair of variables being correlated, regardless of whether the cases have missing values on any other variable in the VARIABLES subcommand.
MEANSUBSTITUTION	*Replacement of missing values with the variable mean.*
INCLUDE	*Inclusion of cases with missing values,* with missing values considered valid.

See the discussion of missing-value treatment and correlation matrices in Chapter 6.

10.68   The CRITERIA Subcommand

You can control the statistical criteria by which NEW REGRESSION chooses variables for entry into or removal from an equation by specifying the CRITERIA subcommand after the VARIABLES subcommand but before the DEPENDENT subcommand. The criteria are

DEFAULTS*	*Includes PIN(0.05), POUT(0.1), and TOLERANCE(0.01).*
PIN(value)	*Probability of F-to-enter.* Used to override the default value of 0.05.
POUT(value)	*Probability of F-to-remove.* Used to override the default value of 0.1.
FIN(value)	*F-to-enter.* The default value is 3.84.
FOUT(value)	*F-to-remove.* The default value is 2.71.
TOLERANCE(value)	*Tolerance.* The default value is 0.01. All variables must pass both tolerance and minimum tolerance before entering the equation. See Sections 10.39 and 10.42.
MAXSTEPS(n)	*Maximum number of steps.*

For example, to change stepwise entry and removal criteria to FIN and FOUT and accept the default values of 3.84 and 2.71 respectively, specify

```
NEW REGRESSION  VARIABLES=LOGBEG,EDLEVEL,SEX,WORK,MINORITY,AGE/
                CRITERIA=FIN,FOUT/
                DEPENDENT=LOGBEG/
                STEPWISE/
```

10.69   An Example Using Stepwise Selection

To produce the stepwise variable selection example discussed in Section 10.47, specify

```
NEW REGRESSION  VARIABLES=LOGBEG,EDLEVEL,SEX,WORK,MINORITY,AGE/
                STATISTICS=R,COEFF,OUTS,F/
                DEPENDENT=LOGBEG/
                STEPWISE/
```

The output from this example is shown in Figure 10.69.

10.70   NEW REGRESSION and Other SPSS Commands

The complete SPSS command file used to run the stepwise example shown in Figure 10.69 is

```
GET FILE        BANK
PAGESIZE        999
COMPUTE         LOGBEG=LG10(SALBEG)
NEW REGRESSION  VARIABLES=LOGBEG,EDLEVEL,SEX,WORK,MINORITY,AGE/
                STATISTICS=R,COEFF,OUTS,F/
                DEPENDENT=LOGBEG/
                STEPWISE/
```

PAGESIZE.   The PAGESIZE command is used to eliminate page breaks that would occur before the step output is complete.

COMPUTE.   This COMPUTE command creates a logarithmic transformation of the beginning salary variable as discussed in Section 10.30 and used throughout this chapter.

Figure 10.69 Stepwise output

```
                        * * * *   M U L T I P L E   R E G R E S S I O N   * * * *
VARIABLE LIST NUMBER   1.  LISTWISE DELETION OF MISSING DATA.
EQUATION NUMBER  1.

DEPENDENT VARIABLE..  LOGBEG

BEGINNING BLOCK NUMBER  1.  METHOD:  STEPWISE

VARIABLE(S) ENTERED ON STEP NUMBER  1..   EDLEVEL       EDUCATIONAL LEVEL

MULTIPLE R          0.68572
R SQUARE           0.47021
ADJUSTED R SQUARE  0.46909
STANDARD ERROR     0.11165
```

--------------- VARIABLES IN THE EQUATION ---------------							--------------- VARIABLES NOT IN THE EQUATION ---------------					
VARIABLE	B	SE B	BETA	F	SIG F		VARIABLE	BETA IN	PARTIAL	MIN TOLER	F	SIG F
EDLEVEL	0.03642	0.00178	0.68572	418.920	0.0000		SEX	-0.34802	-0.44681	0.87327	117.486	0.0000
(CONSTANT)	3.31001	0.02455		18176.766	0.0000		WORK	0.22747	0.30241	0.93632	47.408	0.0000
							MINORITY	-0.08318	-0.11327	0.98234	6.121	0.0137
							AGE	0.15718	0.20726	0.92113	21.140	0.0000

```
                  * * * * * * * * * * * * * * * * * * * * * * * * * * * * * *

VARIABLE(S) ENTERED ON STEP NUMBER  2..    SEX        SEX OF EMPLOYEE

MULTIPLE R          0.75893
R SQUARE           0.57598
ADJUSTED R SQUARE  0.57418
STANDARD ERROR     0.09999
```

--------------- VARIABLES IN THE EQUATION ---------------							--------------- VARIABLES NOT IN THE EQUATION ---------------					
VARIABLE	B	SE B	BETA	F	SIG F		VARIABLE	BETA IN	PARTIAL	MIN TOLER	F	SIG F
EDLEVEL	0.02984	0.00171	0.56183	306.192	0.0000		WORK	0.14425	0.20567	0.77382	20.759	0.0000
SEX	-0.10697	0.00987	-0.34802	117.486	0.0000		MINORITY	-0.12902	-0.19464	0.84758	18.507	0.0000
(CONSTANT)	3.44754	0.02539		18443.279	0.0000		AGE	0.13942	0.20519	0.80425	20.659	0.0000

```
                  * * * * * * * * * * * * * * * * * * * * * * * * * * * * * *

VARIABLE(S) ENTERED ON STEP NUMBER  3..    WORK       WORK EXPERIENCE

MULTIPLE R          0.77066
R SQUARE           0.59391
ADJUSTED R SQUARE  0.59132
STANDARD ERROR     0.09796
```

--------------- VARIABLES IN THE EQUATION ---------------							--------------- VARIABLES NOT IN THE EQUATION ---------------					
VARIABLE	B	SE B	BETA	F	SIG F		VARIABLE	BETA IN	PARTIAL	MIN TOLER	F	SIG F
EDLEVEL	0.03257	0.00177	0.61321	336.772	0.0000		MINORITY	-0.14125	-0.21700	0.75967	23.176	0.0000
SEX	-0.09403	0.01008	-0.30594	87.099	0.0000		AGE	0.07633	0.06754	0.29839	2.149	0.1433
WORK	0.00254	0.5566D-03	0.14425	20.759	0.0000							
(CONSTANT)	3.38457	0.02845		14150.641	0.0000							

```
                  * * * * * * * * * * * * * * * * * * * * * * * * * * * * * *

VARIABLE(S) ENTERED ON STEP NUMBER  4..    MINORITY   MINORITY CLASSIFICATION

MULTIPLE R          0.78297
R SQUARE           0.61304
ADJUSTED R SQUARE  0.60974
STANDARD ERROR     0.09573
```

--------------- VARIABLES IN THE EQUATION ---------------							--------------- VARIABLES NOT IN THE EQUATION ---------------					
VARIABLE	B	SE B	BETA	F	SIG F		VARIABLE	BETA IN	PARTIAL	MIN TOLER	F	SIG F
EDLEVEL	0.03143	0.00175	0.59176	322.412	0.0000		AGE	0.07811	0.07080	0.29784	2.357	0.1254
SEX	-0.09904	0.00990	-0.32223	100.063	0.0000							
WORK	0.00275	0.5458D-03	0.15659	25.444	0.0000							
MINORITY	-0.05225	0.01085	-0.14125	23.176	0.0000							
(CONSTANT)	3.41195	0.02838		14454.042	0.0000							

```
FOR BLOCK NUMBER  1   PIN = 0.050 LIMITS REACHED.
```

Chapter 11

Saving the Bank:
SPSS Command Summary

To present additional SPSS commands and expand the discussion of other commands already discussed throughout this manual, this chapter begins with a complete SPSS job. The file defined and saved with this job is the bank data used in Chapters 4 and 10 and in the exercises in Appendix A.

The data are information about bank employees hired between 1969 and 1971. The variables include the beginning salary and the salary as of March, 1977. Other information is sex, minority status, years of education, years of prior work experience, months of seniority, and a condensed job classification.

The general rules for SPSS command structure and syntax are discussed in Chapter 1. Appendix B shows the complete syntax for each of the commands discussed in this book and a table indicating their order in an SPSS job. Figure 11.1 shows the SPSS command file used to define, analyze, and save the bank data. Line numbers are added for reference.

11.1 LABELING THE RUN, FILE, AND TASK

RUN NAME (line 1).   The RUN NAME command,

```
RUN NAME        BANK EMPLOYMENT STUDY
```

provides a label that is printed at the top of each page of SPSS output. For example, the first line of the output shown in Figure 11.8 includes the label "BANK EMPLOYMENT STUDY" from the RUN NAME command. The RUN NAME label can be a maximum of 64 characters long. Any character that is valid for the computer that you are using can appear in the RUN NAME label. The RUN NAME command is optional. If used, it is usually the first SPSS command in your job.

TASK NAME (lines 36 and 39).   This command provides a subtitle specific to the output of the procedures that follow. The TASK NAME label is printed below the RUN NAME label on the SPSS printed output. For example,

```
TASK NAME        AGE, SEXRACE CROSSTABULATION FOR ENTIRE SAMPLE
```

supplies the label that appears as the second line of the crosstabulation output in Figure 11.8. The TASK NAME label can be a maximum of 64 characters long and can include any valid character for your computer. If you are running a number of procedures in a single job, you can include a TASK NAME command before each procedure to provide a

Figure 11.1   Defining, analyzing, and saving the bank data

```
1    RUN NAME          BANK EMPLOYMENT STUDY
2    FILE NAME         BANK, MIDWESTERN CITY BANK DATA
3    DATA LIST         FIXED(1)/1 ID 1-4 SALBEG 6-10 SEX 12 TIME 14-15
4                                AGE 17-20 (2) SALNOW 22-26 EDLEVEL 28-29
5                                WORK 31-34 (2) JOBCAT,MINORITY 36-37
6    N OF CASES        UNKNOWN
7    INPUT MEDIUM      DISK
8    VAR LABELS        ID, EMPLOYEE CODE/ SALBEG, BEGINNING SALARY/
9                      SEX, SEX OF EMPLOYEE/ TIME, JOB SENIORITY/
10                     AGE, AGE OF EMPLOYEE/
11                     SALNOW, CURRENT SALARY/ EDLEVEL, EDUCATIONAL LEVEL/
12                     WORK, WORK EXPERIENCE/ JOBCAT, EMPLOYMENT CATEGORY/
13                     MINORITY, MINORITY CLASSIFICATION/
14   VALUE LABELS      SEX (0) MALES (1) FEMALES/
15                     JOBCAT (1) CLERICAL (2) OFFICE TRAINEE
16                            (3) SECURITY OFFICER
17                            (4) COLLEGE TRAINEE (5) EXEMPT EMPLOYEE
18                            (6) MBA TRAINEE (7) TECHNICAL/
19                     MINORITY (0) WHITE (1) NONWHITE/
20   MISSING VALUES    SALBEG,TIME TO EDLEVEL,JOBCAT (0)/SEX, MINORITY (9)
21   PRINT FORMATS     WORK,AGE (2)
22   COMMENT           CREATE THE NEW VARIABLE SEXRACE
23   IF                (MINORITY EQ 0 AND SEX EQ 0) SEXRACE=1
24   IF                (MINORITY EQ 1 AND SEX EQ 0) SEXRACE=2
25   IF                (MINORITY EQ 0 AND SEX EQ 1) SEXRACE=3
26   IF                (MINORITY EQ 1 AND SEX EQ 1) SEXRACE=4
27   ASSIGN MISSING    SEXRACE(9)
28   VAR LABELS        SEXRACE, SEX & RACE CLASSIFICATION/
29   VALUE LABELS      SEXRACE (1) WHITE MALES (2) MINORITY MALES
30                            (3) WHITE FEMALES (4) MINORITY FEMALES/
31   COMMENT           TEMPORARY RECODE OF AGE FOR CROSSTABULATION
32   *COMPUTE          AGE=RND(AGE)
33   *RECODE           AGE(18 THRU 29=1)(30 THRU 39=2)(40 THRU 49=3)
34                        (50 THRU 59=4)(60 THRU HIGHEST=5)/
35   VALUE LABELS      AGE (1) 18-29 (2) 30-39 (3) 40-49 (4) 50-59 (5) 60+/
36   TASK NAME         AGE, SEXRACE CROSSTABULATION FOR ENTIRE SAMPLE.
37   CROSSTABS         TABLES=SEXRACE BY AGE
38   READ INPUT DATA
39   TASK NAME         WORK, AVERAGE MONTHLY RAISE SCATTERGRAM OF WHITE MALES
40   *SELECT IF        (SEXRACE EQ 1)
41   *COMPUTE          AVERAISE=(SALNOW-SALBEG)/TIME
42   ASSIGN MISSING    AVERAISE (-1)
43   SCATTERGRAM       WORK WITH AVERAISE
44   COMMENT           SAVE THE SYSTEM FILE
45   SAVE FILE
46   FINISH
```

specific subtitle for each page of your output. Line 36 of Figure 11.1 prints a subtitle for the CROSSTABS output and line 39 prints a different subtitle for the SCATTERGRAM output.

FILE NAME (line 2).   The FILE NAME command has two specifications—the *file name* and the *file label:*

```
FILE NAME       BANK, MIDWESTERN CITY BANK DATA
```

This information is printed below the RUN NAME label and the TASK NAME label at the top of each page printed by SPSS procedures, as in Figure 11.8. The file name and file label are also stored in an SPSS system file when one is saved (see Section 11.10).

The file name must conform to the same requirements as the variable names: 1 to 8 characters long, beginning with a letter, and containing only letters or numbers. The file label can be 64 characters long and can include any valid character on your computer. If you do not include a FILE NAME command in your job, SPSS automatically assigns the file name NONAME to your data file.

11.2 DEFINING THE VARIABLES

DATA LIST (lines 3, 4, and 5).   The DATA LIST command assigns names to the variables and defines the record and column locations for them. It is a required command if you are reading your data from an input data file or from lines included in the SPSS command file. Once you have assigned the names to your variables, you use these names to refer to the variables on all subsequent SPSS commands. The DATA LIST command on lines 3, 4, and 5 of Figure 11.1 combines several of the syntax requirements discussed in earlier chapters (see Chapters 1, 3, and 7).

The first specification, the keyword FIXED, indicates that the data are in fixed-column format. Each variable is located in the same columns in the same record for each case. The second specification, (1), tells SPSS that each case has one record. A slash must follow this specification. Following the slash is the sequence number of the record being defined.

Your data file may contain more than one record per case, and you may need to define variables from several of the records. For example, suppose that the bank data file contained three records per case, and the variables to be defined are located on all three records, as in

```
DATA LIST       FIXED (3)/1 ID 1-4 SALBEG 6-10 SEX 12 TIME 14-15
                       /2 AGE 5-8 (2) SALNOW 10-14 EDLEVEL 15-17
                       /3 WORK 10-13 (2) JOBCAT,MINORITY 30-31
```

The (3) specifies three records per case. The first four variables will be read from the first record, the next three variables from the second record, and the last three variables from the third record. You must separate the definitions for one record from the definitions for the next record with a slash. Following the slash, specify the sequence number of the record you are defining and the variable definitions for that record.

For each variable definition, you must assign a variable name followed by the column location of the variable. If the variable is one column wide, specify the number of the column. If the variable is two or more columns wide, specify the number of the first column followed by a dash and the number of the last column. For example, the DATA LIST command in Figure 11.1 defines the variable ID located in columns 1 through 4, SALBEG, a five-column variable, located in columns 6 through 10, SEX located in column 12, and so forth.

The last two variables, JOBCAT and MINORITY, are defined with one column specification following both names. JOBCAT is located in column 36 and MINORITY is located in column 37. You can define adjacent variables of the same width by listing all of the variable names followed by the beginning column location of the first variable in the list, a dash, and the ending column location of the last variable. You can also assign variable names to adjacent variables by using a special naming convention of the form *alphaxxx* TO *alphayyy*, where *alpha* is the same character string on both sides of the keyword TO, and *xxx* and *yyy* are numbers. The combined length of alpha characters and numbers cannot exceed eight characters. For example, to define 10 adjacent items, specify

```
DATA LIST       FIXED (1)/1 ITEM1 TO ITEM10 5-14
```

where ITEM1 is located in column 5, ITEM2 in column 6, and so forth. You can use the TO naming convention to assign variable names to variables that you otherwise would have difficulty assigning meaningful eight-character names. Although the variable names assigned in this manner are not very descriptive, you can use the VAR LABELS command to assign labels to the variables.

AGE and WORK are variables measuring age of employee and prior work experience in years. Both of these variables have been converted from a measurement in months. Two decimal positions have been retained. However, the decimal point has not been recorded on the data file so that an age of 23.33 has been recorded as 2333 in columns 17 through 20. To define each of these variables with two decimal places, specify the number 2 enclosed in parentheses following the column specification, as shown in the DATA LIST command. Use this specification to indicate the appropriate number of decimal places for nonintegers that are not recorded with the decimal point in the data.

If the coded values of a variable include letters or special characters like an ampersand, you must specify an *A* enclosed in parentheses following the column specification. See Chapter 1 for an example defining an alphanumeric variable. Also, refer to the PRINT FORMATS command discussed in this section.

An excerpt of the first page of output from the sample SPSS job is shown in Figure 11.2. Note that SPSS prints a message below the printback of the DATA LIST command informing you that the 10 variables are defined on one record for each case. The next message on the output shows the FORTRAN format statement that SPSS actually uses to read your data. If you know FORTRAN, this statement will look familiar. However, you need not understand it because SPSS automatically constructs it from your DATA LIST command.

Figure 11.2 First page of output—printing back the definitions

```
SPSS BATCH SYSTEM                                                           07/10/81      PAGE   1

SPSS WITH GRAPHICS OPTION FOR OS/360, VERSION M, RELEASE 9.0, JUNE 10, 1981

SPSS BATCH SYSTEM                                                           07/10/81      PAGE   1

SPSS WITH GRAPHICS OPTION FOR OS/360, VERSION M, RELEASE 9.0, JUNE 10, 1981

                                 CURRENT DOCUMENTATION FOR THE SPSS BATCH SYSTEM
ORDER FROM MCGRAW-HILL:  SPSS, 2ND ED. (PRINCIPAL TEXT)        ORDER FROM SPSS INC.:  SPSS STATISTICAL ALGORITHMS
                         SPSS UPDATE 7-9 (USE W/SPSS,2ND FOR REL. 7, 8, 9)       KEYWORDS: THE SPSS INC. NEWSLETTER
                         SPSS POCKET GUIDE, RELEASE 9
                         SPSS PRIMER (BRIEF INTRO TO SPSS)

DEFAULT SPACE ALLOCATION..    ALLOWS FOR..   102 TRANSFORMATIONS
WORKSPACE    71680 BYTES                     409 RECODE VALUES + LAG VARIABLES
TRANSPACE    10240 BYTES                     1641 IF/COMPUTE OPERATIONS

              1 RUN NAME      BANK EMPLOYMENT STUDY
              2 FILE NAME     BANK, MIDWESTERN CITY BANK DATA
              3 DATA LIST     FIXED(1)/1 ID 1-4 SALBEG 6-10 SEX 12 TIME 14-15
              4                          AGE 17-20 (2) SALNOW 22-26 EDLEVEL 28-29
              5                          WORK 31-34 (2) JOBCAT,MINORITY 36-37

THE DATA LIST PROVIDES FOR  10 VARIABLES AND  1 RECORDS ('CARDS') PER CASE. A MAXIMUM OF   37 COLUMNS ARE USED ON A RECORD.

LIST OF THE CONSTRUCTED FORMAT STATEMENT..
      (F4.0,1X,F5.0,1X,F1.0,1X,F2.0,1X,F4.2,1X,F5.0,1X,F2.0,1X,F4.2,1X,2F1.0)

              6 N OF CASES     UNKNOWN
              7 INPUT MEDIUM   DISK
              8 VAR LABELS     ID, EMPLOYEE CODE/ SALBEG, BEGINNING SALARY/
              9                SEX, SEX OF EMPLOYEE/ TIME, JOB SENIORITY/
             10                AGE, AGE OF EMPLOYEE/
.....        .....
.....        .....
.....        .....
```

VAR LABELS (lines 8-13 and 28). The VAR LABELS command assigns an optional label up to 40 characters long to any variable in your file. The first VAR LABELS command on lines 8 through 13 assigns a label to each of the variables defined on the DATA LIST command.

```
VAR LABELS     ID, EMPLOYEE CODE/ SALBEG, BEGINNING SALARY/
               SEX, SEX OF EMPLOYEE/ TIME, JOB SENIORITY/
               AGE, AGE OF EMPLOYEE/
               SALNOW, CURRENT SALARY/ EDLEVEL, EDUCATIONAL LEVEL/
               WORK, WORK EXPERIENCE/ JOBCAT, EMPLOYMENT CATEGORY/
               MINORITY, MINORITY CLASSIFICATION/
```

For each variable, the variable name is listed followed by at least one blank or comma and the label terminated by a slash. The label can contain any valid character for your computer except a slash or a right or left parenthesis.

The second VAR LABELS command assigns a label to the newly-created variable SEXRACE.

```
VAR LABELS     SEXRACE, SEX & RACE CLASSIFICATION/
```

This VAR LABELS command referencing SEXRACE must follow the commands that created the variable, in this case the IF commands (see Section 11.5). The variable labels for AGE and SEXRACE are displayed on the CROSSTABS output in Figure 11.8.

VALUE LABELS (lines 14-19, 29-30, and 35). The VALUE LABELS command assigns optional labels up to 20 characters long to each value of a variable. Specify the variable name, each value enclosed in parentheses, and the label for the value. Separate one set of labels from the specifications for the next variable with a slash. For example, the first VALUE LABELS command on lines 14 through 19,

```
VALUE LABELS    SEX (0) MALES (1) FEMALES/
                JOBCAT (1) CLERICAL (2) OFFICE TRAINEE
                       (3) SECURITY OFFICER
                       (4) COLLEGE TRAINEE (5) EXEMPT EMPLOYEE
                       (6) MBA TRAINEE (7) TECHNICAL/
                MINORITY (0) WHITE (1) NONWHITE/
```

assigns labels to the values of SEX, JOBCAT, and MINORITY. The second VALUE LABELS command on lines 29 and 30 assigns labels to the values of the newly-created variable SEXRACE.

```
VALUE LABELS    SEXRACE (1) WHITE MALES (2) MINORITY MALES
                        (3) WHITE FEMALES (4) MINORITY FEMALES/
```

This command must follow the IF commands that created the new variable (see the IF commands in Section 11.5). The last VALUE LABELS command on line 35

```
VALUE LABELS    AGE (1) 18-29 (2) 30-39 (3) 40-49 (4) 50-59 (5) 60+/
```

assigns labels to the recoded values of AGE (see the RECODE command in Section 11.6). The value labels for SEXRACE and AGE are displayed on the CROSSTABS output in Figure 11.8. The CROSSTABS procedure prints only the first 16 characters of the value labels (see Chapter 3).

MISSING VALUES (line 20). Very often your data file does not contain complete information on some cases for every variable. For example, in Chapter 1, the day of death is unknown for some individuals. The value 9 is coded for DAY for these "unknown" cases and the MISSING VALUES command flags the value 9 as missing. The SPSS procedures and the ASSIGN MISSING command recognize this flag, and those cases that contain a missing value are handled specially. All procedures provide at least two options for handling cases with missing values. Refer to the earlier chapters in this book for discussions of missing values with each of the procedures.

The MISSING VALUES command on line 20 of the sample SPSS job declares missing values for several of the variables on the bank data file:

```
MISSING VALUES SALBEG,TIME TO EDLEVEL,JOBCAT (0)/SEX, MINORITY (9)
```

The keyword TO is used to reference the variables TIME, AGE, SALNOW, and EDLEVEL that are defined as adjacent variables on the DATA LIST command. The keyword TO can be used on several SPSS commands to reference adjacent variables on your data file. The two sets of missing-value specifications are separated with a slash.

You can instruct SPSS to consider more than one value missing for each variable. For example, if you code 9 for "Refused to Answer" and 0 for "Don't Know" for a variable measuring income, specify

```
MISSING VALUES INCOME (0,9)
```

The values must be separated by a comma. You can specify a maximum of three individual values for each variable. You can also specify a range of values using the keyword THRU. The keywords HIGHEST (or HI) and LOWEST (or LO) used with THRU indicate the highest and lowest values of a variable. For example, to define all values less than or equal to 0 as missing for a variable measuring profit of companies—all companies with no profit—specify

```
MISSING VALUES PROFIT (LOWEST THRU 0)
```

Only one THRU specification can be used for each variable list, and it can be combined with *one* individual value in each value specification list.

PRINT FORMATS (line 21).   The PRINT FORMATS command tells the procedures such as FREQUENCIES and CROSSTABS how to print the values of a variable. PRINT FORMATS does not affect the way the values are read and stored as defined on the DATA LIST command. If you do not specify a print format for a variable, SPSS prints the values as integers. For most variables, this is the correct format. However, if you have defined a variable with decimal places, you usually want to print the values with the decimal places. For example, to print the values of AGE and WORK with two decimal places, use the PRINT FORMATS command shown on line 21:

```
PRINT FORMATS  WORK,AGE (2)
```

Following the variable names, specify the number of decimal places enclosed in parentheses that you want to print. You can define print formats for additional variables in the same manner, separating each specification from the next with a slash.

   If you define a variable as an alphanumeric variable, you must specify the print format for the variable before you use the variable in a procedure that prints the value. For example, the variable HISTORY in the example SPSS job in Chapter 1 is defined as an alphanumeric variable. To define the print format for HISTORY and run FREQUEN-CIES on the variable, specify

```
PRINT FORMATS  HISTORY (A)
FREQUENCIES    GENERAL=HISTORY
```

11.3   DEFINING THE LOCATION AND SIZE OF THE DATA FILE

N OF CASES (line 6).   The N OF CASES command tells SPSS how many cases are in your data file. The UNKNOWN specification tells SPSS to read to the end of the data file. SPSS prints a message informing you how many cases were read from the data file. For example, note the message on page 2 of the output in Figure 11.3. For some implementations of SPSS, the UNKNOWN specification cannot be used if your data are included in the SPSS command file. In that case, you must specify the exact number of cases in your file. In other implementations of SPSS, the END INPUT DATA command can be used to indicate the end of the data if they are included in your SPSS command file (see Chapter 2 for an example). In all implementations, the UNKNOWN specification is accepted if your data are stored in a separate file on tape or disk.

INPUT MEDIUM (line 7).   In Figure 11.1 the data are not included in the SPSS command file. The keyword DISK tells SPSS to search for the data file on a storage device called disk. In most implementations of SPSS, you must supply additional information about the data file on operating-system-level commands for your computer. In other implementations of SPSS, the specification on the INPUT MEDIUM command may be the file name of the data file or may include other information about the file. Check with the consultant at your computer installation for the operating-system-level commands required for your computer and the specifications required for the INPUT MEDIUM command, or refer to the appendix for your computer in *SPSS Update 7–9*.

   If your data are included in the SPSS command file, you do not need to use the INPUT MEDIUM command since the default specification is CARD—the data in the same file as your SPSS commands. Several chapters include examples of SPSS jobs with the data included in the same file as your SPSS commands (see, for example, Chapters 1, 2, 3, and 5).

READ INPUT DATA (line 38).   The READ INPUT DATA command instructs SPSS to read your data file. In the sample SPSS job, SPSS reads the data from the data file defined on DISK. The READ INPUT DATA command *must follow* the first procedure command, in this case the CROSSTABS command. The data are read and the CROSSTABS procedure executed.

Figure 11.3   Second page of output—reading the data

```
BANK EMPLOYMENT STUDY                                        07/10/81      PAGE    2
            36 TASK NAME      AGE, SEXRACE CROSSTABULATION FOR ENTIRE SAMPLE.
            37 CROSSTABS       TABLES=SEXRACE BY AGE

***** GIVEN WORKSPACE ALLOWS FOR  3982 CELLS,  3982 TABLES WITH     2 DIMENSIONS FOR CROSSTAB PROBLEM *****

            38 READ INPUT DATA
AFTER READING    474 CASES FROM SUBFILE BANK    , END OF DATA WAS ENCOUNTERED ON LOGICAL UNIT # 8
```

11.4   TRANSFORMING AND SELECTING THE DATA

The SPSS job in Figure 11.1 demonstrates the three SPSS commands that are the core of the transformation language: RECODE, COMPUTE, and IF. These commands provide the facilities to change existing variables in your data file and to compute new variables from existing variables. The ASSIGN MISSING command is used with the transformation commands to provide special handling of cases containing missing values. The SPSS job also demonstrates the SELECT IF command that selects a subset of cases from your file.

All of the transformations and selection of cases can be applied to the entire SPSS job and saved permanently on an SPSS system file, or they can apply temporarily only to the first procedure following the transformation or selection commands. To indicate a temporary transformation or selection of cases, specify an asterisk in column 1 of the command. Only temporary COMPUTE, RECODE, IF, and SELECT IF commands can follow a procedure. All permanent transformation and selection commands (without the asterisk in column 1) must be placed before the first procedure command.

11.5   Creating New Variables

The *COMPUTE command and the ASSIGN MISSING command on lines 41 and 42 of the SPSS job in Figure 11.1 create the new variable AVERAISE. The asterisk in column one of the *COMPUTE command indicates that the variable AVERAISE will apply only to the next procedure—the SCATTERGRAM procedure. The variable AVERAISE will not be saved on the SPSS system file. Lines 23 through 27 in Figure 11.1 use the IF command and the ASSIGN MISSING command to create a new variable SEXRACE. The variable SEXRACE is created with permanent IF commands (no asterisk in column one) and will be saved on the system file. This variable is used in Chapter 4 to analyze discrimination.

*COMPUTE (line 41).   The COMPUTE command has been used in earlier chapters of this book to create new variables (see Chapter 2). You can use the COMPUTE command to create new variables or change existing variables on the basis of an arithmetic calculation. For example, to calculate the average monthly raise of an employee, specify, as on line 41,

```
*COMPUTE       AVERAISE= (SALNOW - SALBEG)/TIME
```

where AVERAISE is expressed as the difference between present salary and beginning salary, divided by the number of months employed by the bank. So, AVERAISE is the average monthly raise of each employee. The parentheses are used to indicate that the subtraction is to be performed first and the result of the subtraction divided by TIME.

The arithmetic operators and their meanings are

+   Addition.
−   Subtraction.
*   Multiplication.
/   Division.
** Exponentiation.

Only one variable can be named on the left side of the equals sign and only one arithmetic expression is allowed per COMPUTE command. The arithmetic expression can be something as simple as a single value, as in

```
COMPUTE        SEXRACE=1
```

or a more complex expression connected by arithmetic operators, as in the *COMPUTE command on line 41 of Figure 11.1.

Parentheses are used to indicate the order of operations. Expressions within parentheses are evaluated first. If parentheses are not used to indicate the order of operations, the order is

1 Functions

2 Exponentiation

3 Multiplication and Division

4 Addition and Subtraction

Operations of the same level, such as multiplication and division, are executed from left to right in the arithmetic expression. If you are ever unsure of the order of execution, use parentheses to indicate the order.

Several special arithmetic functions can be used on the COMPUTE command. For example, the function LG10 was used in Chapter 10 to calculate the log (base 10) of beginning salary, and the function RND is used on line 32 of Figure 11.1 to round the values of AGE to integers (see Section 11.6). A complete list of functions available on the COMPUTE command can be found in Appendix B. The most commonly used ones are

ABS   Calculates the absolute value of a signed number. The value −4.2 results in the value 4.2.
LG10 Calculates the base 10 logarithm.
LN   Calculates the natural or Naperian logarithm (base *e*).
RND   Rounds the value to an integer.
SQRT Calculates the square root.
TRUNC Truncates the value to an integer without rounding.

IF (lines 23-26).   The IF commands create the new variable SEXRACE by logically combining the values of SEX and MINORITY.

```
IF          (MINORITY EQ 0 AND SEX EQ 0) SEXRACE=1
IF          (MINORITY EQ 1 AND SEX EQ 0) SEXRACE=2
IF          (MINORITY EQ 0 AND SEX EQ 1) SEXRACE=3
IF          (MINORITY EQ 1 AND SEX EQ 1) SEXRACE=4
```

The first specification on the IF command is the *logical expression* enclosed in parentheses. The logical expression is followed by the *assignment specification*. The assignment is executed for a case only if the logical expression is true. For example, the first IF command on line 23 assigns the value 1 to the new variable SEXRACE for all cases that have the value 0 on MINORITY and the value 0 on SEX; that is, for all white males. The next three IF commands assign a value to SEXRACE for other logical combinations of MINORITY and SEX. So the variable SEXRACE has possible valid values of 1 through 4. The ASSIGN MISSING command assigns the value 9 to

SEXRACE for any case that is not evaluated as true for any of the IF commands and for cases that have a missing- value code on either SEX or MINORITY. See the discussion below of the ASSIGN MISSING command for more details.

The assignment specification follows all of the rules and possibilities described for the COMPUTE command. The assignment is executed only if the logical expression is true.

A logical expression can include variable names, constants, relational operators, and logical operators. *Relational operators* are used to compare two values. In the IF commands in Figure 11.1, the EQ relational operator is used to compare the value on a variable (MINORITY or SEX) to a constant. Available relational operators are

EQ Equal to
NE Not equal to
LT Less than
GT Greater than
LE Less than or equal to
GE Greater than or equal to

Two or more relational expressions can be joined logically using *logical operators* AND and OR. For example, the logical operator AND is used in the IF commands on lines 23 through 26 of the SPSS job in Figure 11.1. In the first IF command, a case must have both the value 0 on MINORITY and the value 0 on SEX to be assigned the value 1 on SEXRACE. If you use the logical operator OR, the logical expression is evaluated as true if either of the relational expressions is true. For example, to assign the value 1 to SEXRACE for all cases that are either male or white, specify

```
IF              (MINORITY EQ 0 OR SEX EQ 0) SEXRACE=1
```

The relational operators are evaluated first, then the logical operators. Each IF command is evaluated and executed in order on each case. This means that the order of the IF commands can be important.

```
IF              (SEX EQ 1 OR MINORITY EQ 0) SEXRACE=1
IF              (SEX EQ 0 OR MINORITY EQ 1) SEXRACE=2
```

If a case is coded 0 on SEX and 0 on MINORITY, both of the above IF commands are evaluated as true. However, SEXRACE will be assigned the value 2 since the second IF command overrides the results of the first.

ASSIGN MISSING (lines 27 and 42).   The ASSIGN MISSING command assigns the specified value to variables created with transformations when a value for the result variable cannot be determined or the variables used to create the variable contain a missing value. The specified value is also flagged as a missing value for the variable. In the SPSS job, ASSIGN MISSING commands are used for both new variables— SEXRACE and AVERAISE.

For example, value 9 is declared as a missing value for both MINORITY and SEX (the MISSING VALUES command on line 20). The ASSIGN MISSING command on line 27,

```
ASSIGN MISSING SEXRACE(9)
```

assigns the value 9 to SEXRACE on any case that has the value 9 on *either* MINORITY or SEX. Since SEXRACE is a new variable, the value specified on the ASSIGN MISSING command (value 9) is assigned initially to all of the cases. That is, the value specified on the ASSIGN MISSING command is the *initialized value*. If a case fails to satisfy any of the logical expressions on the four IF commands, the case retains the initialized value 9 for SEXRACE. For example, if a case is coded 2 on SEX, all of the IF commands will be evaluated as false and SEXRACE will be assigned the missing value 9.

The ASSIGN MISSING command on line 42,

```
ASSIGN MISSING AVERAISE (-1)
```

assigns the value −1 to all cases with a missing value on either SALBEG, SALNOW, or TIME. The AVERAISE will be calculated for all other cases.

You can specify only one value for each variable on the ASSIGN MISSING command. The variable name or variable list is followed by the missing-value number enclosed in parentheses. The variable list can include individual variable names and variables referenced with the keyword TO. A slash terminates the specification, and another set of specifications (variable name or list and missing- value specification) can follow.

11.6   Changing Existing Variables

The *COMPUTE and *RECODE commands on lines 32 through 34 collapse the values of AGE for use with the CROSSTABS procedure. The asterisk in column 1 of the command field indicates that the results of the commands apply only to the next procedure in the job—the CROSSTABS procedure.

*COMPUTE (line 32).   In the SPSS job in Figure 11.1, AGE is defined with two decimal places (see the DATA LIST command). The *COMPUTE command on line 32 uses the function RND to round the values of AGE to integers.

```
*COMPUTE        AGE=RND(AGE)
```

For example, an employee 22.66 years of age will have the value of 23 after the *COMPUTE command is executed. See Section 11.5 for additional information on the COMPUTE command, and Appendix B for a complete list of functions available on the COMPUTE command.

RECODE (lines 33 and 34).   The RECODE command on lines 33 and 34 collapses the rounded values of AGE into five age groups. The transformation commands are executed in the order that they appear, so the RECODE command is executed on the results of the COMPUTE command.

```
*RECODE         AGE(18 THRU 29=1)(30 THRU 39=2)(40 THRU 49=3)
                (50 THRU 59=4)(60 THRU HIGHEST=5)/
```

The first specification on the RECODE command is the variable name or list of variables that you want to recode. The variable list can include individual variable names and variables referenced with the keyword TO. The variables must be existing variables, either defined on your DATA LIST command or created by previous transformation commands. The RECODE command does *not* create new variables. Following the variable name or list, each recode specification for one new value is enclosed in parentheses. The old values are specified on the left side of the equals sign and the *one* new value on the right side. Several values can be specified to the left of the equals sign, and the keyword THRU can be used to indicate a range of values. For example, the first recode specification on the *RECODE command recodes the values 18 through 29 to the value 1. A list of individual values can be specified by separating each value from the next by at least one blank or comma, as in

```
RECODE          JOBCAT (1,7=0)
```

where the values 1 and 7 (clerical and technical employees) are recoded into one category with the value 0. Other values of JOBCAT will remain unchanged.

The keywords HIGHEST (or HI) and LOWEST (or LO) can be used to indicate the highest and lowest values of a variable, respectively. These keywords are very useful if you do not know the maximum or minimum value for a variable. For example, to recode the variable SALBEG into two categories—employees with a beginning salary less than

10,000 dollars and those with a beginning salary of 10,000 dollars or more—specify

```
RECODE          SALBEG (LO THRU 9999=0) (10000 THRU HI=1)
```

where SALBEG is measured in dollars.

11.7 Selecting a Subset of Cases

SELECT IF (line 40). The SELECT IF command selects a subset of cases from your data file. The specification field of the SELECT IF command is a logical expression constructed in the same way as the logical expression on the IF command. Refer to the discussion of the IF command in Section 11.5 for the rules of constructing logical expressions.

The SELECT IF command, like the RECODE, COMPUTE, and IF commands, has two forms—permanent and temporary. The SELECT IF command on line 40 is temporary (an asterisk in column 1), and the results apply only to the SCATTERGRAM procedure that follows. The SELECT IF command selects only those cases with the value 1 on SEXRACE; that is, the white males in the file. Only these cases are processed by the SCATTERGRAM procedure. A permanent SELECT IF cannot be used on line 40 since it follows a procedure command (CROSSTABS). If you use more than one SELECT IF command in an SPSS job, a case must be true for the logical expressions on *all* of the SELECT IF commands.

11.8 ANALYZING THE DATA

Two statistical procedures, CROSSTABS on line 37 and SCATTERGRAM on line 43, are included in the sample SPSS job. These procedures and the syntax of the commands are discussed in detail in Chapters 3 and 6, respectively.

Before running the CROSSTABS procedure, the variable AGE is temporarily recoded and new value labels are assigned to the recoded values (see lines 32 through 35). Figure 11.8 shows the crosstabulation table produced by the CROSSTABS procedure. Note the grouped values of AGE and the value labels displayed for each group.

Figure 11.8 CROSSTABS output

```
BANK EMPLOYMENT STUDY                                        07/10/81      PAGE    3
AGE, SEXRACE CROSSTABULATION FOR ENTIRE SAMPLE.
FILE   BANK      (CREATION DATE = 07/10/81)    MIDWESTERN CITY BANK DATA

* * * * * * * * * * * * * * * * *  C R O S S T A B U L A T I O N   O F  * * * * * * * * * * * * * * * * * *
     SEXRACE    SEX & RACE CLASSIFICATION              BY  AGE        AGE OF EMPLOYEE
* * * * * * * * * * * * * * * * * * * * * * * * * * * * * * * * * * * * * * * * * * * *  PAGE  1 OF  1

                        AGE
              COUNT I
              ROW PCT I18-29   30-39    40-49    50-59    60+
              COL PCT I                                                 ROW
              TOT PCT I 1.00I   2.00I    3.00I    4.00I    5.00I       TOTAL
SEXRACE        -------I--------I--------I--------I--------I--------I
          1.   I    38 I   110 I    22 I    13 I    11 I     194
WHITE MALES    I  19.6 I  56.7 I  11.3 I   6.7 I   5.7 I    40.9
               I  25.3 I  67.9 I  33.3 I  21.3 I  31.4 I
               I   8.0 I  23.2 I   4.6 I   2.7 I   2.3 I
              -I--------I--------I--------I--------I--------I
          2.   I    12 I    25 I    17 I     7 I     3 I      64
MINORITY MALES I  18.8 I  39.1 I  26.6 I  10.9 I   4.7 I    13.5
               I   8.0 I  15.4 I  25.8 I  11.5 I   8.6 I
               I   2.5 I   5.3 I   3.6 I   1.5 I   0.6 I
              -I--------I--------I--------I--------I--------I
          3.   I    89 I    21 I    15 I    33 I    18 I     176
WHITE FEMALES  I  50.6 I  11.9 I   8.5 I  18.8 I  10.2 I    37.1
               I  59.3 I  13.0 I  22.7 I  54.1 I  51.4 I
               I  18.8 I   4.4 I   3.2 I   7.0 I   3.8 I
              -I--------I--------I--------I--------I--------I
          4.   I    11 I     6 I    12 I     8 I     3 I      40
MINORITY FEMALES I 27.5 I  15.0 I  30.0 I  20.0 I   7.5 I     8.4
               I   7.3 I   3.7 I  18.2 I  13.1 I   8.6 I
               I   2.3 I   1.3 I   2.5 I   1.7 I   0.6 I
              -I--------I--------I--------I--------I--------I
          COLUMN    150      162       66       61       35      474
          TOTAL    31.6     34.2     13.9     12.9      7.4    100.0
```

The second procedure in the sample SPSS job produces a SCATTERGRAM on WORK by AVERAISE. The variable AVERAISE is created with the *COMPUTE command on line 41 as a temporary variable. It will not be saved on the system file.

11.9 INCLUDING COMMENTS IN THE SPSS JOB

COMMENT (lines 22, 31, and 44).   The COMMENT command allows you to insert comments that explain the transformations and tasks requested. They are for your information only; they are not used by SPSS. They print along with the other SPSS commands on the SPSS output. If you are using several transformation commands to create new variables, you may want to insert a COMMENT command to indicate the intent of the transformation commands.

11.10 THE SPSS SYSTEM FILE

Once you have defined your data file in SPSS, you need not repeat the data definition process. The variable names, variable and value labels, missing-value indications, print formats specifications, and the results of any permanent transformation commands can be saved permanently along with the data on a specially formatted file called the SPSS *system file*.

11.11 Creating the System File

SAVE FILE (line 45).   The SAVE FILE command instructs SPSS to write an SPSS system file. It must be the SPSS command immediately preceding the FINISH command. For example, the SAVE FILE command on line 45 writes a system file containing all of the data and all of the information from the FILE NAME, DATA LIST, VAR LABELS, VALUE LABELS, MISSING VALUES, and PRINT FORMATS commands. In addition, the new variable SEXRACE is saved on the system file. The system file does *not* contain the results of temporary transformation commands or results of procedures. For example, the original values of AGE are saved and all of the cases in the bank data file are included in the system file. The system file is identified by the file name specified on the FILE NAME command. The sample SPSS job saves a system file with the name BANK.

Figure 11.11 shows the last page of output from the sample SPSS job. SPSS tells you that the system file BANK has been saved and lists the variable names and the number of cases saved. The variable names are printed in the order that they are saved on the system file. The first three variables, SEQNUM, SUBFILE, and CASWGT are automatically created by SPSS for all system files. SEQNUM is a variable containing a sequence number for each case with values ranging from 1 to the number of cases. SUBFILE and CASWGT are used by SPSS for special purposes not discussed in this book but discussed in *SPSS*, Second Edition, under the topics subfiles and WEIGHT. Note that the variable SEXRACE created by the IF commands is the last variable on the file. All new variables created with transformation commands are ordered after the variables defined on your DATA LIST command.

The last lines that are printed on the SPSS output tell you that the job was completed successfully and SPSS found no errors. Usually, if you see this message at the end of your SPSS output, it indicates that the job produced the result that you wanted. Of course, SPSS cannot detect all possible errors. See Section 11.13 for a discussion of SPSS error messages.

Figure 11.11   Last page of output—saving the bank

```
BANK EMPLOYMENT STUDY                                          07/10/81        PAGE     7
WORK, AVERAGE MONTHLY RAISE SCATTERGRAM OF WHITE MALES


              45 SAVE FILE

FILE BANK       HAS BEEN SAVED WITH    14 VARIABLES..

SEQNUM    SUBFILE   CASWGT   ID        SALBEG   SEX      TIME     AGE      SALNOW    EDLEVEL
WORK      JOBCAT    MINORITY SEXRACE

                        THE SUBFILES ARE..

                                    NO OF
                        NAME        CASES

                        BANK         474


              46 FINISH

CPU TIME REQUIRED..    0.04 SECONDS

        NORMAL END OF JOB.
          46 CONTROL CARDS WERE PROCESSED.
           0 ERRORS WERE DETECTED.
```

In most implementations of SPSS, you must supply additional information about where to store the system file on operating-system-level commands for your computer. In other implementations of SPSS, the specification on the SAVE FILE command may be the file name assigned by your computer to the system file. Check with the consultant at your computer installation for the operating-system level commands required for your computer and the specifications required for the SAVE FILE command, or refer to the appendix for your computer in *SPSS Update 7–9*.

You can insert any informational text into the system file by including a DOCU-MENT command in an SPSS job that saves a system file. For example,

```
DOCUMENT        THE DATA IN THIS FILE ARE INFORMATION ABOUT BANK
                EMPLOYEES HIRED BETWEEN 1969 AND 1971.
                .  .  .
                .  .  .
                .  .  .
```

is the first two lines of the DOCUMENT command used to save the information printed on page 2 of Figure 11.12b.

11.12   Using the System File

Once you have saved an SPSS system file, you can run your SPSS jobs using the system file. The GET FILE command tells SPSS to read an SPSS system file. This one command replaces all of the data definition commands and all of the permanent transformation commands. For example, to run an SPSS job that reads the system file created by the SPSS job shown in Figure 11.1, specify

```
GET FILE        BANK
```

This command replaces all of the information from the commands on lines 2 through 30 of the SPSS job in Figure 11.1. The SPSS job shown in Chapter 4 reads the system file BANK.

If you are told to run some statistics from an SPSS system file that you have never used before, you will need to know the variables in the file, the missing values declared, print formats, and variable and value labels before you can run the statistics. The LIST FILEINFO command prints all of this information from the system file. Figure 11.12a shows a complete SPSS command file to read the system file BANK and print all of the descriptive information stored on the system file.

Figure 11.12a Using the GET FILE command

```
GET FILE       BANK
LIST FILEINFO  DOCUMENTS COMPLETE
FINISH
```

You can also request only certain information from the system file rather than all of it. Possible specifications on the LIST FILEINFO command are

VARLIST   Print a list of all the variable names in the order they reside on the system file.

SORTVARS   Print a list of all the variable names sorted in alphabetic order.

VARINFO   Print all information about the variables except variable and value labels

LABELS   Print the variable and value labels.

COMPLETE   Print the information produced by VARLIST, VARINFO, and LABELS.

DOCUMENTS Print all the documenting information.

Figure 11.12b shows the output from the SPSS job in Figure 11.12a. After the GET FILE command, SPSS prints a message informing you that the file BANK contains 14 variables and 474 cases. Pages 2, 3, and 4 of the output contain the results of the LIST FILEINFO command.

Page 2 contains the information printed by the keyword DOCUMENTS. This information was saved on the system file using the DOCUMENT command. The text in the specification field of the DOCUMENT command is printed in the same format in which it was entered. The date on which the document information was saved on the file is also printed.

Pages 3 and 4 of the output print the information from the keyword COMPLETE on the LIST FILEINFO command. The file name, file label, creation date, and number of cases in the system file are printed at the top of the page. Following this information is a table of information about the variables in the file. The first column of information about each variable is REL POS, the position of the variable on the file. The second column is the variable name. The third column contains the variable label and value labels if they exist. The fourth column prints the missing values declared for each of the variables. The word NONE is printed in this column if no missing values have been declared for a variable. The final column indicates the print format information for each variable. The print format for a variable is zero (0) unless it has been changed using a PRINT FORMATS command. Note that the print formats for AGE and WORK are two decimal places because we included a PRINT FORMATS command for these variables.

Figure 11.12b   The LIST FILEINFO output

```
                1 GET FILE      BANK


                       FILE BANK    HAS  14 VARIABLES

                       THE SUBFILES ARE..
                                    NO OF
                       NAME         CASES

                       BANK          474


CPU TIME REQUIRED..    0.03 SECONDS



               2 LIST FILEINFO  DOCUMENTS COMPLETE
SPSS BATCH SYSTEM                                                     07/06/81      PAGE    2

FILE   BANK     (CREATION DATE = 07/06/81)   MIDWESTERN CITY BANK DATA

DUMP OF DOCUMENTARY INFORMATION..

07/06/81        THE DATA IN THIS FILE ARE INFORMATION ABOUT BANK
                EMPLOYEES HIRED BETWEEN 1969 AND 1971.

                THE VARIABLES INCLUDE THE BEGINNING SALARY AND THE
                SALARY CURRENT AS OF MARCH, 1977.
                OTHER VARIABLES INCLUDE SEX OF EMPLOYEE, MONTHS OF
                SENIORITY, YEARS OF AGE, YEARS OF EDUCATION, YEARS
                OF PRIOR WORK EXPERIENCE, A CONDENSED JOB
                CLASSIFICATION, AND MINORITY STATUS.
                A COMBINED SEX AND MINORITY STATUS VARIABLE IS ALSO
                INCLUDED.

                REFERENCE:

                ROBERTS, HARRY V. "AN ANALYSIS OF EMPLOYEE COMPENSATION".
                  REPORT 7964.
                  CENTER FOR MATHEMATICAL STUDIES IN BUSINESS AND
                  ECONOMICS, UNIVERSITY OF CHICAGO.

SPSS BATCH SYSTEM                                                     07/06/81      PAGE    3

FILE   BANK     (CREATION DATE = 07/06/81)   MIDWESTERN CITY BANK DATA

DOCUMENTATION FOR SPSS FILE 'BANK    ' MIDWESTERN CITY BANK DATA

LIST OF THE   1 SUBFILES COMPRISING THE FILE

BANK     N=  474

DOCUMENTATION FOR THE   14 VARIABLES IN THE FILE 'BANK

REL  VARIABLE  VARIABLE LABEL                       MISSING PRT
POS    NAME                                         VALUES FMT


  1  SEQNUM                                          NONE    0

  2  SUBFILE                                         NONE    A

  3  CASWGT                                          NONE    4

  4  ID        EMPLOYEE CODE                         NONE    0

  5  SALBEG    BEGINNING SALARY                      0.      0

  6  SEX       SEX OF EMPLOYEE                       9.      0
                          0. MALES
                          1. FEMALES
  7  TIME      JOB SENIORITY                         0.      0

  8  AGE       AGE OF EMPLOYEE                       0.0     2

  9  SALNOW    CURRENT SALARY                        0.      0

 10  EDLEVEL   EDUCATIONAL LEVEL                     0.      0

 11  WORK      WORK EXPERIENCE                       NONE    2

 12  JOBCAT    EMPLOYMENT CATEGORY                   0.      0
                          1. CLERICAL
                          2. OFFICE TRAINEE
                          3. SECURITY OFFICER
                          4. COLLEGE TRAINEE
                          5. EXEMPT EMPLOYEE
                          6. MBA TRAINEE
                          7. TECHNICAL

 13  MINORITY  MINORITY CLASSIFICATION               9.      0
                          0. WHITE
                          1. NONWHITE

SPSS BATCH SYSTEM                                                     07/06/81      PAGE    4


DOCUMENTATION FOR THE   14 VARIABLES IN THE FILE 'BANK

REL  VARIABLE  VARIABLE LABEL                       MISSING PRT
POS    NAME                                         VALUES FMT


 14  SEXRACE   SEX & RACE CLASSIFICATION             9.      0
                          1. WHITE MALES
                          2. MINORITY MALES
                          3. WHITE FEMALES
                          4. MINORITY FEMALES
```

11.13   READING SPSS ERROR MESSAGES

SPSS checks the SPSS commands for syntax errors as they are read. Most of the common errors are syntax errors and can be detected by SPSS. However, SPSS cannot detect misspecification errors such as running a procedure on the wrong variable, incorrect logic in constructing a new variable with the transformation commands, or specifying the incorrect column location for a variable on the DATA LIST command. Therefore, you should always review your SPSS commands carefully before you run a job to verify that you are requesting what you want.

11.14   Misspelled Variable Name

One of the most common errors made by SPSS users is to misspell a variable name on a procedure or transformation command. Once you have assigned a name to a variable, that exact name must be used to identify the variable on all other SPSS commands. Figure 11.14 shows the printed output produced by this type of error. The SPSS job is the same as the one shown in Figure 11.1 except the variable SEXRACE is misspelled on the CROSSTABS command.

Figure 11.14   Error—Misspelled variable name on CROSSTABS

```
BANK EMPLOYMENT STUDY                                             05/26/81       PAGE    2

             35 CROSSTABS        TABLES=SEXRAC BY AGE
THE SYMBOL 'SEXRAC  ' HAS CAUSED AN ERROR
IN HEXADECIMAL, 'E2C5E7D9C1C34040'

ERROR NUMBER..   600. PROCESSING CEASES, ERROR SCAN CONTINUES.


     ***** GIVEN WORKSPACE ALLOWS FOR  5734 CELLS,  5734 TABLES WITH      0 DIMENSIONS FOR CROSSTAB PROBLEM *****


TRANSPACE REQUIRED..       600 BYTES
        6 TRANSFORMATIONS
        6 RECODE VALUES + LAG VARIABLES
       39 IF/COMPUTE OPERATIONS


             36 READ INPUT DATA
FURTHER DIAGNOSTICS WOULD BE MISLEADING, RUN ABORTED.



        ***** LIST OF SPSS ERROR MESSAGES ENCOUNTERED DURING THE RUN *****


        ERRNO= 600
        THE VARIABLE LIST ON THE CROSSTABS CARD IS INVALID

        NORMAL END OF JOB.
          36 CONTROL CARDS WERE PROCESSED.
           1 ERRORS WERE DETECTED.
```

SPSS prints a message on the line below the CROSSTABS command informing you that the symbol in error is SEXRAC. It tells you that the error number is 600. When SPSS detects a syntax error, it stops processing the job but continues to scan all remaining SPSS commands for syntax errors. At the bottom of the SPSS printout, the meaning of all of the SPSS errors encountered during the job are listed. Error 600 means that the variable list on the CROSSTABS card is invalid. These error messages should indicate to you that the "E" has been dropped from the variable name for the variable measuring sex and race.

In some implementations of SPSS, the meaning of the error number is printed at the point at which the error is detected rather than at the end of the SPSS printout.

11.15   Syntax Error on DATA LIST

In order for SPSS to read your data correctly, the DATA LIST command must be correct. As mentioned earlier, some types of errors on the DATA LIST command cannot be detected by SPSS. However, many common types of errors on the DATA LIST command are syntax errors that SPSS can detect. Figure 11.15 shows a partial printout of one such type of error. Again the SPSS job is the same as the one shown in Figure 11.1, except that the DATA LIST command contains a syntax error.

Figure 11.15   Error—DATA LIST command

```
SPSS BATCH SYSTEM                                              05/26/81       PAGE    1

SPSS FOR OS/360, VERSION M, RELEASE 9A, MARCH 5, 1981

                          CURRENT DOCUMENTATION FOR THE SPSS BATCH SYSTEM
ORDER FROM MCGRAW-HILL:  SPSS, 2ND ED. (PRINCIPAL TEXT)      ORDER FROM SPSS INC.:   SPSS STATISTICAL ALGORITHMS
                         SPSS UPDATE 7-9 (USE W/SPSS,2ND FOR REL. 7, 8, 9)          KEYWORDS: THE SPSS INC. NEWSLETTER
                         SPSS POCKET GUIDE, RELEASE 9
                         SPSS PRIMER (BRIEF INTRO TO SPSS)


DEFAULT SPACE ALLOCATION..     ALLOWS FOR..    81 TRANSFORMATIONS
WORKSPACE    57344 BYTES                      327 RECODE VALUES + LAG VARIABLES
TRANSPACE     8192 BYTES                     1314 IF/COMPUTE OPERATIONS

              1 RUN NAME       BANK EMPLOYMENT STUDY
              2 FILE NAME      BANK, MIDWESTERN CITY BANK DATA
              3 DATA LIST      FIXED(1)/1 ID 1-4 SALBEG 6-10 SEX 12 TIME 14-15
              4                          AGE 17-20 (2) SALNOW 22-26 EDLEVEL 28-29
              5                          WORK 31-34 (2) JOBCAT,MINORITY 36-38

THE FOLLOWING SYMBOL HAS CAUSED AN ERROR.. '38      ' (F3F8404040404040 IN HEXADECIMAL).

ERROR NUMBER..  144. PROCESSING CEASES, ERROR SCAN CONTINUES.

   . . .
   . . .
BANK EMPLOYMENT STUDY                                          05/26/81       PAGE    2
AGE, SEXRACE CROSSTABULATION FOR ENTIRE SAMPLE.


             36 READ INPUT DATA

FURTHER DIAGNOSTICS WOULD BE MISLEADING, RUN ABORTED.




      ***** LIST OF SPSS ERROR MESSAGES ENCOUNTERED DURING THE RUN *****


      ERRNO= 144
      INVALID LOCATION RANGE FOR VARIABLE LIST ON 'DATA LIST' OR 'ADD DATA' CARD

      NORMAL END OF JOB.
         36 CONTROL CARDS WERE PROCESSED.
          1 ERRORS WERE DETECTED.
```

At the point where SPSS detected an error (below the DATA LIST command), a message is printed informing you that the symbol in error is "38" and that the error number is 144. After listing and checking for syntax errors in all the remaining SPSS commands, the meaning of the error number 144 is printed. The complete listing of all the remaining SPSS commands is not shown. The error message informs you that a column has been incorrectly specified for a variable on the DATA LIST command. Referring to the DATA LIST command, you see that the last specification is JOBCAT, MINORITY 36–38. Two variable names are listed, but three columns have been specified. The total number of columns must be evenly divisible by the number of variables.

Several syntax errors may be detected in the same SPSS job. Each error is indicated at the point where it occurs, and the meaning of each error is printed either at that point or at the end of the printout. If several errors are detected, some of the later errors may be "spurious"—that is, they are caused by an earlier error. Always interpret and correct the errors in the order in which they occur. Correcting one error may in fact correct several later errors.

Appendix A

Exercises

Most of the exercises suggested in this text use the bank-data file distributed with Release 9 of the SPSS Batch System. The file contains records for 474 employees hired by a midwestern bank between 1969 and 1971. A description of the variables and the commands used to generate the file is in Chapter 11.

The data in the file are part of a larger data base that was used to study possible discrimination by the bank (Roberts). The exercises are organized by chapter and emphasize the procedures described in the chapter.

Many of the exercises require familiarity with the RECODE, COMPUTE, and SELECT IF commands, which are discussed in Chapter 11. You should therefore read the sections of Chapter 11 describing these commands before you attempt the exercises.

A.1   Chapter 1

1   Prepare frequency tables and bar charts for the distributions of the sex, race, education, and job category variables. Write a paragraph describing these characteristics of the sample.

2   (a)Obtain a bar chart for the age variable, truncated to the nearest integer.
(b)Now collapse the age variable into the categories 20-29, 30-39, etc., by dividing age by 10 and truncating the result (removing the fractional part) using the command:

COMPUTE   AGE1=TRUNC(AGE/10)

Obtain a bar chart for this collapsed age variable.
(c)Use the RECODE command to collapse the age variable into three categories: 20-39.99, 40-59.99, and 60-79.99. Construct a bar chart for this collapsed variable.
(d)How much information was lost in the collapsed bar charts? When would a collapsed bar chart be more useful than a bar chart using all the original values of a variable? What considerations should influence your choice of categories when collapsing a variable to obtain a bar chart? Were the categories given in (b) and (c) above reasonable ones for these data?

3   (a)Collapse the beginning salary variable into the categories 3000-3999, 4000-4999, etc., by dividing SALBEG by 1000 and truncating the result:

COMPUTE   SALBEG1=TRUNC(SALBEG/1000)

Construct a bar chart for this collapsed variable.

(b)Use the SELECT IF command to obtain bar charts for the collapsed female beginning salary and the collapsed male beginning salary.

(c)Do the shapes of the bar charts for females and males differ? If the bank discriminates against women, would you necessarily expect the shapes of the bar charts to differ? What sorts of discrimination would produce differently shaped bar charts?

4 Repeat Exercise 3, but this time use nonwhite and white beginning salaries rather than female and male salaries.

A.2   Chapter 2

1 Other variables of possible interest in describing the sample are ages of the employees, work experience, job seniority, beginning salary, and current salary. Calculate summary statistics for these variables. Summarize your findings.

2 (a)Refer to the bar charts obtained in Exercise 3 for Chapter 1. Which, if any, look normal? What deviations from normality are evident?

(b)For the uncollapsed female and male beginning salaries, obtain all summary statistics concerned with the shape of the distribution. Examine the values of these statistics. Are they consistent with your observations in part (a)?

3 For uncollapsed male and female beginning salaries, obtain the mean, median, mode, maximum, minimum, range, and standard deviation. How do these statistics differ for the two groups? In what ways would you expect them to differ if the bank discriminates against women?

4 Carry out Exercise 2, but this time use nonwhite and white beginning salaries.

5 Repeat Exercise 3 using nonwhite and white beginning salaries.

A.3   Chapter 3

1 (a)Prepare a table that shows the number of women and men in each of the first four job categories (use the SELECT IF command).

(b)Construct another table crosstabulating the first four job categories with the sex-race variable.

(c)What do you conclude and why? Justify your answer with a statistical analysis.

2 (a)Collapse work experience into several categories and crosstabulate this collapsed variable with sex. Do sex and work experience appear to be related? Justify your answer with a statistical analysis. Can your choice of categories affect your answer? Why or why not?

(b)If sex and work experience appear to be related, obtain a measure of the strength of the association. What are the disadvantages of the measure you used?

(c)Repeat the above analysis, using race instead of sex.

3 Collapse job seniority into several categories and examine the relationship between job seniority and sex and between job seniority and race, as in Exercise 2.

4 Collapse education into several categories. Are education and sex related at the bank? Are education and race related? Perform an analysis like the one asked for in Exercise 2.

A.4   Chapter 4

1 (a) Describe the distributions of age, educational level, work experience, and beginning salary for the sex-race groups.
(b) Summarize your findings.

2 Collapse education into several categories and describe the distribution of beginning salary for sex-race groupings, controlling for education. Do the results indicate that discrimination may be present? What are the weaknesses of this sort of analysis?

3 Collapse beginning salary into several categories, and describe the distribution of "current" (March 1977) salary across the sex-race groups, controlling for beginning salary. Is there evidence of discrimination?

A.5   Chapter 5

1 (a) Is there evidence to suggest that women and men are not equally compensated? Evaluate the overall difference in beginning salary. Repeat for each of the first two job categories (use the SELECT IF command). Which of these is the better comparison?
(b) Repeat the analysis in (a) for the race variable.
(c) What statistical assumptions are you making?

2 In 1(a) above, what are some arguments in favor of a one-tailed test? What arguments can you state for a two-tailed test? Which test would you use?

3 Repeat Exercise 1, using "current" (March 1977) salary rather than beginning salary.

4 (a) Do the educational backgrounds of women and men appear to be the same? Justify your answer with a statistical analysis.
(b) Obtain bar charts of female and male educational levels. How appropriate does a t-test seem, given the appearance of these bar charts? What does the large sample size here have to do with the appropriateness of the t-test?

5 Repeat Exercise 4, comparing the educational backgrounds of nonwhites and whites rather than women and men.

A.6   Chapter 6

1 (a) Prepare scatterplots for two pairs of variables of your choice. Describe the relationships, if any.
(b) For one of the pairs of variables, prepare separate plots for males and females. Are the relationships similar?
(c) Calculate a correlation matrix for the variables used. Comment on the appropriateness of the correlation coefficient as a summary measure for these pairs of variables.

2 (a) Obtain a scatterplot of beginning salary and education. Compute the correlation coefficient.
(b) Use the COMPUTE command to obtain the logarithm of beginning salary. Plot the logarithm of beginning salary against education, and obtain the correlation coefficient.
(c) How does the relationship between beginning salary and education differ from the relationship between the logarithm of beginning salary and education?

A.7   Chapter 7

1 For job category 1, test the hypothesis that the four race-sex groups are initially equally compensated.

2 (a)Although you would not expect people in different job categories to have the same beginning salaries, you might be interested in examining to what degree average salaries differ for the various job categories and how much variation there is in individuals' salaries within job categories. Perform the appropriate analysis of variance for investigating these questions, using only the first four job categories.
(b)What assumptions are you making? Obtain bar charts of beginning salary for each of the first four job categories. Are these bar charts consistent with your assumptions?
(c)Do salaries appear to be more variable between the first four job categories than within these categories? (Hint: Look at the mean squares.)
(d)What comparisons between means might be of interest? Carry out these comparisons, using one of the multiple comparison procedures.

3 Collapse education into fewer categories and examine the effect of collapsed education on beginning salary, using a one-way analysis of variance. What do your results indicate? Obtain the appropriate bar charts for checking your assumptions.

4 Collapse beginning salary into several categories and perform a one-way analysis of variance to investigate the effect of collapsed beginning salary on "current" (March 1977) salary. Interpret your results. Obtain the bar charts appropriate for checking your assumptions.

5 Choose and test a hypothesis of interest to you, using one-way analysis of variance. State and check your assumptions.

6 Enter the lost-letter data from Chapter 3. Test the hypothesis that overall return rates are the same in cities and towns.

A.8   Chapter 8

1 Examine the effects of the first two job categories and the race-sex variable on beginning salary, using a two-way analysis of variance. Is there an interaction effect? What do your results suggest?

2 Repeat Exercise 1, looking at "current" salary rather than beginning salary.

3 Perform a two-way analysis of variance to examine the effects of collapsed educational level (up to 16 years) and the first two job categories on beginning salary. What assumptions are you making? Summarize your results.

4 Using a two-way analysis of variance, investigate the effects of collapsed educational level (up to 16 years) and collapsed job seniority on "current" salary. Summarize your results.

A.9   Chapter 9

1 (a)Using the Mann-Whitney procedure, test the hypothesis that work experience has the same distribution for women and men. What do your results indicate?
(b)Repeat the above analysis, comparing nonwhites and whites rather than women and men.

2 (a)Use the Kruskal-Wallis procedure to test the hypothesis that the four sex-race groups have the same age distribution. Summarize your results.
(b)What assumptions are you making? Are they satisfied for these data?

3 The cardiac arrest data from Chapter 1 are given below. Use the WEIGHT command to enter these data and obtain a one-sample chi-square test of the hypothesis that the days of the week are equally hazardous for people with a history of heart disease. Repeat the analysis, this time examining people with *no* history of heart disease. What do your results indicate?

	NO	YES
MONDAY	22	16
TUESDAY	7	10
WEDNESDAY	6	10
THURSDAY	13	16
FRIDAY	5	10
SATURDAY	4	13
SUNDAY	6	14

4 Compute the Spearman rank correlation coefficients for the education, sex, work experience, race, and age variables. Compare these with the Pearson correlations given in Chapter 6.

A.10   Chapter 10

1 (a)For one of the job categories (or sex-race groups), develop a regression equation relating beginning salary to some of the other variables. Check your assumptions.
(b)Prepare a brief report summarizing your findings.

2 Repeat Exercise 1, looking at current salary rather than beginning salary.

Appendix B

SPSS Syntax Guide

This appendix provides an abbreviated guide to the SPSS Batch System as of Release 9. It is meant to accompany this book and therefore does not describe the entire language nor the full range of specifications for some of the commands. The *SPSS Pocket Guide*, Release 9, documents the entire system.

Note that implementations on different machines may require additional or alternate specifications. This appendix indicates where you might encounter these differences. The most differences occur in SPSS-11, the SPSS Batch System for the DEC PDP-11. You should not attempt to use this manual without having access to *SPSS-11*, Second Edition, which documents Release 4 of that system.

This appendix is divided into two sections, one on procedure commands and the other on nonprocedure commands, arranged alphabetically within the two sections. In the syntax diagrams, square brackets indicate optional specifications and braces enclose alternative specifications. Ellipses are used to indicate optional repetition. This scheme cannot always exactly describe choices and requirements. If you are in doubt, look at examples in the text. Uppercase specifications should be entered as shown; lowercase specifications show information you must provide.

B.1 NONPROCEDURE COMMANDS

These are not all of the data-definition, data-modification, or run commands available in the SPSS Batch System, but they represent by far the most commonly used. Other than SPSS-11, slight differences among implementations are found primarily with commands used to define files such as FILE NAME, INPUT MEDIUM, etc.

The SPSS-11 implementation has a restricted order of precedence for commands (see the manual). SPSS-11 also has no BINARY specification for the DATA LIST or INPUT FORMAT command. The FIXED specification yields an integer system file and the SPSS-11 REAL specification yields a real system file. Missing values are handled differently from other implementations; see SPSS-11 commands ALL, POSITIVE, NON-NEGATIVE, and NON-MISSING. These commands replace the missing-value treatment options for procedures. SPSS-11 has no ASSIGN MISSING command because it performs that function automatically using a preassigned value. There are no temporary transformations; see SPSS-11 commands CLEAR SAMPLE and CLEAR SELECT. Finally, page control is different in the SPSS-11 implementation.

If you specify the optional asterisk preceding one of the commands indicated with [*], the transformation or selection is in effect only for the first procedure following the command. Such temporary modifications must follow all permanent modifications, and only temporary modifications can be made following the first procedure.

ASSIGN MISSING

```
1                16
ASSIGN MISSING varlistl(missing value)/varlist2.../...
```

Assigns a missing value for computed variables (not SPSS-11). When a case contains missing values for any one of the variables used to calculate a computed variable, that case will assume the assigned missing value for the computed variable. Normally used in place of MISSING VALUES.

COMMENT

```
1                16
COMMENT          any text
```

Allows insertion of user comments anywhere among the commands except between multiple lines of a single command or among the data records.

COMPUTE

```
1                16
[*]COMPUTE       computed variable=arithmetic expression
```

Creates new variables or new values for existing variables by combining existing variables according to one or more of the functions listed below. Only one transformation can be requested per COMPUTE command.

Arithmetic Operators:

+	Addition
/	Division
−	Subtraction
*	Multiplication
**	Exponentiation

Special Functions:

ABS	Absolute value
ATAN	Arctangent
COS	Cosine
EXP	Exponential
LG10	Base 10 logarithm
LN	Natural logarithm
RND	Round to whole number
SIN	Sine
SQRT	Square root
TRUNC	Truncate to whole number
MOD10	Remainder of division by 10
NORMAL(arg)	Generates values from a normal distribution with mean of 0. The argument specifies the standard deviation.
UNIFORM(arg)	Generates values from a uniform distribution with lower bound of 0. The argument specifies the upper bound.

DATA LIST

```
1                16
DATA LIST        {FIXED} (records per case)/record# varlist
                 {BINARY}

                 start position[-end position] [{(n)}]
                                               {(A)}
```

Names variables and specifies their formats. Position specifications can note the location of one variable or the range within which a series of variables of the same column width and type occur. FIXED assumes that all variables are numeric with no implied decimals, unless otherwise informed by variable type notations "A" (alphanumeric) or "n" ("n" decimal places). BINARY assumes that all variables are 4-byte internal format floating point numbers. Binary data have no format specifications. Variable names can be generated with the TO convention when they are of the form "alphannnn TO alphammmm" where mmmm is greater than nnnn and alpha is any alphabetic string. DATA LIST is the alternative to the combination VARIABLE LIST and INPUT FORMAT for entering raw data.

DOCUMENT

```
1               16
DOCUMENT        any text
```

Can be used to insert information into the system file (not SPSS-11). Only one command, with as many continuation lines as needed, can be included in an SPSS run, and it must appear before the first procedure.

EDIT

```
1               16
EDIT
```

Scans the commands for syntax errors, verifies variable references, and produces memory or limitation information. The data are not accessed and no statistical calculations are performed. If you are reading from a system file, SPSS must have access to that file in order to verify the variable names. EDIT must be the first SPSS command.

END INPUT DATA

```
1               16
END INPUT DATA
```

Signals the end of in-stream data (not DEC10/20). Required with specification UN-KNOWN for the N OF CASES command and CARD for the INPUT MEDIUM command.

FILE NAME

```
1               16
FILE NAME       filename  [file label]
```

Names and labels a file. The file name is usually a standard SPSS 8-character name; the optional label usually can be up to 40 characters long. The file name may or may not have to be the same as the actual name of the file if it exists on disk or tape, depending on the machine environment and implementation.

FINISH

```
1               16
FINISH
```

Signals the end of SPSS commands. It is optional.

GET FILE

```
1               16
GET FILE        file name
```

Retrieves a system file. Some implementations of SPSS may require a file name and/or other file specifications on this command. It is required whenever an existing system file is accessed.

IF

```
1                   16
[*]IF               (logical expression)computed variable=arithmetic expression
```

Creates new variables using COMPUTE functions provided the logical expression is true (logical operators are listed below). Only one transformation can be entered per IF command.

Logical Operators:

GE   Greater than or equal to
LE   Less than or equal to
GT   Greater than
LT   Less than
EQ   Equal to
NE   Not equal to
AND   And
OR   Or
NOT   Not

INPUT FORMAT

```
1                16
INPUT FORMAT     {FIXED (formats)}
                 {BINARY (locations)}
                 {FREEFIELD}
```

Describes data formats: organization of cases, type and location of variables. No format is specified for FREEFIELD input. The INPUT FORMAT is required on all runs containing VARIABLE LIST. Common fixed-column format elements on INPUT FORMAT are

Fw.d   Numeric item of width "w" columns counting the sign and decimal if coded and "d" digits interpreted or coded right of the implied decimal point.
Aw   Alphanumeric variable of column width "w". The maximum "w" is machine-dependent (usually at least 4).
nX   Skip "n" columns.
Tn   Transfer to column "n".
/   Skip to the next record.
n( )   Repeat the operation in parentheses "n" times.

(See the "I" format in SPSS-11, Burroughs, and DEC10/20).

INPUT MEDIUM

```
1                16
INPUT MEDIUM     {CARD}
                 {TAPE}
                 {DISK}
```

Identifies the medium through which data are to be entered. The default is CARD. The command is optional when you are submitting data in-stream. It is required on all runs reading data from disk or tape. Some implementations require a file name conforming to host-system naming conventions for external files.

LIST CASES

```
1              16
LIST CASES     CASES= n /VARIABLES= {ALL}
                                    {varlist}
```

Lists values of the selected variables for the first "n" cases. If the CASES=n subcommand (not used in SPSS-11) is omitted, values for the first 10 cases are printed. Must directly precede a procedure command.

LIST FILEINFO

```
1              16
LIST FILEINFO  [COMPLETE] [DOCUMENTS]
```

Lists file data definition information. Used primarily for unfamiliar system files. (SPSS-11 has no specification field).

MISSING VALUES

```
1              16
MISSING VALUES varlist1 (value list1) [varlist2...]
```

Informs SPSS which values are to be considered missing. Blank fields are not automatically considered missing in SPSS. Keyword THRU can be used to indicate a range of missing values; keywords LOWEST (LO) and HIGHEST (HI) can be used in place of values. A maximum of three values can be specified per list including end points of a range.

N OF CASES

```
1              16
N OF CASES     {UNKNOWN}
               {number of cases}
```

Specifies the number of cases in the file. The default is UNKNOWN. Not required for data residing on an INPUT MEDIUM other than CARD, or if END INPUT DATA is used to mark the end of in-stream data.

NUMBERED

```
1              16
NUMBERED
```

Reads only columns 1-72 of the SPSS command lines so you can use columns 73-80 to number your SPSS command lines.

PAGESIZE

```
1              16
PAGESIZE       {n of lines}
               {NOEJECT}
```

Specifies the number of lines to be printed per output page. NOEJECT specifies continuous printing (over perforations, etc.).

PRINT FORMATS

```
1              16
PRINT FORMATS  varlist1 {(n)} /varlist2.../...
                        {(A)}
```

Specifies special printing formats. Must be used when the file includes alphanumeric variables, specified by "A", and is also used to note the number of decimal places to be printed, specified by "n" (maximum is 5; default is 0). It is required for alphanumeric variables, but optional for numeric variables. When it is not used with numeric variables, no decimal digits are printed. (Required in DEC10/20 implementations only for recoded or computed variables).

READ INPUT DATA

```
1               16
READ INPUT DATA
```

Instructs the system to begin reading input data. Required when processing from raw data or adding variables or cases to a system file. Used only once during a run.

RECODE

```
1               16
[*]RECODE       varlistl ( {value listl} =newvaluel)
                         {BLANK}

                ({value list2} =newvalue2)          .../varlist2...
                 {ELSE}
                    or
                (CONVERT)
```

Recodes variable values. Adjacent values can be listed implicitly with keyword THRU. Keywords LOWEST (LO) and HIGHEST (HI) can be used instead of numeric values. ELSE recodes all values not otherwise assigned. BLANK assigns values to blank data fields, which are otherwise treated as zero (for SPSS-11 and DEC10/DEC20 implementations, see the ASSIGN BLANKS command). CONVERT recodes alphanumeric values into numeric values.

RUN NAME

```
1               16
RUN NAME        label
```

Supplies a run name of up to 64 characters in length to be printed at the top of each page of output.

SAMPLE

```
1               16
[*]SAMPLE       {sampling fraction}
                {sample size FROM file size}
```

Selects a random sample of cases without replacement. The probability of selection for each case is given by the sampling fraction, which must be a number between 0 and 1. Or, to extract an exact-size random sample, enter the sample size desired, the keyword FROM, and the exact file size (not SPSS-11).

SAVE FILE

```
1               16
SAVE FILE       [filename] [file label]
```

Saves raw input data with all definitions; optional name and label override those provided with FILE NAME. Some implementations of SPSS may require a file name and/or other file specifications on this command. It is required when raw data definitions and/or data modifications to an existing system file are to be retained.

SEED

```
1                  16
SEED               {a large integer}
                   {PRINT}
```

Used in conjuction with the SAMPLE command. Gives SPSS a seed number for a random sample. Used in some implementations to reproduce same sample, in other implementations to change default seed (SPSS-11, Burroughs, DEC10/20). Keyword PRINT prints the seed used by SPSS.

SELECT IF

```
1                  16
[*]SELECT IF       (logical expression)
```

Selects for processing only those cases that meet the criteria specified in the logical expression (logical operators are EQ, LE, LT, GE, GT, NE, AND, OR, NOT). Cases must satisfy the criteria on each SELECT IF command included in a run in order to be selected.

TASK NAME

```
1                  16
TASK NAME          label
```

Supplies a task name of up to 64 characters in length to be printed below the run name. Remains in effect until the end of the run or until the system encounters a new TASK NAME command.

VALUE LABELS

```
1                  16
VALUE LABELS       {varlist1} (value1)label1 (value2)label2.../ varlist2...
                   {ALL}
```

Associates a label of up to 20 characters with each value for the variables specified.

VAR LABELS

```
1                  16
VAR LABELS         varname1 label1/varname2 label2/...
```

Associates a variable label of up to 40 characters with the variables specified.

VARIABLE LIST

```
1                  16
VARIABLE LIST      list of variables
```

Names variables in the order defined on the subsequent INPUT FORMAT command. With INPUT FORMAT, it is the alternative to DATA LIST when data are to be read from a raw data file.

WEIGHT

```
1                  16
[*]WEIGHT          varname
```

Weights cases based upon the named variable (not SPSS-11). A value of 1 for the named variable will not affect the case and a value of 0 (or less) will eliminate the case. Any other value will be used to weight the case.

B.2   PROCEDURE COMMANDS

These syntax summaries are for procedure commands described in the chapters of this book. The SPSS-11 implementation does not provide the NEW REGRESSION procedure but does have the REGRESSION procedure that features the forward inclusion method. Procedure ONEWAY is not available in SPSS-11.

ANOVA

```
1                 16
ANOVA             dependent varlist1 BY independent varlist1(min,max)

                  independent varlist2(min,max)...[WITH covariate list]/

                  dependent varlist2.../...
```

Analysis of variance for factorial designs up to five factors and five covariates. Can handle unequal cell sizes, different methods of entering effects and interactions, multiple classification analysis, and output of regression coefficients.

Options:

1   Include cases with missing data.
2   Don't print variable or value labels.
3   Delete all interaction terms from the model.
4   Delete three-way and higher interaction terms.
5   Delete four-way and higher interaction terms.
6   Delete five-way interaction terms.
7   Process covariates concurrently with main effects for nonmetric factors.
8   Process covariates after main effects for nonmetric factors.
9   Regression approach. Overrides Options 7 and 8.
10 Hierarchical approach.
11 Restrict printed output to 80 columns.

Statistics:

1   Multiple classification analysis (not with Option 9)
2   Unstandardized partial regression coefficients for covariates
3   Means and counts table (not with Option 9)

BREAKDOWN

Integer Mode (not SPSS-11):

```
1                 16
BREAKDOWN         VARIABLES=varlist1 {(min,max)}         varlist2.../
                                     {(LOWEST,HIGHEST)}
                  {TABLES}     =varlist BY varlist BY.../...varlist...
                  {CROSSBREAK}
```

General Mode:

```
1                 16
BREAKDOWN         TABLES=varlist BY varlist BY.../varlist BY.../...
```

Features up to five independent variables; means, variances, and subgroup counts; oneway analysis of variance; test of linearity; and table, tree diagram, or crosstabulation formats.

Options:

1   Include cases with missing data.
2   Exclude cases with missing data on the dependent variable only.
3   Don't print labels.
4   Modified tree-diagram format (general mode only).

5   Don't print cell frequencies (CROSSBREAK only).

6   Don't print sums (CROSSBREAK only).

7   Don't print standard deviations (CROSSBREAK only).

8   Print variable labels but not value labels (CROSSBREAK only).

Statistics:

1   One-way analysis of variance (not for CROSSBREAK)

2   Test of linearity (not for CROSSBREAK); also request Statistic 1

3   Chi-square (CROSSBREAK only)

4   Phi for 2 x 2 tables, Cramer's V for larger tables (CROSSBREAK only)

5   Contingency coefficient (CROSSBREAK only)

6   Lambda, symmetric and asymmetric (CROSSBREAK only)

7   Uncertainty coefficient, symmetric and asymmetric (CROSSBREAK only)

8   Kendall's tau-b (CROSSBREAK only)

9   Kendall's tau-c (CROSSBREAK only)

10 Conditional gamma (CROSSBREAK only)

11 Somers' d, symmetric and asymmetric (CROSSBREAK only)

12 Eta (CROSSBREAK only)

CONDESCRIPTIVE

```
1              16
CONDESCRIPTIVE {varlist}
               {ALL}
```

Provides summary statistics for interval data. Features statistics for central tendency and dispersion, minimum and maximum values, and compact output.

Options:

1   Include cases with missing data.

2   Don't print variable labels.

3   Write out Z-scores.

4   Print a reference index.

Statistics:

1   Mean

2   Standard error

5   Standard deviation

6   Variance

7   Kurtosis

8   Skewness

9   Range

10 Minimum

11 Maximum

12 Sum

CROSSTABS

Integer Mode (not SPSS-11):

```
1              16
CROSSTABS      VARIABLES=varlist(min,max) varlist(min,max).../
               TABLES=varlist BY varlist.../varlist BY varlist.../...
```

General Mode:

```
1              16
CROSSTABS      TABLES=varlist BY varlist.../varlist BY varlist.../...
```

General purpose procedure for two- to n-way crossclassification. Features two- to eight-way tables, control of information printed in cells, and many measures of association.

Options:

1 Include cases with missing data.
2 Don't print labels.
3 Don't print row percents.
4 Don't print column percents.
5 Don't print total percents.
6 Print variable labels but not value labels (integer mode only).
7 Include missing values in tables but not statistics (integer mode only).
8 Print tables ordered on row variable values, highest to lowest (integer mode only).
9 Print an index of tables.
10 Write out non-empty cell contents.
11 Write out all cell contents.
12 Suppress printed output.

Statistics:

1 Chi-square
2 Phi for 2 x 2 tables, Cramer's V for larger tables
3 Contingency coefficient
4 Lambda, symmetric and asymmetric
5 Uncertainty coefficient, symmetric and asymmetric
6 Kendall's tau-b
7 Kendall's tau-c
8 Gamma (partial, zero-order gamma only in integer mode)
9 Somers' d, symmetric and asymmetric
10 Eta
11 Pearson's r

FREQUENCIES

```
 1              16
 FREQUENCIES    GENERAL= {varlist}
                        {ALL}
```

Tables and statistics for univariate distributions. Features tables of counts and percentage distributions, bar graphs, statistics, options for condensed output and an index of table locations.

Options:

1 Include cases with missing data.
2 Delete value labels from frequency tables.
3 Print output in 8 1/2 by 11 inch space.
4 Write output on a permanent print file.
5 Print tables in condensed format.
6 Condense only tables that fill more than one page.
7 Delete tables and print only requested statistics.
8 Print a bar graph.
9 Print an index of tables.
10 Print tables in descending order of values.
11 Print tables in descending order of frequency.
12 Print tables in ascending order of frequency.

Statistics:

1   Mean
2   Standard error
3   Median
4   Mode
5   Standard deviation
6   Variance
7   Kurtosis
8   Skewness
9   Range
10 Minimum
11 Maximum

NEW REGRESSION

```
1                16
NEW REGRESSION MISSING=[LISTWISE]           /
                      [PAIRWISE]
                      [MEANSUBSTITUTION]
                      [INCLUDE]

               DESCRIPTIVES=[DEFAULTS] [MEAN] [STDDEV] [CORR]/
                            [VARIANCE] [SIG] [BADCORR] [COV]
                            [XPROD] [N] [NONE]

               VARIABLES=varlist  /

               CRITERIA=[DEFAULTS]    [MAXSTEPS(n)]  [TOLERANCE(value)]      /
                        [PIN(value)] [FIN(value)] [POUT(value)] [FOUT(value)]

               STATISTICS=[DEFAULTS] [R] [COEFF] [OUTS] [ANOVA]      /
                          [CHA] [BCOV] [XTX] [ZPP] [CI] [SES] [COND]
                          [LABEL] [F] [HISTORY] [END] [TOLERANCE] [ALL]

               {ORIGIN}   /
               {NOORIGIN}

               DEPENDENT=varlist /

               {STEPWISE} [=varlist] /...
               {FORWARD}
               {BACKWARD}
               {ENTER}
               {REMOVE}

               RESIDUALS=[DEFAULTS]    [{LARGE}]  [{HISTOGRAM}(temp varlist)]/
                         [ID(varname)] {SMALL}    {OUTLIERS}
                         [DURBIN]                 {NORMPROB}

               CASEWISE=[DEFAULTS]             [{DEPENDENT}] /
                        [OUTLIERS(n)]           {temp varlist}
                        [PLOT(temp varname)]    {ALL}

               SCATTERPLOT=[{SMALL}] [(varname,varname)... /
                            {LARGE}
```

Multiple regression analysis procedure with various equation development methods and
residuals analysis. The minimum required syntax is one VARIABLES= subcommand,
one DEPENDENT= subcommand, and one method (STEPWISE, FORWARD, etc.)
subcommand.

NONPAR CORR

```
1                16
NONPAR CORR      varlist  [WITH varlist]/varlist...
```

Spearman and Kendall's tau-b rank-order correlations. Features one- or two-tailed
significance tests.

Options:

1   Include cases with missing data.
2   Exclude cases with missing data listwise.
3   Apply a two-tailed test of statistical significance.
4   Write out a matrix for lists not specified with WITH.
5   Compute Kendall's tau-b correlations.
6   Compute Kendall's tau-b and Spearman correlations.
7   Select a random sample of cases if insufficient memory.

B.42 NPAR TESTS

```
1                 16
NPAR TESTS        CHI-SQUARE=varlist(min,max)/[EXPECTED={EQUAL}      ]/
                                                        {proportions}

                  K-S({UNIFORM[,min,max]}   )=varlist/
                      {NORMAL[,mean,stddev]}
                      {POISSON[,mean]}

                  RUNS({MEAN}   )=varlist/
                       {MEDIAN}
                       {MODE}
                       {value}

                  {MCNEMAR} =varlist WITH varlist/
                  {SIGN}
                  {WILCOXON}

                  {COCHRAN} =varlist/
                  {FRIEDMAN}

                  {MEDIAN(value)} =dependent varlist BY
                  {M-W}
                  {K-S}                 independent var(valuel,value2)/
                  {W-W}
                  {MOSES(value)}
                  {K-W}
```

Fourteen nonparametric tests (Siegal, 1956). Features choice of statistical tests and condensed output.

Options:

1   Include cases with missing data.
2   Exclude cases with missing data listwise.
3   Sequential pairing of variable list.
4   Select a random sample of cases if insufficient memory.
5   Restrict printed output to 75 columns.

Statistics:

1   Mean, maximum, minimum, standard deviation, number of cases

B.43 ONEWAY

```
1                 16
ONEWAY            dependent varlist BY independent var(min,max)/

                  [POLYNOMIAL=n/] [CONTRAST=coefficient list/CONTRAST=.../...]

                  [RANGES={LSD}      (alpha)./]
                          {DUNCAN}
                          {SNK}
                          {TUKEYB}
                          {TUKEY}
                          {LSDMOD}
                          {SHEFFE}
                          {ranges values}
```

One-way analysis of variance with optional tests for trends across groups, user-specified a priori contrasts, and a posteriori contrasts.

Options:

1   Include cases with missing data.
2   Exclude cases with missing data listwise.
3   Don't print variable labels.
4   Write out the number of cases, mean, and standard deviation for each group.
6   Label groups with first 8 characters of independent variable value labels.
7   Read in group frequencies, means, and standard deviations.
8   Read in group frequencies, means, pooled variances, and degrees of freedom.
10 Use the harmonic mean for all groups in range tests.

Statistics:

1   For each group, the number of cases, mean, standard deviation, standard error, minimum, maximum, and 95% confidence interval for the mean
2   Fixed- and random-effects measures
3   Homogeneity of variance statistics: Cochran's C, Barlett-Box F, and Hartley F-max

PEARSON CORR

```
 1              16
PEARSON CORR    varlist [WITH varlist]/varlist...
```

Bivariate correlation analysis with Pearson's r. Features simple descriptive statistics, significance tests, crossproducts and covariances, optional output displays, matrix output.

Options:

1   Include cases with missing data.
2   Exclude cases with missing data listwise.
3   Two-tailed test of significance.
4   Write a matrix for lists not specified with WITH.
5   Don't print number of cases and significance.
6   Print nonredundant coefficients only.

Statistics:

1   Means and standard deviations for each variable
2   Cross-product deviations and covariance for each pair

SCATTERGRAM

```
 1              16
SCATTERGRAM     varlist1 {(min,max)}          varlist2 {(min,max)}
                         {(LOWEST,HIGHEST)}             {(LOWEST,HIGHEST)}

                [WITH varlist3].../...
```

Produces a bivariate plot. Features control of the axis scale, control of the grid pattern, and produces simple regression statistics.

Options:

1   Include cases with missing data.
2   Exclude cases with missing data listwise.
3   Don't print variable labels.
4   Don't print plot grid lines.
5   Print diagonal grids.
6   Apply a two-tailed test of statistical significance.

7 Scale variable values to integers.
8 Select a random sample of cases if insufficient memory.

Statistics:

1 Pearson's r
2 r-squared
3 Significance of r
4 Standard error of the estimate
5 Intercept with the vertical axis
6 Slope

T-TEST

Independent Samples:

```
1                    16
T-TEST               GROUPS= {varname(value)}              /VARIABLES=varlist
                            {varname (value1,value2)}
                            {value1,value2}
```

Paired Samples:

```
1                    16
T-TEST               PAIRS=varlist [WITH varlist]/varlist...
```

Student's t test of differences between means for independent or paired samples. Provides between group and between variable t tests.

Options:

1 Include cases with missing data.
2 Exclude cases with missing data listwise.
3 Don't print variable labels.

B.3   ORDER OF SPSS COMMANDS

The following table of SPSS commands shows a correct order, not *the* correct order. Many violations are acceptable, some are logical and necessary.

RUN NAME

GET FILE — Use this command in place of DATA LIST, INPUT MEDIUM, N OF CASES, and READ INPUT DATA if you are reading an SPSS system file.

FILE NAME

DATA LIST — Use VARIABLE LIST and INPUT FORMAT FREEFIELD if you are reading freefield format data.

INPUT MEDIUM
N OF CASES
COMPUTE
RECODE
IF
SELECT IF
WEIGHT
DOCUMENT
*COMPUTE
*RECODE
*IF
*SELECT IF
VAR LABELS
VALUE LABELS
MISSING VALUES
ASSIGN MISSING
PRINT FORMATS
LIST FILEINFO
LIST CASES

first procedure command — Use any of the procedure commands available in SPSS, such as FREQUENCIES, CROSSTABS, and so forth.

OPTIONS
STATISTICS
READ INPUT DATA
data lines

END INPUT DATA — Use this command only if your data are included in the SPSS command file.

temporary data transformations — Additional *COMPUTE, *RECODE, *IF, or *SELECT IF commands can be included. You can also include VAR LABELS, VALUE LABELS, MISSING VALUES, PRINT FORMATS, and ASSIGN MISSING commands to define the transformed variables.

procedure commands — Additional procedure commands can be included before the SAVE FILE command.

SAVE FILE
FINISH

An order is not shown for the COMMENT command since it can appear anywhere except between the READ INPUT DATA command and the lines of data. The order shown for data transformations is arbitrary. These commands should appear in the order you want the transformations executed. Temporary transformation commands can appear between procedure commands, and several sets of temporary transformation commands and procedure commands can be used in an SPSS job.

Bibliography

Anderson, R., and S. Nida. Effect of physical attractiveness on opposite and same-sex evaluations. *Journal of Personality,* 46:3 (1978), 401-413.

Berk, K. N. Comparing subset regression procedures. *Technometrics,* 20 (1978), 1-6.

————. Tolerance and condition in regression computation. *Journal of the American Statistical Association,* 72 (1977), 863-866.

Blalock, H. M. *Social Statistics.* New York: McGraw-Hill, 1979.

Borgatta, E. F., and G. W. Bohrnstedt. Level of measurement once over again. *Sociological Methods and Research,* 9:2 (1980), 147-160.

Cedercreutz, C. Hypnotic treatment of 100 cases of migraine. In F. H. Frankel and H. S. Zamansky, Eds. *Hypnosis at its Bicentennial.* New York: Plenum, 1978.

Conover, W. J. Some reasons for not using the Yates continuity correction on 2 X 2 contingency tables. *Journal of the American Statistical Association,* 69 (1974), 374-376.

Cook, R. D. Detection of infuential observations in linear regression. *Technometrics,* 19 (1977), 15-18.

Everitt, B. S. *The Analysis of Contingency Tables.* London: Chapman and Hall, 1977.

Fienberg, S. E. *The Analysis of Cross-Classified Categorical Data.* Cambridge: MIT Press, 1977.

Frane, J. W. Some simple procedures for handling missing data in multivariate analysis. *Psychometrika,* 41 (1976), 409-415.

————. A note on checking tolerance in matrix inversion and regression. *Technometrics,* 19 (1977), 513-514.

Goodman, L. A., and W. H. Kruskal. Measures of association for cross-classification. *Journal of the American Statistical Association,* 49 (1954), 732-764.

Greeley, A. M., W. C. McCready and G. Theisen. *Ethnic Drinking Subcultures.* New York: Praeger Publishers, 1980.

Haberman, S. J. *Analysis of Qualitative Data,* Vol. 1. London: Academic Press, 1978.

Hansson, R. O., and K. M. Slade. Altruism toward a deviant in city and small town. *Journal of Applied Social Psychology,* 7:3 (1977), 272-279.

Hocking, R. R. The analysis and selection of variables in linear regression. *Biometrics,* 32 (1976), 1-49.

King, M. M., et al. Incidence and growth of mammary tumors induced by 7,12-dimethylbenz(a) anthracene as related to the dietary content of fat and antioxident. *Journal of the National Cancer Institute,* 63:3 (1979), 657-663.

Kleinbaum, D. G., and L. L. Kupper. *Applied Regression Analysis and Other Multivariable Methods.* North Scituate, Massachusetts: Duxbury Press, 1978.

Lee, E. T. *Statistical Methods for Survival Data Analysis.* Belmont, California: Lifetime Learning Publications, 1980.

Loether, H. J., and D. G. McTavish. *Descriptive and Inferential Statistics: An Introduction.* Boston: Allyn and Bacon, 1976.

Mantel, N. Comment and a suggestion on the Yates continuity correction. *Journal of the American Statistical Association,* 69 (1974), 378-380.

Meyer, L. S., and M. S. Younger. Estimation of standardized coefficients. *Journal of the American Statistical Association,* 71 (1976), 154-157.

Miller, J. B., Jr., and P. Bush. Host selling vs premium TV commercials: an experimental evaluation of their influence on children. *Journal of Marketing Research,* 16 (1979), 323-332.

Neter, J., and W. Wasserman. *Applied Linear Statistical Models.* Homewood, Illinois: Richard D. Irwin Inc., 1974.

Nie, N. H., et al. *SPSS: Statistical Package for the Social Sciences.* Second edition. New York: McGraw-Hill, 1975.

Norušis, M. J. *SPSS Statistical Algorithms.* Chicago: SPSS Inc., 1978.

Overall, J. E., and C. Klett. *Applied Multivariate Analysis.* New York: McGraw-Hill, 1972.

Rabkin, S. W., F. A. Mathewson and R. B. Tate. Chronobiology of cardiac sudden death in men. *Journal of the American Medical Association,* 244:12, (1980), 1357-1358.

Richardson, J., and A. L. Kroeber. Three centuries of women's dress fashions: a quantitative analysis. *Anthropological Records,* 5:2 (1940), 111-153.

Roberts, H. V. *An Analysis of Employee Compensation.* Rpt. 7946, Center for Mathematical Studies in Business and Economics, University of Chicago: October 1979.

————. Statistical bases in the measurement of employment discrimination. In E. Robert Livernash, ed. *Comparable Worth: Issues and Alternatives.* Washington, D.C.: Equal Employment Advisory Council, 1980, 173-195.

Robinson, D. E. Fashions in shaving and trimming of the beard: the men of the *Illustrated London News,* 1842-1972. *American Journal of Sociology,* 81:5 (1976), 1133-1141.

Siegel, S. *Nonparametric Statistics for the Behavioral Sciences.* New York: McGraw-Hill, 1956.

Sigall, H., and N. Ostrove. Beautiful but dangerous: Effects of offender attractiveness and nature of the crime on juridic judgement. *Journal of Personality and Social Psychology,* 31 (1975), 410-414.

Snedecor, G. W., and W. G. Cochran. *Statistical Methods.* Ames, Iowa: Iowa State University Press, 1967.

Somers, R. H. A new symmetric measure of association for ordinal variables. *American Sociological Review,* 27 (1962), 799-811.

Stevens, S. S. On the theory of scales of measurement. *Science,* 103 (1946), 677-680.

Theil, H. *Economics and Information Theory.* Chicago: Rand McNally, 1967.

Winer, B. J. *Statistical Principles in Experimental Design.* New York: McGraw-Hill, 1971.

Wynder, E. L. Nutrition and cancer. *Federal Proceedings,* 35 (1976), 1309-1315.

Wyner, G. A. Response errors in self-reported number of arrests. *Sociological Methods and Research,* 9:2 (1980), 161-177.

INDEX